Theory Can Be More than It Used to Be

Theory Can Be More than It Used to Be

*Learning Anthropology's Method
in a Time of Transition*

Edited by Dominic Boyer, James D. Faubion,
and George E. Marcus

Cornell University Press
Ithaca and London

First published 2015 by Cornell University Press
First printing, Cornell Paperbacks, 2015
Printed in the United States of America

Library of Congress Cataloging-in-Publication Data

Theory can be more than it used to be : learning anthropology's method in a time of transition / edited by Dominic Boyer, James D. Faubion, and George E. Marcus.
    pages cm
Includes bibliographical references and index.
ISBN 978-1-5017-0007-1 (cloth : alk. paper)
ISBN 978-1-5017-0008-8 (pbk. : alk. paper)
1. Anthropology—Methodology. 2. Anthropology—Philosophy.
I. Boyer, Dominic, editor. II. Faubion, James D., editor. III. Marcus, George E., editor. IV. Boyer, Dominic. Portable analytics and lateral theory. Container of (work):
  GN33.T44 2015
  301.01—dc23   2015018642

Cornell University Press strives to use environmentally responsible suppliers and materials to the fullest extent possible in the publishing of its books. Such materials include vegetable-based, low-VOC inks and acid-free papers that are recycled, totally chlorine-free, or partly composed of nonwood fibers. For further information, visit our website at www.cornellpress.cornell.edu.

Cloth printing   10 9 8 7 6 5 4 3 2 1
Paperback printing   10 9 8 7 6 5 4 3 2 1

CONTENTS

Theory Can Be More than It Used to Be

INTRODUCTION

New Methodologies for a Transformed Discipline

Dominic Boyer and George E. Marcus

We aim here to offer a different kind of book about "theory in anthropology." Generally speaking, one would expect from such a project a gathering of theoretical narratives more and less recent, a discussion of major arguments and paradigms, the kind of retrospective or futurological canon-making of which Sherry Ortner's well-known article (1984) remains an exemplary case. Another variation, although perhaps less common in our relatively ecumenical era, is the programmatic manifesto arguing more or less explicitly that "this is what theory should look like in anthropology." But our objective here is not to promote theory or any theoretical approach as such. Nor do we offer an analysis of the latest trends—this book does not explain why, for example, new materialisms, vitalisms, and ecological phenomenologies are roaming anthropological ethnography so boldly of late. Rather, this book tries to take a step back from the assumption that we know *what* "theory" is to investigate *how* "theory"—a phenomenon we regard equally as a matter of concepts, of analytic practice, of medium of value, of professional ideology—operates in anthropology and its kindred human sciences today. We are specifically interested in what kind of object "theory" becomes within the anthropological research process and standard protocols of training anthropologists-in-the-making, where norms, for better or worse, remain focused on individual scholars producing works of ethnography from fieldwork.

This work is a companion to *Fieldwork Is Not What It Used to Be* (Faubion and Marcus 2009), and much like its predecessor, it explores the changing conditions of knowledge-making in anthropology today. Above all, both works are methodological reflections, soundings of how the classic norms and objects of anthropological research and training have become unraveled and reordered in the late twentieth and early twenty-first centuries. The pivotal transformational period began a bit earlier than is often recognized, between 1950 and 1975 when the postwar expansion of higher education and Cold War geopolitical concerns spurred strong growth in, and thematic refocusing of, anthropological research. Although sociocultural anthropology began the middle of the twentieth century as a field science still strongly anchored by community-level and holistic culture studies, less than a generation later the number of practicing anthropologists, the variety of their research engagements, and the scales and processes to which they paid analytical attention had all expanded exponentially. Anthropology, like other human sciences of the era, was enriched through this abundance but also suffered the sense that its disciplinary core was receding or disappearing. Tensions between what the anthropological research community had been and what it was becoming were inevitable. New institutions came to replace the professional conditions that had given us signature ancestors such as Franz Boas, Bronislaw Malinowski, and Margaret Mead. For example, as late as the 1960s advisors could place their advisees in jobs through a phone call and tenure could be earned without a single publication; forty years later, hundreds of applicants compete in a "job market" for every advertised position, and the expectations for scholarly research productivity seem only to grow and grow.

The 1980s offered the first concerted stock-taking of the new conditions of anthropology and anthropologists-in-the-making. The results (e.g., Clifford and Marcus 1986; Marcus and Fischer 1986) were highly important and, at least in retrospect, predictably controversial, although perhaps less for the new anthropological norms to which they were helping to give shape and substance than for a perceived criticism of norms of anthropological writing and thinking past. Interventions such as *Fieldwork,* and now *Theory,* would have been impossible without these opening controversies that legitimated new frameworks of reflexive inquiry. But the present volumes also move toward a fuller reassessment of the methodological implications of the transformation of anthropology. Taken together, *Fieldwork* and *Theory* address how the sacred trinity of anthropological practice—fieldwork, ethnography, and theory—have all changed from the ground up, not least in their relations with each other.

Fieldwork, for example, surfaced and analyzed traditional conceptions of geographically remote and temporally bounded field research in the search for a new "ethics of connectivity" (Faubion 2009). In a parallel way, this volume seeks to trouble a certain expected division of labor between "theory" and "ethnography" in anthropological knowledge (and, by extension, in other disciplines that also make similar distinctions). In this relationship, analytical and representational practices are treated as somehow incommensurable with, and frequently unequal to, each other, creating a robust but often misleading polarization of conceptual and empirical poles of knowing. The consequences of this polarization are unfortunate. By framing discourse on anthropological knowledge, they tend to credit either (1) the prioritization of ethnographic narrative over analytical practice or (2) the functional absorption of ethnographic "data" into some pregiven theoretical paradigm. Both consequences, we think, underuse the epistemic possibilities of this crucial juncture in anthropological knowledge, the rich terrain in the interstices among conceptual/analytical schemata, representations/narratives, and the experiential continuum of fieldwork. Beyond diagnosing a certain impasse in the theory-ethnography relation today, the contributions in this volume begin to experiment with what we might term alternative analytical ethics and to consider what norms might prosper were we to leave a polarized theory-ethnography relation behind in our training practices and in the normal course of professional performance. Our argument is, therefore, that theory can be more than it used to be.

The issue of training is critical because it is the space in which present ethical selves encounter future ethical selves. It is thus a key space of investment for rethinking and remaking our profession's ethical futures. *Fieldwork* focused on the pedagogical context of first research projects and their outcomes in early professional development. This period is also a focus of the present volume, particularly its second half. But we seek, as well, to illuminate the theory-ethnography relation in other contexts of knowledge-making, for example in processes of research design and in the composition of anthropological writing. And, although we most often refer to the professional culture of anthropology in what follows, we believe that this relation resonates widely in other contexts and disciplines. Consequently, we have recruited fellow travelers from disciplines such as science and technology studies and sociology to join us in the first half of the volume.

Theory Matters

"Theory" is obviously a gloss. What counts as theory and theoretical practice is no less obvious and incontestable than what counts as "the field" and fieldwork. But such glosses make for reasonable points of departure in a process of methodological reassessment in that they are already organically interwoven into the contexts into which we seek to intervene. That is to say, for all its limitations, "theory" has the advantage of constituting a well-known coordinate in anthropological practice and pedagogy and a term that a great many anthropologists (as well as other humanists and social scientists) deploy frequently in the routine practices (e.g., researching, writing, reviewing, and mentoring) of professional life. Theory belongs to a cluster of key evaluative categories in trade-talk that pervade the corridors of departments and professional meetings, and that carry even greater weight in the intimate pedagogy of the seminar room and meetings with mentors. Does the job candidate have "theoretical agility"? Is the journal article "theoretically original"? Does the grant application position itself well in terms of "relevant theory?" In other words, like it or not, "theory" matters—not only does it signal the conceptual frames and contexts for the reception of every research project, not only does it index the analytical process that accompanies the often anarchic and kaleidoscopic character of fieldwork activities, but "theory" and "theoretical" also serve as reservoirs of semiotic value and political power in their own right.

So, to reiterate, this volume should not be read as a call for, to, from, or against theory in anthropology. It is, further, not a review of theoretical influences and orientations past or present. Our point of departure is, rather, that theory is a social fact of contemporary anthropological practice, a fact with wide and multiple anchorage in anthropological institutions, routines, discourse, and self-understandings, a fact that we are all, to varying extents, invested in and that we should therefore be interested in as an anthropological problem in its own right, not least because theory plays a vital role in the production and reproduction of anthropological disciplinarity. We note, for example, that every PhD program and a great many undergraduate majors in the United States involve some kind of designated, self-identifying "theory course," in which students are exposed to both a canonical set of texts and to certain modes of conceptual and analytical engagement that are deemed an essential part of an anthropological education. Some of these courses, like the famous Systems sequence at the University of Chicago, are treated as the foundational pedagogical experience of an entire training program.

The importance of theory as social fact in discourse and knowledge demands questions such as: What passes for theory in anthropology and the human sciences today, and why? What is the relation of theory to ethnography? How are students trained to identify and respect anthropological theorization, and how do they practice theoretical work in their later career stages? What is the range of theoretical experiments, languages, and institutions available to us in the human sciences? All these questions point toward how we might consider theory as part of a practical schematics of analytical engagement rather than as a set of ideas, an esoteric discourse of power, a norm of intellectual life, or an infinitely contestable canon of texts.

This seems to us an optimal time to reflect on the status of theory in relation to ethnographic research in anthropology and related disciplines. Reflections, critical and otherwise, on ethnographic and field methods have multiplied over the past twenty-five years, but theory and its entitlements have been less self-consciously probed (see, however, the fascinating and revealing Cerwonka and Malkki 2007). This relative silence is somewhat surprising given the aforementioned importance of theory in disciplinary practices and self-imaginations and given the contemporary expansion of research on professions and other "cultures of expertise," which has provided encouragement for reflexive work on our own modes and methods of knowledge. But the silence is also understandable given the aforenoted polarizing and alienated position of theory in the human sciences. Theory is very often treated as something external to the main enterprise of human scientific research; where it is not indulged outright as a kind of floating world of more fundamental insights and purer concepts, it often appears on the back-end of research projects in the form of citational afterthoughts.

Yet, especially after the inflationary period of interest in "reading theory" (meaning most often certain strands of continental philosophy) from the late 1970s through the mid-1990s, there has been considerable subsequent talk of theoretical impasses and exhaustion of late in our disciplines, talk that has highlighted a certain restlessness with the status quo of our theoretical practices and commitments. This volume takes the latter restlessness seriously (see Boyer and Howe, this volume) but interprets it to some extent as a symptom of the previous absence of metamethodological awareness of theory as a social fact, how it operates in the constitution of research projects and the production of knowledge. At least since the 1980s, it is very clear that theory does not simply inform research but that it is deeply interwoven within all phases of its practice. Paying greater attention to the practice and pedagogy of theory is a crucial completion of the process of methodological reassessment that began in the 1980s, following reflections on ethnography and fieldwork, of anthropology's coming to terms with professional conditions (and an external world!) strikingly different than those in which it developed its classical ambit and method within the human sciences.

As a final (introductory) framing for the work of the volume, we offer a matrix of six categorical distinctions about the uses of theory in contemporary research in anthropology as rough and ready coordinates with which to triangulate the reflections that follow. These categories cross-cut more familiar categorizations in use today: feminist theory, identity theory, globalization theory, postcolonial theory, political economy, and so on. The first three categories concern the positioning of theory within the anthropological research process; the second three emphasize how theory becomes objectified as a thing unto itself.

First the processual positions:

1. Theory as fully inside the research process and not distinguishable from it as a separate function or activity. This is theory merged into method—doing, asking, conversing, reading, amid other research tasks, such as observing and recording. This is theory in lowercase

letters, diagnostic and analytic practices that resist bundling into a singular process.

2. Theory as a separate and superordinate informing discourse and space of epistemic production held in oppositional relation to the granular data collection of fieldwork and to the storytelling of ethnographic case studies. Although theory may be identified as having a presence in fieldwork and ethnography, it has its own separate authority, discipline, and scholarship. The theorist is ultimately someone performing a different kind of productive labor from the fieldworker and ethnographer. The theorist thinks across case studies, finding the transparticular linkages and resonances that lend broader importance to particularities of individual research projects. In contrast, the ethnographer who theorizes is to some extent classified an amateur or at least recognizes theory as its own authoritative sphere.

3. Theory as particular lines of inquiry that make anthropological research distinct. Anthropology has traditionally offered certain sorts of "'big questions"—for example, What is the nature of race? or How do gifts and exchange create social bonds?—that have helped to define it as a discipline that puts ethnography to use to solve important problems. These "big questions," although multiple, subject to many projects of investigation, and changing over time, together offer a distinctive theoretical enterprise that makes ethnography anthropological.

Next, the overlapping categories concerning the objective status of theory:

4. Theory as a body of topical theories specific to anthropology, which has emerged in the long-term reception of specialized ethnographic bodies of work with their distinctive objects and subjects: culture, kinship, ritual, myth, exchange. Figures such as Clifford Geertz or Claude Lévi-Strauss can be viewed as exemplars of anthropological theory, perhaps even as culminations, although the ethnographic archive defines these topics as always renewable and potentially lively frames for renewing the mission of anthropological theory.

5. Theory as the exegetical work of anthropologists within social thought and philosophy on their own voyages of discovery in relation to their ethnographic projects. Here anthropologists are

informed, amateur, and perhaps idiosyncratic interlopers into theory traditions that are the products of other specialized scholarship, especially in philosophy and literary theory. This is called "high theory," connected to the research questions of anthropology but remaining a distinctive separate activity ("doing theory") and claim to knowledge within the discipline.

6.   Theory as specifically connected to the hyperactive period of theory interest across the human sciences from the 1970s through the mid-1990s, a definable cross-disciplinary theory project or two that came to define deeply at a particular juncture what served as "theory" in anthropology—for example, poststructuralism and its derivations. This period defined a theory-driven academic movement with which anthropology became deeply affiliated (before more recently experiencing its post-theoretical backlash).

With these coordinates, we offer a compass for exploring the diversity of ways in which theory is engaged, voiced, and objectified in anthropological research practice today. As we all know, research practice is highly heterogeneous, composed of diverse thematic interests and queries, and a real kaleidoscope of different durations and intensities of effort. Theory can be a central concern in research practice, but more often than not, it remains latent, introduced in the form of cited problems and concepts to help strengthen the authoritative discourse of the ethnographic narrative. Despite this latency, there is more or less continuous informal reflection about this or that theorist "being fashionable" in the discipline at any given moment. There is also, as we hear clearly in the second half of this volume, a strong intuitive sense that, even though theory is important to anthropological and ethnographic knowledge, it exists in an abstract relation to it, a plane of concept and arguments that may be sewn together with ethnography but that do not enjoy an obvious organic relationship to it.

Such ad hoc assessments are important because they constitute the everyday understandings in professional life that orient and legitimate practices. Their rough and ready judgments, however, rarely do factual justice to the diversity of concept work and analytic practice that exists within the discipline (itself not a unitary phenomenon but, rather, a matter of multiple intersecting centers and peripheries). Because we continue to lack serious mappings of current dynamics of anthropological disciplinarity, a major benefit of this volume's attention to how theory operates in anthropological research is to highlight the heterogeneity of anthropological knowing and to reflect on whether anthropology still has order, or points of order, in its proliferation of interests. Invocations of "theory," or "theory talk" as we prefer to say, posit a certain ordering influence in their promise of the existence of higher levels of truth claims beyond the particularities of fieldwork experiences and ethnographic narratives. But when looked at as a matter of analytical practice or method, do these claims hold up? Are there really distinctively anthropological modes of theorization any longer? Or is the more relevant scale of order larger (e.g., the human sciences) or smaller (e.g., the subdiscipline)? We leave these questions unanswered here because they are ruminated upon at greater length and with greater care in the contributions that follow. We simply suggest here that the collaboration of *Fieldwork* and *Theory* on reevaluating fieldwork-ethnography-theory relations provides provocative insights into the complex intellectual history-of-the-present of anthropology.

Organization of the Volume

The organization of the volume is an experiment in its own right. This project began in a symposium held at Rice University in 2009 and simmered for many years through conversations among the contributors before reaching its final form. We strive to capture some of that conversational spirit here on the printed page. The first part of this volume consists of five position papers authored by participants in the original symposium. Each paper offers its own unique point of departure for exploring what to make of "theory" given contemporary conditions of anthropological and ethnographic research. All consider the possibility of a theory of theory-in-use with regard to ethnography and/or fieldwork, but all also strive to perform new analytical ethics.

The specific stakes and arguments of the contributions, as one might expect, vary but overlap in many places. Andreas Glaeser views the theory-ethnography relation as potentially crucial and transformational of human scientific research and public knowledge; thus he calls symmetrically for ethnography to take a central role in theory development and for theory to push ethnography beyond narration. Dominic Boyer and Cymene Howe discuss the mobilization of theory-forms and attempt to rethink theoretical practice for the digital era, sounding new patterns of conceptual mobility and connectivity as anthropological knowledge-making is drawn ever more deeply into a new ecology of information and a new ethics of connectivity. Kim Fortun beautifully narrates how theory can be made to emerge collaboratively within the iterative learning process of ethnographic research design. Likewise, Kaushik Sunder Rajan explores what theorization means in the context of conversation and collaboration, using ethnographic encounters and para-ethnographic entanglements with the biomedical paradigm of "translational research" as his muse. James Faubion offers a provocative, trenchant typology of the elementary forms of theoretical life. George Marcus, in turn, engages Faubion's model of programmatic theory as a "disciplined technology of question formation," launching his own reflections on new electronic and nonelectronic research experiments that can be used to stimulate theoretical imagination and innovation in anthropological knowledge.

All the contributions are further joined by a common spirit of inquiry. Sunder Rajan articulates this well: "I am less interested in what theorists *say* than in what they *do*. I am not concerned with canonization, and even less with the generation of branded concepts that can be packaged into citable modules and circulated as academic currency. Rather, I am interested in *processes of elucidation*—in *theorization.*" A desire to explore theory-in-process and theory-in-practice as modes of knowing that can be unmade and remade, rather than as epic and imposing Knowledge, is the red thread running throughout the first half of the volume.

The second part of this volume circles back to the work of *Fieldwork* in examining the role theory plays in professional training and pedagogy. It consists of three sections. First, we offer six response papers by relatively recent PhDs in anthropology reacting to a set of questions, posed by the editors, prompting our respondents to look back and reflect on the role that "theory"—substantively, ideologically, and affectively—has played in shaping them as scholars from their initial phases of professional formation to their present situations and interests. The opening prompts solicit narratives of first encounters with theory in graduate school and how it was made to relate to the research process in the training context of first fieldwork. Further, we ask how, in our colleagues' various experiences, their ideas about and relations to theory may have changed in the postdoctoral period, however it is spent, and especially what roles and significance theory takes as their careers begin to take shape. We editors are curious about how our interlocutors view the status and privilege of theory talk in contemporary anthropology and whether it seems to them more epistemically significant than "tales of the field" or the critical reception of new ethnographies. Finally, we invite them to explain to us what, in their views, could and should be changed about the relation of anthropology to theory.

Second, we provide three excerpts from a teleconference between the editors and the six authors, in which we collectively work through the issues raised by the papers. What comes across very strongly in the conversations are deep-rooted senses of alienation, ambivalence and anxiety regarding theory as an object of professional entitlement and a goal of professional discipline. The ethics of the turn away from anthropological culture theory and toward resources, such as German critical theory or French poststructuralism in the 1970s and 1980s, no longer seem to be the ethics of contemporary anthropology. "Theory" no longer seems redemptive of the anthropological project in the way it once might have. In response, the third and final section of part II is a short editorial afterword that explores alternative ethics and institutions of pedagogy and training in theory, especially how we might displace the traditional graduate "theory course" from professional training and replace it with greater attention to "analytical method," including both a reflexive-historical approach to engaging works identified as "theory" and an iterative and reflexive design process of analytical experimentation that encourages a more organic interrelationship among field knowledge, ethnographic writing, and concept work.

Part I

Ethnography, Fieldwork, Theorization

1

PORTABLE ANALYTICS AND LATERAL THEORY

Dominic Boyer and Cymene Howe

Anthropological knowledge sprawls, incorporating a dazzling variety of thematics, theoretics, and arguments. What varies less is that this knowledge is always in transit. Anthropologists compose documentations and analyses based on their field travels and then set them into communicative motion, hoping that their work will be engaged, absorbed, cited, and rerouted along invisible trajectories. Epistemic transit itself is not distinctive to anthropology. Citationality and circulation are practices of any number of intellectual professions. What differentiates anthropological knowledge is the crucial expectation that it moves along a continuum where one pole is the elite publicity of northern and western social science and the other is the intimate understanding of some other bundle of life experiences. Anthropology transacts in mobile revelation. Its epistemic movements are designed to surprise, confound, and occasionally even delight the paradigms of northern-western social science by leveraging what Lévi-Strauss once aptly termed "the other message," the knowledge of the not-here that still, fortunately enough, speaks a northern-western language.

Two institutions have helped to cement mobile revelation as a key institution of anthropological knowledge. The first was the general acceptance of Malinowskian field research and field reporting as standards of professional legitimacy in the course of the twentieth century. This standard has proved remarkably durable into the twenty-first century despite the fact that what is understood to be fieldwork has changed significantly (Faubion and Marcus 2009). "The field" can now exist down the block; it can be accessed by a computer interface; it can unfold in surreal montage rather than in neatly bounded realist narrative. In some respects, the epistemic horizons of anthropology have never been wider. Yet what remains crucial is that one reports from an environment that is not entirely one's own, that one mediates or translates between X and Y. Anthropologists individually and anthropology as a disciplinary field consistently delegitimate research that refuses to position itself at an analytical distance from the norms of northern-western social science. For, without distance, however slight and however precarious, there is nowhere to go, no capacity for surprise. Thus, even following the pluralization of anthropological research sites, methods, and objects since the 1970s, we continue to pride ourselves on a capacity for other-messaging, even when "the field" is the office next door and the research subject an intellectual professional very much like oneself.

The second institution is, in a way, the extroversion of the first. When one observes closely what counts as "legitimate anthropological knowledge"—that is, when one reads between the lines of peer reviews and grant-proposal feedback or listens in on departmental meetings, evaluations of job applicants, and the corridor talk of one's colleagues—one realizes quickly that the Malinowskian field report is necessary but never in itself sufficient to guarantee anthropological legitimacy. The field report in its singularity is a case study. It can move, to be sure, but its revelatory power is inactive until it sheds the particularity of the field conditions that gave it form and becomes instead *transparticular*, a study that speaks with other studies, a study that operates as a cryptological key to a larger information set or that repatterns the light and shadow around some broader problem. There are various ways of describing this process of achieving transparticular import, but in the spirit and letter of this volume, we refer to it here as "theory." Anthropological theorization, in our view, is not so much the management of a certain body of concepts as the process of wresting away from an ethnographic case study the cluster of insights that are worth mobilizing. Anthropologists have long recognized a comparative method as an essential and distinctive feature of their knowledge. Even if that method operates now in a more ad hoc fashion, the movement of insights between ethnographic cases still helps to cohere anthropology as a distinctive field of discourse. Anthropological theory thus thrives on the mobilization of transparticular ethnographic insight. When an article or grant proposal is judged to be "theoretically inadequate," what is usually being said is that this case study is either unwilling or unable to give and receive insights of transparticular import. The offending text is not deemed to be just naïve but also, at some level, a sociopath, refusing to recognize that anthropological knowledge demands not only integrity in its case studies but also a restless desire to bridge heres and elsewheres.

Recognizing (1) that anthropological knowledge is designed to travel and (2) that a process of transparticular theorization is a crucial part of its epistemic mobilization raises the question, both analytical and ethical, as to how theory does and should travel in anthropology. In this chapter, we diagnose and discuss some common tendencies of theoretical travel in anthropology today. We take seriously the models of theoretical motion already available to us in the human sciences (especially Edward Said's "traveling theory" and Jean Comaroff and John Comaroff's "theory from the south") and reflect on growing criticism of how theory (particularly grand theory of the philosophical variety and culture theory of the 1970s and 1980s anthropological variety) operates in contemporary anthropological knowledge. In our own performance of mobile revelation, we argue that the current impatience with theory is closely related to new ecologies of digital information. That is, we show how criticism of theory in anthropology today mirrors a wider contemporary disavowal of the radial (e.g., hub-spokes) model of epistemic organization typical of the mid-twentieth century and its reliance on centralized communication infrastructure. We identify in calls for more theory from below or even for the dissolution of theory the rise of a new "lateral" sensibility signaling the desirability of peer-to-peer meshes and mashes of communication that are better adapted to the epistemic potentialities of emergent digital infrastructures such as the Internet and social/mobile media (see, e.g., Golub 2011; Jackson 2012; Kelty 2012). Along the way, we develop our own model of experimental conceptual practice, portable analytics, in which analytic concepts that emerge from within specific ethnographic contexts are mobilized to help

provoke new insights into the forms and forces at work in other ethnographic contexts. The stakes, we believe, are how to allow anthropological
fieldsites and fieldknowledges to interilluminate each other more effectively, generating new revelatory sparks and trajectories in a thickening
mesh of digital-lateral connectivity.

We begin with an example of how anthropological research on epistemic mobility can both confirm the Saidian model of "traveling theory"
and also open the door to portable analysis.

Traveling Theories and Para-theoretical Mobilities

We know through ordinary experience and intuitively that ideas are mod-
ular and concepts have a transmissional life. Acts of transposition across
space and time often yield new insights about the analytic process itself
and, perhaps more important, provide a novel view on something that
seems abundantly familiar. The Greeks used the term *theōros* to designate the man sent by the polis to witness ritual events in other cities. His
travels always began and always ended in the same place, his home. For
the Greeks, theory was "a product of displacement, comparison and a certain distance" (Clifford 1998, 1), but it was also, interestingly enough, tethered to the familiar epistemic space of home. In Edward Said's influential
1982 essay, "Traveling Theory," we find a parallel reflection on the routes
and directions of theoretical passages. Charting an epistemic path through
Europe during the first half of the twentieth century, Said's coordinates
form a theoretical topography that moves from Georg Lukács's Hungary
to Lucien Goldmann's Paris to Raymond Williams's London. He develops a model of knowledge transmission in which theory moves unidirec-
tionally, between senders and targets and from one epistemic location to
another. There is no recursiveness to Said's travel tale; routes never fold
back on themselves. The modes of transmission are linear, cartographi-
cally charted as they move from man to man and author to author, with
each authorial actor relatively secure in the knowledge that his works will
be read and, for the most part, by whom.

But perhaps the "theory effect," as Pierre Bourdieu once put it (1989,
21), is not always exchanged through the influence of authorship. Often

theories cannot be so neatly tracked by a series of citations and evolving academic discussions. Nor are they summarily unilinear in their paths. They
originate somewhere, among some constellation of people, but it is their
transposition that allows for analytic insights on social dynamics in places
near and far. Traveling theories operate in a particular intellectual uni-
verse, largely an academic one, which has its own investments, purposes,
and points of departure. What we describe next as portable analytics, in
comparison, may be, at least initially, less self-consciously theoretical. Indeed, portable analytics are very often para-theoretical; that is, they may do
conceptual work without being explicitly designated, by their originators
or by others, as theoretical projects. They are just as likely, for instance, to
have very pragmatic, political purposes or artistic and aesthetic end points.
However, before elaborating on portable analytics further, let us return,
briefly, to Said's model of traveling theory, which is surely one of the most
elaborated commentaries on theoretical movement available to us.

In his much-acclaimed essay, Said discerned a recurrent pattern among
traveling theories and found that they shared four stages of transmission
and emergence. First, he wrote, "there is a point of origin, or what seems
like one, a set of initial circumstances in which the idea came to birth or entered discourse." Second, "there is a distance transferred, a passage through
the pressure of various contexts as the idea moves from an earlier point
to another time and place where it will come into a new prominence."
Third, "there is a set of conditions—call them conditions of acceptance or,
as an inevitable part of acceptance, resistances—which then confronts the
transplanted theory or idea, making possible its introduction or toleration,
however alien it might appear to be." And fourth, "the now full (or partly)
accommodated (or incorporated) idea is to some extent transformed by its
new uses, its new position in a new time and place" (1982, 226–27). As an
experiment in ethnographically operationalizing Said's model, we turn to
a case study: sexual rights activism in Nicaragua. The theory in motion
is "sexual liberalism." Although many other examples could be retrofit-
ted with the diagnostic apparatus of traveling theory, in this instance we
are seeking to map not only how theories travel both inside and outside
anthropology, and inside and outside particular social settings, but how
mobilizing theory in the north, seeing it reconfigured in the south, and
then turning it north again can inform a more lateralist turn in our theory

work. Put another way, in the case study we chart here we map the Saidian turns at each juncture with the objective of making a reconstituted theoretical "traveler" capable of portable analysis.

Case 1: Sexual Liberalism in Motion

Beginning with the 1979 Sandinista revolution and continuing through the 1980s, Nicaragua was recognized, for a time, as a beacon of anti-imperial resistance. But after the experiment with social and economic equality, Nicaragua instituted socially conservative policies and more profound neoliberal economic restructuring. In 1992, two years after the electoral defeat of the Sandinistas, Nicaragua instituted the most repressive anti-sodomy law in the Americas. Partly in response to the draconian law, sexual politics—in particular liberal rights claims on behalf of *lesbianas, gays, homosexuales, bisexuales, trasvestis,* and others—became an increasingly visible element of the Nicaraguan social ecology. Because Nicaragua had a very explicit history with transnational discourses such as Marxism and liberation theology, among others, the emergence and dissemination of sexual liberalism and sexual politics is not in itself particularly novel. Rather, it is another instance in a series of routes and passages where knowledge and ideological models are appropriated, managed, and reframed. But in this process of distillation, we suggest, a set of propositions are formed that can themselves be ported to new epistemic locations provoking distinctions, juxtapositions, and parallels.

(one) "Coming to Birth/Entering Discourse"   In the global north, the early days of gay and lesbian liberation were founded on principles of both social tolerance and radical transformation. In the 1950s, the homophile movements in the United States and Europe quietly and rather cautiously sought tolerance for homosexuality. This changed dramatically with protests against police repression at the Stonewall bar in New York City in 1969. Gay and lesbian rights proponents began to demand liberation in increasingly public and vocal forms. In so doing, activists employed many of the tools of the second wave of feminism, and more broadly, evoked the political openings and transformations that the civil rights era had begun to achieve. The assertion that individual rights ought to triumph over and against conservative institutions such as the nuclear family and what

Adrienne Rich called "compulsory heterosexuality" (1980, 9) were fundamental aspects of the liberal narrative that animated these politics. Ultimately, claims for equality became codified under the keyword of lesbian and gay pride, a concept that continues to exert its discursive force in contemporary lesbian-gay-bisexual-transgender (LGBT) politics. Indexing categories of family and acts of kinship have been an equally generative political repository in the battle for sexual rights. Like Said's reproductive metaphor suggesting that discourse is "birthed," the thematics of kinship have been influential in framing many of the debates around sexual rights, subjectivity, and policy demands, especially most recently in calls for marriage equality.

(two) "Passage through [to a New] Time, Place, and Prominence"   Nicaragua in the 1980s was a revolutionary place, pursuing a Marxist and nationalist program that was, ideologically, deeply committed to principles of social equality even if these goals were never fully executed. In the mid-1980s, while the country was being besieged by a counterinsurgency war sponsored by the United States, a small group of lesbian and gay identified women and men founded the Nicaraguan Gay Movement. Their meetings involved discussing their lives and the limitations placed on them for their sexual difference. Partly influenced by their interactions with gays and lesbians from North America and Europe who had traveled to Nicaragua in support of the revolution, the group sought to establish new, respectable identity categories to counter the derogatory monikers of *cochón* ("fag") and *cochona* ("dyke"). Beyond claiming a "lesbian" or "homosexual" identity personally, members of the Nicaraguan Gay Movement were also invested in locating a space for sexual rights within the political ideology of the greater Sandinista state project. The relatively quiet sexual politics of the 1980s were replaced with more overt claims for sexual justice when, following the end of the Sandinista state in 1990, the country ushered in a series of neoliberal governments and a set of reforms to the penal code that raised the penalties, and the stakes, for same-sex sexuality. The 1992 anti-sodomy law indicted not only men but women as well; the scope of the law was vast, including even those who were "promoting" or "propagandizing" (and of course practicing) same-sex sexuality. Although the law saw little enforcement, it became a rallying point for diverse activists, from feminists to disenchanted Marxists, and protest against the law

galvanized the contemporary sexual rights *lucha* ("struggle") in Nicaragua (Howe 2013). In Said's terms, liberal rights had achieved, under the sign of sexuality, a new "prominence" through two different sorts of passages: one in an ideological register of rights and the other in the penal potency of law.

(three) "Acceptance, Resistance, Introduction, and Toleration"   By the 1990s, Nicaraguan sexual rights activists had expanded their demands for equality. The country was being inundated with development projects of various stripes, many of them animated by human rights principles. Perhaps unsurprisingly, activism for sexual equality and tolerance gravitated toward the elusive beacon of modernity and liberal thought that human rights seemed to hold. For some Nicaraguan activists, the terms of gay and lesbian pride (*orgullo lésbico-gay*) offered a promising set of ideals and social principles. Clearly, this move shared more than a little discursive kinship with the political rhetoric that was, and continues to be, important in the United States. In a very public and visible way, this was a period when the concept of sexual equality, identity and rights became the subject of various forms of "acceptance, resistance, introduction, and toleration" across the Nicaraguan political milieu. This toleration was, it is important to note, not manifested in full social equality for sexual minorities. Discrimination remained within families, in the schools, and in many places of employment. Nevertheless, in a discursive and traveling theoretical mode, these logics had settled in.

(four) "The Accommodated Idea Is Transformed by Its New Uses and Position in a New Time and Place"   As traveling theories of sexual liberalism became resituated in a new time and place, the struggle for sexual rights in Nicaragua became more complex. Some Nicaraguan sexual rights activists adopted discourses of Lesbian and Gay Pride and, in addition, harnessed the moral values associated with human rights. Other activists engaged a formulation that proved to be the most efficacious register for sexual rights advocacy in Nicaragua, which they called *"una sexualidad libre de prejuicios"* ("A Sexuality Free from Prejudice"). Sexuality Free from Prejudice makes an easily assimilable proposition, namely (and according to a document regularly circulated among activists to frame their project) that "there is sexual diversity among human beings" and "this diversity is an

undeniable right." Rather than emphasizing discrimination against sexual minorities or focusing attention on gay and lesbian subjectivity in a definitional form, many sexual rights advocates instead favored a broader approach. In part, this multiculturalist impulse can be read through the lens of liberalism and its progeny. But Sexuality Free from Prejudice equally reflects the Marxist values that fueled the Sandinista revolution. It is predicated on broad social transformation and an attempt to create a tolerant sexual logic for the Nicaraguan nation as a whole rather than simply ensuring the rights of individual marginalized sexual subjects. Sexuality Free from Prejudice takes a step beyond, or adjacent to, Lesbian and Gay Pride by insinuating that some form of sexual pride is part of the general human condition. It is a biopolitical move to establish that everyone not only has "a" sexuality but, more important, a right to it. As it turns out, the composite projects of sexual rights activists, from pride to prejudice, appear to have yielded results. Following a decade and a half of political work and advocacy, the anti-sodomy law was ultimately overturned by the Nicaraguan National Assembly, and new legal codes now prohibit discrimination against sexual minorities. Nicaragua has adopted the trappings of a "new time and place" for sexual rights. Is it free from prejudice? Not quite. Yet it is a place that has seen its share of traveling theories and that has also demonstrated, at the political level, the ability to recast their forms and functions.

The fact that liberal politics and rights have been an important component of civil society activism is a story that could be retold in many sites and idioms. It is, on one level, a diffusionist tale that is not remarkable or unexpected. That political rhetorics and strategies have a global life of their own and are amenable to the quadripartite definition that Said inscribed three decades ago is a testament to the accuracy (and amplitude) of his schema, just as it is a testament to the circulatory powers of neoliberalism and globalization. But it is also clear that the political forms articulated in Nicaragua have their own migratory merit, ways in which their reconstituted logics can be reported to other contexts and perform evaluative work in those settings. The trick is to find points of transparticular correspondence. Since the emergence of the comparative method, from the early twentieth century to the present, anthropologists have often been surrogates for the movement of native theories. But extracting ethnographically particular knowledges and declaring their legibility and legitimacy in other settings is a complicated proposition. Most anthropologists would refuse to be complicit in simply mapping one set of temporal and locational sensibilities to another place and time without fully elaborating the contingencies of each. These transpositions are never simple, yet we believe it is important to make the effort. In the case of Nicaragua, for example, how might Sexuality Free from Prejudice encourage us to re-imagine queer politics in the global north? How might sexual subjectivity that has emerged through Marxist praxis and refuses explicit identitarian ascription be a useful analytic to reframe the parochial limits of western liberalism and theorizations of sexuality elsewhere?

The story of same-sex marriage offers a case in point. Marriage equality has been a focal battle fueling the politics of sexuality in the United States, constituting one of the front lines in the so-called "culture wars." Whether same-sex marriage ought to be legal and whether this issue ought to be the primary goal of the contemporary LGBT movement are questions that have, from very different political perspectives, caused a fair amount of discord. Marriage equality has been institutionalized in many parts of the world, including several European countries and South Africa, Argentina, and Brazil, among others. Individual states in the United States have also found variable success in legislating same-sex marriage provisions, with the 2013 Supreme Court ruling on the Defense of Marriage Act opening further possibilities for modifying marriage law. Each of these cases, whether national or state-legislated, has ensured that same-sex couples have a legal right to marry, allowing them to access the legal, fiscal, and moral benefits that follow from this status. As queer theorists and queer political activists have pointed out for some time, however, leveraging the efforts and resources required for marriage equality is a very particular investment, one that may come at the expense of other queer political priorities, such as addressing poverty among queerfolk; preventing homelessness for queer youth; or ameliorating racism, sexism, and capitalist domination more generally. For some, the drive toward marriage equality simply re-iterates a "heteronormative" (Rubin 1975; Warner 1991) impulse, a set of values that privileges heterosexual pairings and institutions, and naturalizes their rights and entitlements (Berlant and Warner 1998; Cohen 2005). Ultimately, this may foster the production of a mimetic form of politics, "homonormativity," in which dominant heteronormative assumptions and institutions are upheld and sustained (Duggan 2003, 50). Advocates of a queered politics of subjectivity and sexuality have questioned the wisdom of devoting so much energy to obtaining the right to participate in a heterosexually inscribed, legally encumbered, and (de facto) monogamous dyadic pairing instead of promoting a more general tolerance for sexual diversity. Why not rally for a sexuality that is not dependent on identity and promote a form of sexual tolerance that is more expansive than that allowed under the aegis of marriage and other reproductive logics? Or taking the formulation of Nicaraguan activists, why not advocate for Sexuality Free from Prejudice?

The grammar of sexual rights in Nicaragua demonstrates how liberal theories of gay liberation and human rights emerged in the north, traveled south, and ultimately found a new articulation, adaptation, and purpose. To take this pivot one turn further—to port the analytic—is to imagine how these theories might effectively recondition the way that sexuality is imagined, theorized, and given political life elsewhere. Mobilizing theoretical labors of the south and pushing them northward is not in itself an entirely new project. Jean Comaroff and John Comaroff, among others, have charted a similar passage. Following in the postcolonial intellectual tradition of Homi Bhabha, Dipesh Chakrabarty, Achille Mbembe, and Gayatri Spivak, they have revived a call to theorize from the south. This involves a substantial repositioning of the generative project of theory making to, as Homi Bhabha puts it, its "ex-centric" sites (1994, 177). For the Comaroffs, the African continent is a paradigmatic case where daily life, history, and social genealogies are not securely tethered to the (suspect) veracity of the Enlightenment project. As they see it, modernity has always been a north-south collaboration, even if deeply disparate in its origins and outcomes. Writing against modernist conceits, they ask, what would happen if, instead of treating the quotidian realities of social and political life in the global south as "raw fact," we instead imagined its possibilities for "theory work" (Comaroff and Comaroff 2011, 6)? Reading the contingencies of the global south against the contemporary crises of Euro-America allows us to recursively reframe the teleological march of capitalist modernity, among other things. With portable analytics, however, we are advocating the further lateralization of these movements to probe the transparticular potentialities of various ethnographic specificities—sometimes moving from the south to the north, or from the east to the west, but just as easily going north, south, and then north again.

As it responds to queer critiques of hetero- and homonormativity (and, at least in the Nicaraguan case, has been efficacious in changing social policy), Sexuality Free from Prejudice offers a recombinant form of sexual subjectivity in both political and theoretical registers. Many lesbian and gay rights politics and advocacy practices have sought to guarantee the right to choose a sexual and affective life that is not bound by prejudice. But several global sexual rights movements currently in circulation have also invested in the protection of property rights and securing the financial interests of queer people. Sexuality Free from Prejudice offers a challenge to these sorts of autologics and their emphasis on fiscal matters and liberal individualism. Mobilizing the conceptual possibilities offered by Sexuality Free from Prejudice allows for a different set of sensibilities, fostering a relationality that is not based on dyadic pairs, financial obligations, and ascriptions to identity. It instead responds to networked logics of human relationships and reckons liberation in ways that go beyond individual subjects and individual couples. At the same time, Sexuality Free from Prejudice departs from more radical tenets of queer theorizing and politics because at its core it is a quest for social and legal assimilation. In this way, Sexuality Free from Prejudice offers more than a political tactic; it presents a unique analytic position of its own. It is not reasoned solely through lesbian and gay minority politics or grounded in the idioms of identity. But is it not precisely queer either.

The portable analytic that we mobilize in Sexuality Free from Prejudice is a peripatetic intellectual resource because it uncovers the paradoxes and tensions of two very different sorts of sexual rights discourses—both queer and liberal identitarian. It signals destabilizations and cracks in each of their naturalizing logics and, in turn, disrupts the concentrated authorities of northern and western liberal epistemologies. It performs an intellectual exercise by translating a Marxian paradigm into the register of human rights that lets us test, query, and experiment with political and intellectual formulas. Appropriations of Marxism and liberal rights in the Nicaraguan case are, in one instance, traveling theory and, in their passage back, "theory from the south." But in aggregate, this case suggests an analytic that can be transported laterally in a variety of directions. Portable analytics, as we are imagining them, are more flexibly directional than theory from the south and less bound to the world of letters than traveling theory. Rather than an optic from the antipodes or a telephone game between great minds, portable analytics follow ethnographic life, inviting a lateral meshwork of thought respun to create agile links, not only across space and time but across different kinds of intellectual practice, academic and otherwise, including political tactics, artistic interventions, and other varieties of creative assemblages.

Lateralist Discontent and Portable Analytics

As already noted, something seems awry with theory today. One hears increasing unease among anthropologists about the legacy of the 1980s and 1990s' turn away from distinctively anthropological theory—a tradition often imagined as culminating in the 1960s and 1970s culture theory of figures such as Clifford Geertz, Marshall Sahlins, and David Schneider—and toward continental (particularly French) theory as the dominant conceptual apparatus of the field. A popular vein of criticism is that the sacrifice of a distinctively anthropological tradition of theory has undermined our disciplinary ability to practice unique forms of concept work within the human sciences. David Graeber provides an excellent example of this position in the context of his announcement of a new open-access online journal, *HAU,* a project that also seeks to reinvigorate anthropological or "ethnographic theory" as a distinctive epistemic practice:

> Contemporary anthropology often seems a discipline determined to commit suicide. Where once we drew our theoretical terms—"totem," "taboo," "mana," "potlatch"—from ethnography, causing Continental thinkers from Ludwig Wittgenstein to Sigmund Freud and Jean-Paul Sartre to feel the need to weigh in on the resulting debates, we have now reduced ourselves to the scholastic dissection of terms drawn from Continental philosophy (deterritorialization, governmentality, bare life . . .)—and nobody else cares what we have to say about them. And honestly, why should they—if they can just as easily read Deleuze, Agamben, or Foucault in the original? A project like *HAU* is exactly what's needed to begin to reverse this bizarre self-strangulation. It is a journal that dares to defy the Great Man theory of intellectual history, to recognize that most ordinary human beings, the world over, have just as much to say about love, time, power, and dilemmas of human existence as any paid philosophers, and that sometimes, their reflections can be decidedly more interesting. It proposes anthropologists

return to the kind of conversations with which we began, except this time, as equals, and that we have a moral responsibility to make the results freely available to everyone, the world over.[1]

On the one hand, this is a far from uncontestable representation of the current state of affairs in anthropology. Is "disciplinary suicide" not an overdramatization of a field that, regardless of what is happening with its theory, continues to enjoy robust intellectual activity and relevance across the world? But such complaint rather misses the point. Graeber's discourse, articulated not incidentally by one of the more impressive theorists of his generation (e.g., Graeber 2011), is a rallying cry. It invokes traditional anthropological suspicions regarding the epistemic parochialism of northern-western Great Men. But, most important from our perspective, it also captures the Zeitgeist of disenchantment with theory in anthropology. His particular vision may sound somewhat nostalgic for an era ended. But nostalgia is a politics of the future (Boyer 2006), and this Zeitgeist has more obviously presentist and futurist expressions as well. For example, another important theorist of his anthropological generation, Bill Maurer, criticizes the search for "(dated) grand theory about something" (2005, 35) and instead emphasizes the need to look more deeply into the "dense lateralizations that obtain between subjects and objects of inquiry" (xv). Maurer defines this space of "transacting . . . parallel knowledges" as the focus of properly anthropological experimentation. Here, too, theory is problematic if it interrupts ethnographic adjacency and singularity, if it performs a "monopoly in the market for truth" (16) rather than a status of one kind of mobile "lateralization" (17) among many. Paul Rabinow has advocated a move from theory to the analytic temporality of "adjacency," by which he means "neither the overdrive of the universal intellectual nor the authoritative precision of the specific. Rather: the space of problems. Of questions. Of being behind and ahead. Belated or anticipatory. Out of synch. Too fast or too slow. Reluctant. Audacious. Annoying" (2007, 39). Remarking on the incapacity of Sahlinsian culture theory to handle novel happenings in the world, Rabinow writes that "it is only that so much effort has been devoted in the name of social science to explaining away the emergence of new forms as the result of something else that we lack adequate means to conceptualize the forms/events as the curious and potent singularities that they are" (1999, 182). Indeed, Rabinow's position seems to be the inverse

of Graeber's. For Rabinow, the worst thing anthropology can do is to continue to pretend as though anthropological culture theory constituted a
universalist achievement and monopoly on truth; this would be damnation
through eternal repetition.

So what, if anything, unites this field of discontent? We argue that these
three examples share a dissatisfaction with a practice of theory in which a
limited set of theoretical categories (whether drawn from culture theory or
French poststructuralism) are used to define and bind the possible forms
of anthropological knowledge. *Theory* is defined in each case as a monopo-
lizing epistemic authority, whether in the form of the universal authority
of European philosophy or in the name of the professional authority of
anthropological tradition. One finds here the rejection of what we would
term a radial organization of theory, a model in which a surplus of epistemic authority emanates from a limited number of broadcast points, generating largely hub-spokes, unidirectional flows of messaging. Such flows
might have their uses. For example, their conceptual and citational econo-
mies of scale could offer communicative coherence to a field of knowledge.
But the critics hold that what we are terming radial theory ultimately un-
dermines the anthropological enterprise. Why? Because radial theory is
believed to restrict epistemic innovation and distinctiveness (especially in
the margins of northern-western sociality in which anthropologists often
conduct their business) while reinforcing at the same time the norms and
forms of northern-western epistemic authority. Radial theory, in other
words, can explain everything, but it is always the same answer. Thus,
however "grand" it may purport to be, it seems an increasingly tedious
and suspect exercise. The discontent expressed articulates a desire for theory that is better attuned to the knowledges emerging from the work of
ethnography, for theory that, to use Maurer's phrase, "lateralizes" more
effectively. We argue that this is an increasingly doxic feeling today in anthropology. But why, and why now?

Put plainly, this is critique for the digital era. Today's theoretical criticism in the human sciences is not the same as Said's, for whom, as we
have noted, the directionality and organization of messaging remained
relatively unproblematic. Said was most interested in highlighting the
contingencies of meaning and the processes of reappropriation as theory
moved along its radial corridors. But for the anthropologists we have just
discussed, the underlying problem is the organization of messaging itself.

In our view, the institutionalization of Internet-based communication has prompted new practices and aspirations for anthropological knowledge-making, new epistemic dispositions, if you will (see Kelty et al. 2008). It is thus not incidental that Graeber's intervention appears in the context of an open-access, online journal, a project that is precisely seeking to multiply lateral lines of research communication beyond a radialist credentialing cartel of "journals of record," most of whose content is captured by the paywalls of corporate publishing. What seems nostalgic about Graeber's vision for *HAU* could be viewed instead as a kind of steampunk appropriation of older anthropological theory in the name of arriving at the same kind of experimental ethos that Maurer and Rabinow call for.

Because, to the best of our knowledge, no one has yet directly connected the rising dissatisfaction with the state of theory in anthropology to the rising awareness of the possibilities and realities of anthropological knowledge-making in the Internet era, we reiterate: a lateralist revolution in anthropological knowledge is arriving, building on the multi-directional, peer-to-peer capacities of the Internet, social media, and mobile media. There was a broadcast era of academic knowledge that is currently being undermined from within and without by a new media ecology, just as other broadcast institutions (e.g., newspapers, television, and radio) find themselves today in a state of crisis and reimagination. As a conservative intellectual profession like many others, anthropology has been relatively late in recognizing its own process of transformation. Yet the messages coming from anthropologists deeply engaged in digital culture have been unequivocal that the practice and organization of knowledge is being reshaped, in some ways profoundly, by the saturation of all aspects of northern professional intellectual life with digital communication and information technology (Boellstorff 2008; Boyer 2013; Coleman and Golub 2008; Kelty 2009; Miller 2011). Anthropologists are now screenworkers as much as fieldworkers, relying on digital data archives, on computers, on word-processing software, and search functions; and using e-mail, social media, and mobile telephonic data devices continuously. Anthropological research unfolds in a fast-time informatic continuum in which the lines between fields, offices, and homes are increasingly blurred. At the level of mundane practice, the impact of the digital revolution on the techniques of anthropological research and communication has been enormous. Yet the changes have transpired so quickly that it has been difficult to come to terms with their broader implications for the epistemic practice of anthropology. The open-access issue—the question of how to share all published anthropological knowledge—is an excellent case in point; we have been slow to disrupt an inherited conservative radiality that seems drastically at odds with the oft-stated desire for anthropological knowledge to travel more widely and impactfully in the world.

If one accepts that the unease regarding theory in anthropology today expresses a lateralist chafing against the legacies of radial institutions of knowledge-making, then the next question is to ask, what might lateral theory look like? We do not feel that an answer to this question has yet crystallized, although experiments in lateral theorizing appear to be multiplying rapidly (e.g., Choy et al. 2009; Fischer 2007; Helmreich 2009; Ingold 2011; Fortun, this volume). Although we do not pretend to be able to imagine lateral theory as a singularity (that would be a radialist exercise in itself), in the remainder of this chapter we further unpack the experimental modality of lateral theory that we term portable analytics. As previously noted, the goal of portable analytics is to help elicit the desired mesh of lateral analytical flows with the effect of helping to disperse the surplus authority of any particular theoretical tradition and language. The basic procedure of portable analysis is to locate analytical concepts within ethnographic contexts that help us to objectify or epitomize the forces and forms at work there, and then to dislocate and mobilize these concepts for experimental use elsewhere. We think that nurturing such mobility and linkages has the potential not only to generate new and distinctively anthropological concept work but to offer unusually provocative insights, especially when the common polarities of epistemic travel are reversed (just as the Comaroffs and Graeber advocate).

What follows is a second case of portable analysis in action.

Case 2: *Stiob* as Portable Analytic

In another collaborative research project with Alexei Yurchak, Dominic Boyer has been exploring the juxtaposition of late socialist aesthetics of parody with contemporary U.S. popular and political culture (Boyer and Yurchak 2010). The relevant portable concept here is *stiob*, which is a Russian slang term for a particular late-Soviet technique of parodic overidentification, the method of which was to inhabit the form of authoritative discourse so perfectly that it was impossible to tell whether the imitative performance was ironic or sincere. *Stiob* was particularly germane to late Soviet socialism because of the communist party-state's obsessional emphasis on the formal orthodoxy of its discourse. As Boyer has discussed elsewhere (2003) with respect to censorship in East Germany, late socialist states typically invested considerable energy into the formalization of languages of political communication as a means of constituting perfected socialist consciousness. Yet the main achievement of late-socialist authoritative discourse was most often the expert overcrafting of every aspect of language. Reading front-page articles in *Pravda* or *Neues Deutschland* or any other central party newspaper in the 1970s, one encountered an exceedingly technical, cumbersome, and not seldom absurd language filled with long sentences, proliferating nominal structures, perplexing passive constructions, and repetitive phraseological formulations. If one listened to speeches of local communist youth leaders, one heard texts that sounded uncannily like quotations from previous texts written by their predecessors (which is, in fact, precisely how they were produced). The pressure was always to adhere to the precise norms and forms of already existing authoritative discourse, and to minimize subjective interpretation or voice. Yurchak (2006) terms the result of this pressure "hypernormalization," a snowball effect of the layering of the normalized structures of authoritative discourse on themselves. Political discourse largely ceased to have an indicative relationship to external reality and became increasingly absorbed with its own performance.

Under such conditions, an aesthetics of *stiob* made sense. Faced with authoritative discourse that already caricatured its alleged purpose, *stiob* did not engage it on the level of literal meanings (because socialist discourse often had little indicative relationship to the world around it). Instead, the *stiob* parodic technique of overidentification mirrored the discursive overformalization of the socialist state. There was also a tactical advantage in that, although the state easily identified and isolated any overt form of oppositional discourse as a threat, recognizing and disciplining the critical potential of overidentification was more difficult because of its formal resemblance to the state language. Also, unlike more overt forms of dissidence and critique, overidentification with state rhetoric did not require one to wholly distance oneself from communist idealism. For this reason, *stiob* rarely occupied or promoted recognizable political positions—it operated outside the familiar axes of political tension between party and opposition, between socialism and liberalism, aware of these axes but uninvested in them.

The hypernormalization of discourse in the late socialist party-state can thus be interpreted as enabling the performativity of *stiob*. Boyer and Yurchak then mobilize their analysis of late-socialist *stiob* to explore its capacity to expose the norms of forms in late liberal political discourse as well. Using *stiob* as a kind of conceptual compass, they work through a variety of recent instances of overidentifying parody in western popular and political culture (e.g., "fake" news television shows such as *The Daily Show* and *The Colbert Report*, the activist hoax group The Yes Men, the parody newspaper *The Onion*, and so on), which they term experimentally, "American stiob" (Boyer and Yurchak 2010). They conclude that the lateral mobilization of *stiob* helps to reveal how the changing institutional and mediational organization of political culture in the United States (and elsewhere) has consolidated discursive conditions analogous in certain respects to late socialist hypernormalization. For example, Boyer and Yurchak highlight that the increasing monopolization of broadcast media production and circulation and the adaptation of news journalism to digital media have actually made political and economic news content significantly more homogeneous and experientially repetitive. They examine how the general professionalization of political life and the rising importance of 24/7 news cycles for political communication have made political performance in the United States increasingly calculated and formalized, invested more in repetitive messaging than in riskier forms of political debate and communicational improvisation. Finally, they look at how in the 1970s and 1980s the increasing delegitimation of both socialism and social democracy led (neo)liberal political discourse into ever tightening loops of monological self-reference. Liberalism has increasingly meant the freedom to express a limited set of convictions as witnessed, for example, in the 2012 U.S. presidential election when two fundamentally economically neoliberal and politically conservative parties struggled to perform difference elsewhere in their platforms.

The authors do not claim, however, that late-socialist *stiob* and "American stiob" are exactly analogous, just as the political forces generating hypernormalization in the two cases differ considerably. Much as Said noted, theory should and does transform through travel. Moreover, portable analysis does not seek to transmit exact conceptual replicas from point to point, as in radial theory. Like other lateralist experiments in anthropology, the purpose of porting analytics is to stage collaboration between fieldsites and fieldknowledges, to reveal differences as well as samenesses, through precise but partial illumination. For example, in the case of *stiob*, its mobilization from late Soviet Russia to the late liberal United States allows us to develop analytic homologies between the ethnographic case studies that we might not otherwise see without a conceptual spark jumping ahead to guide our way. When *stiob* is embedded in the ethnography of contemporary U.S. political culture, it contains enough diodic glow to illuminate how discursive hypernormalization is rising in late liberalism, producing the very kinds of repetitive messaging and standardized modes of political performance and communication on which *stiob*-esque metapolitical parodists such as Colbert and The Yes Men thrive.

Portable analysis is exploratory and experimental in this way; and, as noted, it should be mobilized in multiple directions for best results. For example, porting *stiob* to another elsewhere we find that there is also "Icelandic stiob," a further mutation in the form of what was perhaps the world's most successful "joke party," Besti Flokkurrin (the Best Party), whose self-described "anarcho-surrealist" leader, Jón Gnarr, was elected mayor of Reykjavík in 2010. In the aftermath of a terrifying collapse of the Icelandic banking system, currency, and economy in 2008, Gnarr described the Best Party as an effort to provoke a "cultural revolution" in Iceland. All the major political parties in Iceland had, in one form or another, supported the political establishment that had engineered the collapse. A conservative government had deregulated the banks and allowed them to take on massive debt. The succeeding government then tried to hold the Icelandic people accountable for the debts amassed by the bankers. As in late socialism, it seemed as though Icelandic liberal democracy had ceased, in any way, to be accountable to its citizens or to offer any alternative to creditor-friendly neoliberal policy. This situation, Gnarr explained, is what provoked him and his colleagues to action: "Political discourse is all dead and vapid. I've never been interested in governance or politics. . . . I've listened to all the empty political discourse, but it's never touched me at all or moved me, until the economic collapse. Then I just felt I'd had enough of those people. . . . I started reading the local news websites and watching the news and political talk shows—and it filled me with so much frustration. . . . So I wanted to do something, to fuck the system. To change it around and impact it in some way" (Magnússon 2010).

A *stiob* sensibility in Gnarr's and his collaborators' language is quite clear—the assertion of the emptiness of political discourse, the disinterest of the Best Party in traditional political labels and ideologies, the recourse to overidentifying parody (or, in Gnarr's terms, "fun") as a more efficacious mode of disrupting an ossified political system than conventional opposi- tional politics. These emphases carried over into what news media often glossed as a "mock" political platform. The Best Party's ten-point platform was composed of thirteen points and included statements such as "3. Stop corruption: We promise to stop corruption. We'll accomplish this by par- ticipating in it openly" and "10. Free access to swimming pools for everyone and free towels: This is something that everyone should fall for, and it's the election promise we're most proud of." Gnarr repeatedly promised a polar bear for the Reykjavík zoo. The Best Party platform was popularized through an Internet campaign video to the tune of Tina Turner's *Simply the Best* that circulated widely in Iceland. In the video, collaboratively produced with several prominent Icelandic musicians, the Best Party either satirizes the traditional form of the political campaign video or presents a sincere po- litical message. At the climax of the video, Gnarr is seen shouting from the top of a building in Reykjavík that represented the worst spending excesses of the precrash period, demanding a "Drug Free Parliament by 2020."

Over time, in a variety of other speaking engagements, it became evident that several elements of the Best Party platform obliquely referenced signifi- cant social, political, and environmental issues facing Iceland and the world. The polar bear for the zoo addressed, for example, climate change and the current Icelandic policy to shoot polar bears that swam to Iceland to avoid melting ice farther north. The free towels at swimming pools was aimed at developing European tourism, invoking an obscure EU regulation that, for a pool to be classified as a "spa," free towels had to be provided. The drug-free parliament referenced an extended rhetorical analogy that Gnarr later elabo- rated that the relationship of Icelandic political culture to the nation was one of a substance-abusing father to his injured yet enabling family. But Gnarr consistently refused to state, either before or after winning the election, that the Best Party held any political ideology in the conventional sense. In his first presentation of a city budget in December 2010, Gnarr commented, "What kind of party is The Best Party? I don't really know. We are not a proper political party. We are maybe more of a self-help organization, like Alcoholics Anonymous. We try to take one day at a time, to not overreach our boundaries and to maintain joy, humility and positive thinking. . . . Our motto is: humanity, culture and peace. We do not foster any other ideals or political visions. We do not share a predetermined, mutual ideology. We are neither left nor right. We are both. We don't even think it matters."

Today the Best Party no longer exists. But there are still observers in Iceland and beyond who debate whether the Best Party was a serious political intervention or some form of protest performance art. Gnarr himself continues to refuse the idea that any clear distinction can be drawn between parody and sincerity in the political practice of the Best Party. The analytic of *stiob* helps us to pinpoint the tactical character of this ambivalence as a means of highlighting (and perhaps remediating) the monopolization of political discourse. Gnarrian *stiob* seems at once a genuine effort to inhabit the norms and forms of liberal representational politics yet also a performative denial of the adequacy of those forms for guaranteeing democratic rights and freedoms. In the Best Party's turn toward a ludic model of political action, we perhaps even see, as in the Nicaraguan case, a new epistemic mutation of liberalism.

So, to close, the experiment of using *stiob* as a portable analytic allows for the "interillumination" (Bakhtin 1981) of the conditions and effects of overformalized political discourse in late-socialist and late-liberal societies. It enables anthropologists to explore how and why authoritative discourse in contemporary U.S. and Icelandic political cultures has come to enable a *stiob*-like performativity of its own, a project that Boyer and Yurchak hope will allow for more extensive study of the phenomenon of form in contemporary northern political cultures. This opening was created by the lateral mobilization of categories and concepts originating outside North America and Western Europe as a means of providing fresh insight into their political cultures. In a simple sense, the United States and Iceland have not, or not yet, originated their own native terms for *stiob*. Yet when the Russian concept is ported into these contexts, homologies become visible that then permit deeper mapping, exploration, and comparison.

Conclusion: Lateral Theory and Radial Remains

We have sought in this chapter to both diagnose and advocate emergent theoretical trends in anthropology. On the diagnostic front, we have discussed why the epistemic work of theory remains crucial for anthropology, yet explored reasons why theory of a certain kind seems increasingly problematic today. On the advocatory front, we have argued that because a transformation of theory is already underway in anthropology—with the critique of universalist (radialist) theory being an important part of the transformation—what is needed now is more self-awareness and experimentation in the development of new lateralist modalities of theory.

We hope that it is by now obvious why we do not want to close our discussion of portable analysis—our own modest contribution to the broader field of lateralist experiments already underway in anthropology—with a universalist model of lateral theory. Our objective here has not been to define a new concept "lateral theory" so much as to suggest a language through which to discuss a phenomenon already in the making. In an important respect, lateralization means rebalancing the relationship between concept and method in our analytical work. It is not that concepts are no longer important in anthropological analysis; rather, their provisional and processual character is highlighted, meaning that the method of doing generative concept work becomes more important than the integrity of any concept or paradigm per se. The long-term goal is not to innovate new universal categories or to perfect paradigms. Rather, the point is to further develop and refine anthropological theorization today as the effort to work between transparticular and particular knowledges, developing techniques of frame formation and frame dissolution, as an art in itself. Anthropologists today are beginning to adapt their epistemic enterprise of transparticular connectivity to the potentialities of our new media ecology. This ecology offers unprecedented capabilities of informational archiving and searchability, textual plasticity and intertextual linkage, and fast-time physical and informational mobility. Theory in the radial mode incorporated the fixity of print language and the signal strength and purity of broadcasting. Theory in the lateral mode is growing into the informational elasticity, speed, and noise of the digital era. One could, of course, lament this state of affairs. But one could also work to extend and improve what seems to us to be a very creative process of transformation that has the potential to expand the reach and impact of anthropological knowledge massively.

To focus once more on our examples of portable analytics, we have already shown their potential to interlink the epistemic work of artists, political actors, and anthropologists. There is no reason to stop there.

The procedure could just as easily be used to make connections between the epistemic work of religion and of science or between any number of other ways of knowing. Like other experiments in lateralization, portable analysis prioritizes flexible, multidirectional, and plural connectivities that can help accelerate epistemic exchange and partnership between anthropologists and their interlocutors, both in the field and elsewhere in the humanities, social sciences, and sciences. As per Graeber's call, it can make everyday knowledge theoretical, but it can also spark new synapses between different cultures of expertise by mobilizing concepts in unexpected directions and at unusual velocities. Lateralization thus has the capacity to broaden and deepen flows of knowledge between anthropologists and their research subjects, to support new designs of knowledge-making.

Our final point is cautionary: even though the content of anthropological theory is rapidly incorporating lateralist sentiments, we should not be too quick to congratulate ourselves. The potential of greater lateral connectivity guarantees little on its own without the development of new institutions to support it. At the moment, the broader implications of lateral theory continue to be muted by the enduring strength of radialist (and preradialist) institutions such as, for example, disciplinary standards of solo proprietary authorship and a model of research communication that remains reliant on a limited number of privileged, paywalled journals. We believe that, for lateral theory to actually become something other than a lateralist aesthetics of radial theory, it needs to become an ethical as well as a conceptual intervention. This is not just a question of confronting the ethics of theory as much as what Faubion (2009) has called the broader "ethics of connectivity" in anthropology today. Portable analysis and lateral theory would be optimalized in an intellectual environment oriented by open-access institutions (meaning that all anthropological research communication should be freely and publicly available) and supportive of multiresearcher collaboration and multiauthor experimentation. True to its digital environs, lateral theory wants to share analytic code, to mash and to mesh, to use techniques such as portable analysis to actually make fieldsites and field-knowledges co-present and interactive in ways that will transform and enrich anthropological epistemic practice. In short, we need to make more of the dense lateralizations that are becoming possible both inside and outside our theoretical work.

2

ON PROGRAMMATICS

James D. Faubion

In concluding *An Anthropology of Ethics* (Faubion 2011), I identified four general conceptual apparatuses—referential, model-theoretic, tendential, and diagnostic—that singly or in combination have become part of our anthropological legacy. I made the effort for several reasons. The first was apologetic (read "self-justificatory"). *An Anthropology of Ethics* is a generalist enterprise. It is the sort of enterprise that was common and comprehensible enough in social and cultural anthropology through the 1970s. It is a rare enterprise, perhaps bordering on the exotic, and very often regarded with considerable skepticism today, especially among cultural anthropologists and especially (though not exclusively) in the United States. The prevailing rationale for such skepticism can be traced to Clifford Geertz's critique of the quest for cultural universals, first published in 1966 (in the same year, ironically, as his entirely generalist essay on religion as a cultural system; both essays appear in Geertz 1973). It takes on further force with the nominalist epistemology of Paul Rabinow's *Reflections on Fieldwork in Morocco* (1977) and the similarly nominalist epistemology of Johannes

Fabian's *Time and the Other* (1983). Although on different grounds, Rabinow and Fabian converge in insisting that fieldwork is the only source of anthropological knowledge and that the knowledge gained from it is particularistic in every case (see also Rabinow 1988). The position was already entangled with the critique of the inherent conservatism of structure-functionalism (although its generalism was less in focus than its love affair with homeostasis; see, e.g., Hymes 1972; Asad 1973). It became a juggernaut, and it is still very much afloat.

To my mind, it has also led to throwing out quite a few babies with the bath (which has become something of an anthropological habit). The problem is not the turn to nominalism, which is very often the only proper epistemological order of the day and which in any case does not preclude arguments of comparative scope (more on this later). The problem is rather one of settling into epistemological complacency (of which, it should be added, neither Rabinow nor Fabian can for a moment be accused), and all the more so when such complacency devolves into an anthropological subconscious, with all its defenses in tow. Fight or flight: it is a familiar (all too familiar) syndrome. It is the inevitable companion of dogmatism. It is also symptomatic of two further disciplinary shortcomings that have tended to make *theory* a largely hollow term and the sort of conceptual work that might yield a genuinely programmatic result—a genuinely generative technology of disciplined question formation—an increasingly lost (or at least underappreciated) art. One of these are the sorts of "theory courses" that Boyer and Marcus have already called into question—courses that deposit one or another recognized example of theory at students' doorsteps but neglect to include cogent users' guides. The second is conceptual cherry-picking, which often more nearly resembles the picking of apples and oranges. The collection might have an appealing palette, but it might also—and often does—run the risk of amounting to little more than a still life. A pedagogy more devoted to the epistemological and ontological lineaments of what has usually passed as theory (and less devoted to perfunctory endorsements and dismissals) might ameliorate these shortcomings. It might, if only it could effectively be put into operation—not just in a "theory course" but across our now Balkanized curricula.

It was this, with all due immodesty, that I proposed in *An Anthropology of Ethics,* and so, in the same spirit, I continue here, revisiting the apparatuses that I thought worth distinguishing from one another and adding a few further notes on their applicability, combinatoric possibilities, virtues, and shortcomings. All of the apparatuses are schematics. The specificity of the questions they generate depends on the specificity of the substantive domains to which they are addressed. I turn first to referential apparatuses. Their original philosopher is Francis Bacon. Their logic is inductive. Their methodology is extrapolative. They permit and demand the decontextualization of particular empirical events and entities, and their eventual classification as tokens of purely general types. They further demand that tokens be unambiguously commensurate with the types that (accordingly) subsume them. They are one of the kinds of apparatuses central to the ascendance of the natural sciences and remain very close to the center of the epistemic authority of the natural and applied sciences today, especially of those touted as being "data-driven." Although at the cost of compromising the unambiguous commensurability of tokens and types, they serves statisticians very well. Whatever their specific substantive domain might be, their cardinal epistemic virtue is reliability, of which replicability is the acid test and to which even a single counterexample can prove fatal. Biological anthropologists and anthropological archaeologists are their primary intradisciplinary champions, but many cultural anthropologists have embraced one or another of them as well. A referential apparatus was the kind of apparatus that informed Clyde Kluckhohn's quest for cultural universals (Kluckhohn, McCombe, and Vogt 1951) and, undaunted by Geertzian objections, Donald Brown's later quest for the same (Brown 1988, 1991). Anthropologists (and other social scientists) who continue to champion referential apparatuses without qualification are almost sure to be scorned by the sociocultural vanguard for being "positivists." Geertz had a different complaint to file against the universalists—that their results were largely vacuous. In more current terminology, the complaint could be cast as a failure of robustness, of the capacity to generate further questions from questions already answered. The infernal variability of human affairs tends to lend the complaint considerable force. In sociocultural anthropology at least, referential apparatuses tend not to reach very far beyond the particular cases on which they are based.

Logically and methodologically, referential apparatuses are a thing apart from model-theoretic apparatuses, one of which is featured (in combination with a diagnostics and with a bit of the tendential thrown in as well) in *An Anthropology of Ethics*. Logically, such apparatuses are hypothetico-deductive. René Descartes's *Discourse on Method* is an exemplary philosophical primer, but Descartes was well aware that he was following (loosely) in the footsteps of Aristotle. Methodologically, any such apparatus must be grounded first of all in principles, axiomatic (for Descartes) or provisionally axiomatic, from which hypotheses capable of being evaluated directly in light of empirical evidence can be inferred. Model-theoretic apparatuses are well suited to those generalist enterprises that have the articulation of the systematicity of one or another systemic phenomenon as their goal. They are technologies appropriate for the analysis of kinship, structurally if not pragmatically. Like Marcel Mauss before him, Claude Lévi-Strauss is one of the great model-theoreticians of the discipline, of kinship and ever so many other putatively systemic phenomena. They are not incompatible with referentialist research, but such research can only be a propaideutic to their construction, never their redemption. Hence their unpopularity with referentialist purists, who are likely to find them too speculative, too much a putting of the cart before the horse.

Anthropologically model-theoretic apparatuses are (or had better be) empirically informed, and in the past, they were also the pretext of many an ethnographic pursuit of variations of what they thematized. The anthropology of kinship is again illustrative. Understandably, fieldworkers today are not very often interested in merely exploring a variation of themes already established. Moreover, any particular fieldworker's fieldwork—and this goes for any other sort of propaideutic as well—can at best inspire the construction of a model-theoretic apparatus. Put more technically, it can at best invite the quasi-intuitive abduction that carries the observer from the particularities of a particular case to the general principles that might— just might—account for it. Referentialist purists would think this an illegitimate generalization from a statistically nonsignificant sample. But then, model-theoretic apparatuses *qua* model-theoretic apparatuses are not constrained by the referentialist requirement of commensurability between token and type. Logical coherence trumps referential rigor; counterexamples can often be treated as (mere) exceptions to the rule. Robustness trumps reliability. Model-theoretic apparatuses are the other sorts of apparatuses central to the natural sciences, present and past, but they have by no means vanished from the social sciences. Jürgen Habermas's axiomatics of communicative action (1984, 1987) is model-theoretic, as are Pierre Bourdieu's axiomatics of the logic of social reproduction (more widely, but less instructively, known as his "theory of practice"; 1977, 1990) and Niklas Luhmann's axiomatics of the social system (1996). Do not trouble Bourdieu (too much) with the "facts." Although the concept of the habitus, the fulcrum of his analysis, is the concept of a systematic set of dispositions embodied in full particularity in each of us, his axiomatics are a statistical distillation from particular cases and does not refer to individuals as such. Do not trouble Luhmann too much with the facts, either. As he himself puts it, his apparatus "can be a far-reaching, elegant and economical instrument" of analysis, but "whether it is correct is another matter" (1989, 35).

Model-theoretical apparatuses completely detached from any reference to the domains they are designed to model are, of course, highly suspect. Tendential apparatuses similarly detached are suspect as well. Like their model-theoretic counterparts, however, they do not stand or fall, logically or methodologically, on their strict conformity to the actual states of affairs they engage. They cannot possibly do so because (by definition) they offer general schematizations of currents, trends, and lines of force and flight that are not (because they are merely currents, trends, and lines of force and flight) fully determinate and so not fully definable. In contrast to their model-theoretic counterparts, they work not to elucidate the systematicity of systems but instead to draw out the distinctive character and (at their most robust) at least some of the causes and some of the actual or potential effects of dynamic processes that may or may not be processes internal to a system as such. This said, most of the tendential apparatuses currently operative are intrasystemic. The only proviso is that the systematicities within which they are embedded must always be open rather than closed. (Closed systems have no trends; if they register temporality at all, they register it recursively and reversibly.)

A great many tendential apparatuses are in fact currently operative across the various arenas of social and cultural thought. They are symptomatic of our widespread preoccupation with globalization, neoliberalization and the increasing pace and breath of capitalist deterritorialization and reterritorialization, biopoliticization, postcolonization, and other processual phenomena that are as consequential and vivid as they are hard to pin down. I reiterate here the examples and exemplars to which I gestured in *An Anthropology of Ethics*. More of a model-theoretician in *The Constitution of Society* (1986), Anthony Giddens turns tendentialist in *Modernity and Self-Identity* (1991) and *The Transformation of Intimacy* (1993). Ülrich

Beck follows his lead (or vice versa) in *Reflexive Modernization*, the two joining together with Scott Lash to sketch out the trend toward a critical post-traditionalism among the European middle classes (Beck, Giddens, and Lash 1994). Peter Sloterdijk is a tendentialist in his *Critique of Cynical Reason* (1987), identifying and lamenting the rise of an ethos of "making do" in his native Germany (and presumably elsewhere) from the Weimar period forward. David Harvey has his analytical eyes on a trend toward the entrenchment (although how deeply and how permanently he cannot say) of an economic regime of "flexible accumulation" in his *Condition of Postmodernity* (1990). Michael Hardt and Antonio Negri are at least aspiring tendentialists in their effort to elucidate the characteristics of an emergent modality of sovereignty in *Empire* (2000). I could easily add anthropologists to the list—but frankly, there are too many to mention.

Tendential apparatuses share with model-theoretic apparatuses the weighting of robustness over reliability. At a minimum, their legitimacy rests on their identification of at least some of the more or less general parameters of the trend or trends they highlight. Their legitimacy increases the more that they facilitate a causal account of a trend, and it increases all the more should they facilitate a plausible projection of the course and career that a given trend might have. At their best, they also get everything more rather than less right. More or less: it needs repeating. Properly wrought, tendential apparatuses preserve the ambiguities not merely of trends but also of the open-ended and so fuzzy environments in which they unfold. (The referentialist purist would once again not approve.) They do not and cannot produce the whole picture. They are inherently partial and so always a partial failure from a model-theoretic point of view.

Last but not at all least, diagnostics: Geertz originally deploys the term in "Art as a Cultural System," borrowing it from medicine at a time (the essay was published in 1976) when medical diagnostics had yet to become predominantly experimental and was still largely clinical, attending to the always ontologically particular case. He distinguished it, perhaps too ardently, from a semiotics confined to the consideration of "signs as means of communication, code to be deciphered" and put it forward in contrast as:

> a science [*sic*] that can determine the meaning of things for the life that surrounds them. It will have, of course, to be trained on signification, not pathology, and treat with ideas, not with symptoms. But by connecting incised

statues, pigmented sago palms, frescoed walls, and chanted verse to jungle clearing, totem rites, commercials, or street argument, it can perhaps begin at last to locate in the tenor of their settings the sources of their spell. (Geertz 1983, 120)

Geertz is concerned here, as elsewhere, with capturing the dynamics of interpretative contextualization. Only a few years previously, he had resorted to Gilbert Ryle's conception of thick description as a frame for those dynamics, which he proceeded to liken not to the work of the "cipher clerk" but instead to the work of the "literary critic" (Geertz 1973, 9). Diagnostics strikes me as the more effective term. All diagnostics are contextualizing and are like literary criticism in just that respect. Not all of them settle for readings that merely identify motifs and relations of discursive coherence. Venturing beyond the bounds of the literary *stricto sensu*, even some literary critics (psychoanalytic or Marxist) and most medical diagnosticians also have etiological ambitions, looking to connect symptoms to what is causing them. They're not required to do so (in every last case), and sometimes know in advance that they cannot do so, but their etiological orientations point to modes of diagnostics that are logically and methodologically extra-aesthetic.

More recently, Paul Rabinow and Gaymon Bennett have formulated and refined a diagnostics of cases that has its initial provocation in the role that Foucault (1997, 117–18) assigns to "problematization" in genealogical inquiry. Problematization *à la foucauldienne* is, however, a process of large scale, well beyond the vision of the fieldworker. With the aid of John Dewey's more intimately scaled characterization of thinking and Foucault's characterization of conceptual-practical "equipment" as "the medium of transformation of *logos* into *ethos*" (Rabinow 2003, 1; Foucault 2005, 327), Rabinow and Bennett proceed to trim and tailor a diagnostics of problematization to a scale better suited to the fieldworker's or fieldworkers' abilities and limitations. The result is also a modestly tendential diagnostics, directed toward inquiry into processes emergent in the recent past and very likely to extend at least into the near future—hence the building blocks of an "anthropology of the contemporary" (Rabinow 2008).[1]

Geertz defended at length one of the aspects of diagnostics that referentialists and their fellow travelers could hardly countenance. Like tendential apparatuses, diagnostics are referentially underdetermined and can provide only interpretations as a consequence. Or, as Geertz summarily cast anthropological writings, they are "fictions; fictions, in the sense that they are 'something made,' 'something fashioned'—the original sense of *fictio*—not that they are false, unfactual, or merely 'as if' thought experiments" (1973, 15). His apology (again, read "self-justification") did not persuade everyone, and diagnosticians can continue to anticipate encounters with the unpersuaded—certainly in the present and in all likelihood in the near future as well. They do not satisfy model-theoreticians any more than they satisfy (hard) scientists. Diagnosticians can nevertheless claim to share with model-theoreticians and tendentialists alike the valorization of robustness over reliability. Like all their fellow conceptual apparatuses (which would otherwise not merit the label of "conceptual apparatuses"), diagnostics all on their own can provide the basis of research designs of most impressive comparative compass. Diagnostically inflected comparison is, however, comparison with a twist. Because it always must begin with a case, and because no case offers the guarantee of being detachable from its context, a diagnostics can in principle foster comparison merely of an analogical sort. Only an etiologically oriented diagnostics whose etiological aspirations are fulfilled can offer comparisons of a more scientifically palatable sort. Unmotivated by any such aspirations, diagnostically inflected comparison is comparison by analogy. Rabinow has dared to speak the name of its logic: "casuistics" (2003, 131–33). One can already hear trouble brewing in the wings.

As I have mentioned, the conceptual apparatus that I fashioned in *An Anthropology of Ethics* is a combination of the model-theoretic, the diagnostic, and the tendential. I could not have fashioned anything of the sort were the system I sought to model (the ethical domain) a closed system. The closed system and the tendential are, to reiterate, not compatible with one another. Because I sought to show the fruitfulness of bringing a general model of the ethical domain to the contextualization and interpretation of particular ethical subjects in particular climes and times, I could not do without a diagnostics. The upshot is an apparatus that licenses comparisons of two distinct sorts. At the level of the model-theoretic—which is the level of the second order—it licenses comparisons resting in the identification of common features among various cases. At the level of the diagnostic, it licenses comparisons resting on analogy alone. It is an eclectic apparatus, and every eclectic apparatus requires compromising the integrity of some of the parts of which it is composed. In my revision of Luhmann's model-theorization of systems that are organizationally closed into a model-theorization of a system organizationally open, I admit to going beyond compromise. I did violence, and I admitted to it (in so many words; Faubion 2011, 60). Doing violence is not, however, being inconsistent. A conceptual apparatus that is inconsistent should simply be put out of its misery.

3

THE AMBITIONS OF THEORY WORK IN THE PRODUCTION OF CONTEMPORARY ANTHROPOLOGICAL RESEARCH

George E. Marcus

James Faubion's crucial move in the preceding chapter is to link the question and standing of theory in the practice of anthropological research today to the relation of theory to "the programmatic," which I take to be its systematic reception and development in a collectivity, usually conceived as a community of interested scholars, experts, and professionals. In short, theoretical work is significant to the extent that someone else makes something systematically of it.[1] When we observe the work of theory in anthropology, in whatever discursive form or genre (e.g., typically, as it provides a frame and structure for both argument and narration in much contemporary ethnographic writing), we should ask: In relation to what generative project? Or to what, as Faubion terms it, "technology of disciplined question formation"? Without some systematic connection to a notion of the programmatic, the substance of theory making, in its manifestation— concept work—in mainly ethnographic research/fieldwork-based inquiry in anthropology, is much reduced in value as a foundational category for evoking what holds a discipline together.

The substance and significance of an interest in theory in any particular research project are thus linked to its reception and the contribution that it makes to the collective thinking of a community, a public, or publics. The question today is whether theory as it applies to individual research in anthropology can have such robust programmatic significance, especially with reference to a disciplinary or scholarly professional community; and if this is in doubt (as I believe it is, and as it certainly is for Faubion as well), then is there an alternative and distinctive sense or process of inquiry, perhaps specific to anthropology in its modern tradition as a field science developing through ethnography, in which the work of theory in the production of research can be considered programmatic? Faubion suggests that there is by engaging in an acute typological exercise.

The first sense of the programmatic that Faubion evokes—the referential—is the most mythic (at least for the positivist-minded social sciences), thoroughly deconstructed (at least in anthropology), but still powerfully influential one: the status of theory work dependent on its relation to empirical methods of some demonstrable reliability. These are theories that grow and are changed by studies, controlled experiments, reproducible investigations, and growing accumulations of variable-defined, factual materials. In its central tendencies, anthropology has not tried to literally produce this sort of project for a very long time (except perhaps in some subspecialties such as latter-day sociobiology, semiotics, and linguistic anthropology; but even these, although often formal in concept and deeply empiricist, are tolerably unruly in their research projects). There are indeed legacy-form comparative projects in the history of anthropology to take up again (but it is very unclear in the present era of data science whether they would ever be taken up referentially again), in which the value of the ethnographic study could be theorized in terms of a research program in the positivist ethos (as isolating limited variables and proving a hypothesis, with some logic of replicability).

Faubion then discusses two derived types of the relation of theory work to the condition of the programmatic. Both might be uncharitably understood as hedges, as what theoretical practice for individual projects can be when the conditions for operating in the realm of the referential programmatic are absent. These are the model-theoretic and the tendential. The former is not practiced much, at least in social/cultural anthropology, where theory work in reports, essays, or monographs would be a formal abstract exercise of constructing models in which to organize and narrate the data of an ethnographic report. It gestures toward comparison and appeals to rigorous, factorial thinking, but it mostly remains the distinctive mark or signature of a particular researcher. The model-theoretic, which was the common form of producing work when I came of age as an anthropologist (during the late 1960s through the 1970s), sets up thinking for the programmatic without following through.

What Faubion terms the tendential is the most common form that theory work takes in contemporary anthropological research. It gestures even more remotely to the conventional idea of the programmatic. In its practice, it is highly variable in the way that it uses theory to set ethnographic work within a form of argument, narration, and description sensitive to emplacement in a particular location, condition of fieldwork, and historical or contemporary context. At best, the tendential use of theory does a lot of imaginative, creative work in the making of argument out of the exploration of a case or problem found in fieldwork. The tendential mode of theory making creates concepts close to materials, develops an analytics (yet not approaching a model) around it, and stands for an ethnographic work discursively as it travels in recognition and discussion. Nevertheless, the tendential is very far indeed from a referential notion of the programmatic. It gestures toward such a classic notion of the programmatic but is furthest from it. The diverse efforts, of varying longevity, to build topical research programs in anthropology today mostly circulate arguments, connections, and associations through the power of theoretical usages developed in the tendential mode within the frame of exemplary presentations of ethnographic material. As such, the tendential mode of theory work is a weak source to establish a condition of the programmatic that sustains disciplined systematic inquiry.

Still, it should be noted that, for the tendential to thrive as widespread disciplinary practice, to be effective in the pedagogy of apprentice anthropologists, and to serve, stimulate, and reward the diversity and variety of research initiatives of varying ephemerality that characterize anthropology today, a seat of programmatic knowledge about traditions, genealogies, currents, and fashions of theory, in the mode of scholarly projects and commitments associated with intellectual historians and philosophers, is indeed necessary to inform the practice of the tendential and keep it going. But this specific and necessary programmatic function exists, I argue, alongside, or laterally, to most research projects. It serves to fire up the engine of the tendential, so to speak.

So, there are deep and close readers of theoretical traditions and innovations (e.g., Faubion, Boyer, and Glaeser, among others) who follow them systematically for their own interest and within the frame of evolving questions that anthropology asks. This kind of systematic theory interest on the part of some anthropologists helps to give theory work a powerful standing in the production of individual research projects, especially in graduate school curricula, but it does not serve to define the programmatic in its classic referential sense, collectively pursued by a discipline. This off-side exercise of the programmatic when it comes to the intellectual history of theory is thus of immense importance in giving theoretical competence to students to produce the tendential in their projects, but it does not make the projects programmatic in any of the senses that Faubion evokes as defining the significance of theory in contemporary anthropological research.[2]

Finally, Faubion explores a fourth type or potential source of the programmatic condition of theory work that differs in kind from the other three in not depending on a derivation from, or relation to, the referential type. He labels it the diagnostic (perhaps with an inflection from where the influence of Foucault has led the application of anthropological thought in recent decades) but also folds into it the more commonly known and practiced interpretive tradition of theory in anthropology, associated most famously and recently with Clifford Geertz. What is bold in Faubion's inclusion of this otherwise familiar, even standard type of theory work in his typology is his suggestion that such work can be strongly programmatic as well—that it can be more than the theory work in the tendential pose and that it can have broader, more intensive, and lasting reception than is otherwise supposed or expected.

This move of expecting a disciplined technology of question formation in such projects of ethnographic research and a different mode of reception for them, both within the realm of the field of fieldwork activity and within the realm of their professional scholarly community consideration, suggests a different ambition (modality) for theory work in contemporary ethnographic research, on which I want to focus.

Faubion's delineation of this fourth type folds the question of the possibility of programmatic theory work into questions of method, but it is perhaps unhelpful to use this category because *method* is traditionally understood in distinction to *theory,* with some version of the referentially programmatic in mind. What Faubion instead suggests is that the strength of theory work in contemporary ethnographic investigations is in the possibility of producing a sustained and diverse reception for them in their production. How theory travels in research as analytics (an idea key to Boyer and Howe, this volume) is critical to forging the programmatic contexts of the remarkably diffuse and varied explorations of anthropological research today. What is lacking are the forms and means in research practice to establish a programmatic context for it, project by project.

The diagnostic, as a structure of research, incorporates diverse audiences and receptions for its pursuit (in analogy with theater, it breaks the "fourth wall" of the imagined, enclosed mise-en-scènes of anthropological fieldwork taking place elsewhere), involving design strategies (and increasingly, new digital-based technologies) of intervention, scenarios, or events in which different modalities of theory work blended into fieldwork can literally take place. (See, analogously and suggestively, Saunders 2008, for a deeply ethnographic account of disciplined diagnostic intrigue and its elaborate production in the interpretation of computed tomography scans). Theory work, or analytics, then, would not be so much the product of this research, blended into ethnographic writing and forms of argument, as its means. It needs accessible forms for reception that are performative, more raw, and prototypical (Marcus 2014) in relation to ways that anthropologists have articulated theory in conventional reporting genres to the academy—the ethnographic-based text or article. Such collective diagnostic thinking, which each project makes accessible, becomes programmatic in the field before it becomes programmatic in disciplinary discussion. At present, however, this programmatics of and within the field remains a potential—largely invisible, anecdotal, or relegated to the now almost canonical reflexive framing of ethnographic writing.

Research results are thus what different communities of reception do with them, including the professional one that is incorporated as a second-order, still perhaps authoritative community, that now must take reception itself as a theorized and empirical dimension of what is presented to it as research, as ethnographic cases. This suggests that a lot more is going on of a theoretical nature in many projects than anthropology currently has a vocabulary for or genres of access to. (Fischer 2003 gestures in this direction through his evocation of "third spaces," but in my case, there is a more material, and literal concern with the design of such spaces as research practices, within long-standing norms of fieldwork; Marcus 2012.)

Clarifications of the changing forms of questions, thought of as analytics or theory in play, thus become the sustained programmatic endeavor of the myriad morphing diagnostic projects of research that abound in contemporary anthropology. The task of the programmatic played out in the field in professional reception and pedagogy is to systematically and recursively reprocess and rearticulate the questions on a moving contextualized ground—to create a collective and sustained discourse and framework for organizing such apparently unruly arrays of individual inquiries.[3]

This alternative notion of the programmatic is indeed a viable collective research program, centered on a disciplinary tradition in which explanation in its classic ambition, as Faubion says, plays no role. The work of theory or analytics in ethnography is to pose continuously and empirically the questions as they are asked and articulated (of course, the posing of questions situationally is never just that, although it is a sustaining fiction of theory work). This view of the collective work of contemporary anthropology depends on the connectivity of the many research projects of diffuse curiosity that anthropologists are pursuing in the contemporary under the long-established regulative professional norms of fieldwork research. This diagnostic programmatic still depends very much on the sort of theory work and interest that anthropologists have developed for themselves to shape and revitalize in recent decades the ethnographic form and argument of their discipline as writing genres, but the forms that this theory work take in fieldwork itself are very different—platforms, stages, and designed interventions as necessary for falling into the liveliness, variety, and collective curiosities that compose the empirical stuff of ethnographic research projects so much in evidence over the past three decades.

The contemporary ethos or spirit of the way that theory informs inquiry is well captured in a remark by Jamer Hunt, a participant in the discussions of our volume, who has made a distinctive career teaching design methods informed by the same sources of theory that have now inspired several generations of ethnographic research in anthropology: "theory is a frame for anthropology intervening in arenas new to it." Indeed, such a remark is a spur for anthropologists to ask questions both new and relevant to the contexts in which they work and for them to enter distinctively into arenas of social and cultural life that have been already diversely represented (or even theorized) by actors on the ground, including other kinds of experts who have gotten there earlier. But what theory becomes in practice and product in the course of research—as fieldwork or, in Hunt's case, design projects—very much depends on its specific scenes of emergence in fieldwork, its recursive circulations, as the fieldworker himself moves his research to different sites and locations and, finally, to its second-order disciplinary receptions, which are both continuous with and self-defining from the theory work in and as fieldwork research.

In the following section, I outline briefly what forms—both digital and conventional—seem to be developing that make theory work both programmatic, in the sense of the diagnostic potential for it that Faubion evokes in his typology, and a more explicit core activity of contemporary fieldwork. But with which paradigm of classic fieldwork in mind? Is there any other one than the dominant Malinowskian exemplar, which despite the actual complexities of its conduct by Bronislaw Malinowski himself, has nonetheless shaped the regulative ideals that have guided field research in the Anglo-American tradition for generations in the direction of the referential type of the programmatic or one of its derived variations? Is there an alternative tradition of fieldwork to evoke in inventing the diagnostic type of the programmatic that Faubion has proposed?

Here I am inspired by an essay by Matti Bunzl (2004) who, under the influence of Foucault, revives and reimagines an alternative Boasian paradigm of fieldwork that serves much better than the dominant Malinowskian one as a frame to think through and propose forms of field research that accommodate at its core a project of collaborative theory work.[4] Boasian fieldwork never became methodological doctrine because it served most explicitly museum and linguistic science (rather than social science), in which the reference of the programmatic was to the patient accumulation, classification, and interpretation of collections in temporal frames of history and evolution. Yet in Bunzl's Foucauldian revival of its core mise-en-scène of anthropologist-subject relation, Boasian regulative norms of research are a better version to think with than the dominant Malinowskian ones in proposing the development and accessibility of prototypical forms of the diagnostic type of programmatic potentiality in the conduct of contemporary fieldwork. In short, they imagine more open and dynamic dialogic conditions of inquiry that encourage the kinds of constructions and interventionist forms that create ethnographic data as theory work that punctuate and extend fieldwork as a programmatic exercise.

Platforms, Para-Sites, Installations, Prototypes, and the Like. . . . Toward the Condition of Programmatic Theory Work in Ethnography as Technologies of Disciplined Question Formation

The key innovation in method is that reception is folded into ethnographic strategies of inquiry and thus requires making accessible to real and imagined publics for a project (who might also serve as its subjects) of sustained and variable concept work alongside norms and expectations of investigation. New forms of enabling, applied theoretical discourse—as granular public discourse in formation—thus become the primary discourses-in-use of the actual conduct of inquiry and investigation. These forms become the latter's basis for paths of circulation and reception that it continually incorporates until the projects stops, wears out, or merges with another. At present, such a research process can be imagined only in terms of a referentialist-derived notion of the programmatic. It needs something else.

The professional scholarly and expert community that practically exercises authority and control over research (through controlling the channels of funding, recognition, and career prestige and determining what is to count as knowledge, etc.) finds itself, if not just another public in reception, then a second-order one, obliged to think through, making programmatic, a body of research, not just through what the researcher argues and offers but through being presented with, and perhaps integrated into, a lively arena of primary and derived receptions that an ethnographic inquiry ignites and spreads merely by being in the field. Still, although this might be the reality of contemporary research—embedded in the conditions of the "found field," however it is constructed as fieldwork for research—it is not how it is presented or received in traditional genres of ethnographic writing and reporting, or how these are received and rewarded professionally.

Forms are thus needed to make visible and accessible these levels and recursions of reception as fieldwork moves and develops. The lateralist analytics as evoked by Boyer and Howe in their chapter is one such imaginary of form; diagnostics is another in Faubion's chapter, though he insists on a more complex eclecticism amid his typology to characterize his own writing practice. Intermediate expressions of knowledge, collaboratively and sometimes self-consciously composed and designed, are necessary to expose the kinds and forms of thinking that a contemporary fieldwork project assimilates. These expressions take the form of debates, proofs, and experiments in the field—designed interventions, more than single-authored data recording and interpretation of field notes, which are produced alongside them. Ultimately, these forms capture layered receptions for cumulative theory and concept work that have various mise-en-scenes of their own that run parallel to the more solitary theory work that comes from the traditional recording and observing of classic fieldwork, and that eventually reach back to the academy and encourages it to think differently about how knowledge presented to it in raw and prototypical forms is certified, if it is, or continues on as a lively programmatic of question asking that establishes novel sorts of relationships with long-standing modes of receiving ethnographic cases as the basis of theoretically defining anthropology.[5] How does the academy participate in projects that it is pulled into by forms of promoting and developing theory work as fieldwork—not just in a location but in its recursions and trajectories of movement among granularly defined publics of reception, of which the receiving authority of academic debate and assessment is one, but perhaps not the final one?

What stabilizes knowledge-making in such projects is precisely the crafting of forms of interventions where emerging claims, concepts, and ideas can be received. Much depends on skills of curating and organizing ethnographic forums that punctuate and move alongside the sort of classic probing by the individual's research in the traditional vision of how fieldwork proceeds. The problem is how to coordinate and relate the two. Over the past decade, and continuing, there are two modalities—the first, necessarily narrow and directed in its range; the second, more diffuse and expansive—in which I have been interested, primarily from the vantage point of activities sponsored by the Center for Ethnography (founded in 2005) at the University of California, Irvine. The first modality experiments with the developing affordances of digital technology to create commons of organized research and participation; the second modality operates conventionally with the protocols of doing research but experiments with incorporating, on one hand, forms and exemplars that recognize affinities with varieties of design thinking and methods and, on the other, arts such as theater, museum curation, site-specific installation, conceptual and performance genres, and the craft of filmmaking.

Of digital experiments, I have been most interested in those that structure the entire project through the construction, care, and tending of platforms as the core apparatus of a research project. Although such a project may be, minimally, a modality of dynamic, continuous archiving or, more, the engine of a topically conceived research project that accumulates vast sources and types of data for it, for my interest here the platform is a greatly enhanced ethnographic/fieldwork project of the ambition and variety that have been expressed in the most original but conventional ethnographic writing over the past three decades. In a sense, platforms can literally develop the kinds of expanding receptions and engagements that ethnographies now can only imagine.

At the core of such platform experiments are novel theoretical imaginations and applied theory work that is challenged by the care and development of a variable and expanding commons of participation, without conventional boundary or reach (such as "a readership" or the evaluation of peers in the academy). This is work engineering the spread of the sort of commons that Chris Kelty (2008) so attractively terms "recursive publics" and in conceiving contemporary online communities of mutual interest, participation, and co-construction. A platform is thus a machine for knowledge-making in the wild that generates research, brings together its subjects and others as publics, and creates the means of novelty in individual and collective participatory thinking with recognizable connections to the diagnostic (tendential?) theory and concept work so prevalent in post 1980s ethnography. And in terms of the interest of this essay in the means for establishing the grounds of the programmatic in independent fieldwork research, platform projects operate through imaginaries and means for the production of disciplined technologies of question asking—a core theoretical function within research protocols that otherwise have been difficult to achieve in current exemplars of ethnographic research practice.

How practical is it to produce such a modality of research today and under what conditions? I have followed two projects of particular interest to me. One is "The Asthma Files," developed by Kim and Mike Fortun[6] over the past seven years on the basis of very little funding but strong and expanding networks of collaboration (see K. Fortun 2012b; Fortun, this volume). Although asthma might seem a very specialized topic—which indeed it is, although expansive in its empirical manifestations—it becomes much less so when developed through the platform affordances designed by the Fortuns and their collaborators. To develop these has involved both a continuing practical education and the recruitment of expertise in digital technology, and also the rethinking and reforming of the modalities of theory work that so influentially shape ethnographic texts (indeed, it is an interesting exercise to follow the quite original way that theory is used to compose Fortun's highly regarded 2001 ethnographic work, *Advocacy after Bhopal*, and how related and extended techniques of theory work emerge as aspects of the design, making, and protocols of use and participation in "The Asthma Files" platform). Eventually, the activities of research, reception, and concept work in "The Asthma Files" forums, incorporating traditional concepts of the field and fieldwork, will attract the distanced critical attention of the authorizing discussion of the academy and evolve new modes of incorporating them as well. At least, this is its promise.

The other platform project of continuing interest that I have discovered more recently is Bruno Latour's "An Inquiry into Modes of Existence." It is not only ironic but indexical of the times that many in academia will discover this dynamically online platform project that has invented attractive protocols of participation by first gaining notice of it in a largish tome recently published by Harvard University Press (Latour 2013). The book is more a reporting (a reception?) of the theory work and research of the platform than yet another theoretical meditation on the career evolution of a famous mode of inquiry, and it distinctively opens with "A User's Manual for the Ongoing Collective Inquiry." This text thus might be understood as both the culmination of and the transition from Latour's long series of texts, many evoking or performing the ethnographic voice of reporting on fieldwork-like researches, of his own and others. What is important to note here is that theory work for Latour has not so much reached an end, an exhaustion, climax, or final version or synthesis of older ideas (this might already have indeed happened a while back for him in his prolific output within the terms and means of the conventional genres of discourse and textuality available) but a new medium of making, and certainly new communities of reception, and therefore new stakes, ambitions, continuities—and, foremost, forms (or in Faubion's term, disciplined technologies of question asking) and partners for working through those ideas. Although prominent in his example, the stakes for any such shift of an established line of theory in ethnography to platform affordances would be the same. With the development of platforms for inquiry and theory making, researchers become intellectually project managers and members of recursive overlapping communities of varying commitments and agendas.

In both examples, the participatory ethos of the two platform experiments are the same, as are the centrality of open theory work and the idea of a coming alternative modality of method. There are also significant differences. The Fortuns' platform is built collectively and with minimal resources on volunteer labor and learning as they go; Latour's is the production of considerable funding support and prestigious institutional connections and reputation. Characteristic of the digital age, who—and whether a significant number—can be attracted to what protocols are what the programmatic ethnographic value of these projects depends on. Practically, they depend on social capital and reputation of the traditional sort, as well as considerable continuous funding and patronage (although the Fortuns impressively show what can be done in the kind of recursive community or commons that Kelty evokes; they actively are moving toward creating a technology that moves beyond their originating project and that can be applied to any number of modest projects conceived as ethnographic inquiry).

Most important, both projects squarely make shifts in the gravity of theory making, depending on how the platforms granularly develop publics of participation, and they both challenge the traditional academy in its standard-keeping to adapt to its role as second-order reviewers of, and indeed late-entry participants into, the knowledge-making processes emergent in how platforms operate socially. Perhaps when the technologies for producing platforms are more streamlined, cheaper, and easier to implement, the question will be how they will become method in pedagogy and more advanced research practice. Their central product is not only the data that they can amass, organize, and concentrate but the constant invention of theoretical and conceptual frames for giving them diagnostic/interpretive shape.

So platforms, then, are one interesting development of the ethnographic method that we have known beyond its textual genre and its tendential gesture toward the programmatic. A second such, perhaps more accessible, development lies in the relation of ethnographic practices to—by alliance, kinship, and incorporation—more experimental forms appropriate to their long-standing disciplines.

Without working with and through digital technologies as the primary forms of research and theory work, one has, then, the many sources of inspiration in collaborations with designers and artists that might inspire studio or installation interventions integrated into, or significantly alongside, the conduct of fieldwork according to its regulative ideals (of a preferred Boasian rather than Malinowskian origin). In terms of experiments with implementing forms toward a diagnostic programmatic for contemporary fieldwork research, one might view ethnographic practice as shifting between two poles of attraction today: that of design (see Gunn, Otto, and Smith 2013), and that of traditions of site-specific installation and conceptual art, and their curation (see, e.g., Papastergiadis 2012). Each has forms—imagined, adapted, and theorized spaces and materialities— to offer ethnographic research a means to develop a programmatics within its present protocols of research. Dubbed "para-sites" by me (see Deeb and Marcus 2011; but see especially Sunder Rajan, this volume, for a thorough and critical working through of a para-site in his research), "third spaces" by Fischer (2003), and zones of "lateral reason" by Maurer (2005), such interventions in fieldwork (usually in collaboration with designers, installation artists, or theater- and filmmakers, who know what they are doing!), spaces are forged and occasions are designed that permit the systematic creation of the middle-range, prototypical exposure of thinking, and theory making in fieldwork, making it visible and accessible, giving it extended publics and receptions , and setting research on a path (literally and figuratively) with theory work as its core activity, creating nested levels of constituencies, collaborations, and receptions along the way.

My own recent experience of a project that has thought through a range of the kinds of design- and art-world-derived experiments in form, within and in relation to ethnographic research, would be an excellent case to illustrate this second realm of creating forms for the expression of theory and concept work in (and as) the field if its climax had not occurred recently and if I were not presently in the throes of considering how to present or report on it to a conventional readership. So, in the notes of this chapter, I offer some extended (and indulgent) notes about it. This concerns a second act or after-life period of research at the World Trade Organization in Geneva, following a collaborative team ethnography project extending from 2008 to 2010 and organized by Professor Marc Abélès at the invitation of Pascal Lamy, director-general (D-G) of the World Trade Organization (WTO) until the end of June 2013 (see Abélès 2011).

Lamy had a special intellectual fascination with anthropology and a certain despair about the state and purpose of the WTO during his two-term tenure as D-G (including the 2008 world economic crisis and the WTO failure to conclude a long-awaited [since 2001] global trade agreement, the Doha Round). To the puzzlement and annoyance of many of his colleagues, he thought for a time that anthropological ethnography might locate, define, and suggest the means by which the WTO could shift and broaden its functions by showing, through ethnographic observation and insight, where this might already or potentially be happening.

There were some interesting methodological questions about how the ten of us in the project worked both individually and collaboratively, but only I used the project as an opportunity to experiment with the para-site form as a sort of metacontext to our challenging work of understanding the everyday life of trade as diplomatic and bureaucratic thinking and operations—that is, how a certain postwar vision and theory of world order (of the General Agreement on Tariffs and Trade, GATT) matured and evolved through the microconcept work of the WTO. Toward the end of the project, I staged a series of seminar-like meetings with D-G Lamy (creating the right mood or tone for these as something different from the usual genres of meeting at the WTO—an interview, a conference, a committee report, and so on—required the skills of scenographers and installation artists whom I consulted) that tried to articulate and probe his stakes in anthropology and his own deeper thinking that lay within his notion of anthropology and its relevance. The results (see Deeb and Marcus 2011) were interesting to all concerned but were inconclusive and, rather, were left dangling by the project coming to end.

That is where I left it until 2012, when in the midst of my increasing interest in the concerns described in this chapter (the making of forms to do theory work inside or alongside fieldwork projects) I became motivated to produce an experiment at the WTO that would create a collaborative project between art and anthropology, and that would run for a duration along parallel and intersecting lines in the same space of research and exhibit, with possibilities of creating quite different as well as overlapping constituencies or publics for the cooperating projects of fieldwork and installation art. Our time constraint was that Lamy was leaving the WTO at the end of June 2013, and it is not clear that after that any more research of an experimental kind could be done. Further, one of his *chefs de cabinet* had a taste for such a project and, therefore, was willing to facilitate it in June.

Perhaps the varied discussions around this project—planning for it and imagining scenarios that might work among various artists, designers, museum curators, anthropologists formerly associated with the research, and others who were not, with whom I consulted—was the most valuable experience for me in producing it. These discussions have richly filled in with content and detail my schematic thinking about a theory of producing forms (such as para-sites) in the course of fieldwork projects. Finally, there were five developed scenarios considered for producing an anthropology-art event at the WTO that would occur during the last three weeks of June 2013 at the Centre William Rappard in Geneva. The one we settled on entailed the production off-site (at Pace University in New York City) of three scenarios enacting problems of trade at the WTO, performed by improv dancers. Films of these scenarios were projected continuously at the WTO headquarters for three weeks, curated on site by the theater artists with whom we collaborated, while two of us, Jae Chung and myself, conducted intensive interviews, conversations, and had reunions with those we had worked with before as well as with new interlocutors. We did not meet face to face with Lamy again. The WTO was at a remarkably different place than it had been when we left in 2010, and we registered but stayed away from the current tense politics, especially about the future of the organization, as Lamy left and many of the veterans from the time of GATT retired.

In any case, this all is to be written up in the tradition and current styles of ethnographic reporting (e.g., I am imagining an account with the title "Lamy's Charge . . ."). But in parallel to this convention, the 2013 art-anthropology intervention has established its own trajectory and requires its own accounting, focused on the form we created and what it produced, what connections it opens up, and where it is still to move. The ethnographic reporting is a summation of the former project, but it is still a lively medium in relation to what the intervention generated. When we were still in Geneva, as both a summary of our thinking and a memo to ourselves, we produced a document that Jae Chung thought to call "Our Theory of the WTO Case"—considered as a kind of token or presentation, a parting gift, to Lamy (Chung, Hegel, and Marcus 2013).[7] His simple response to us, the fact that he cc'd it to his still most trusted and respected staff, and the fact that he indicated that he had already "said it" was almost a ritualistic endorsement from our patron of the entire project, from 2008 onward, about which he had remained officially silent (he had written a bland preface to Abélès's book). Certainly it was not the last word for us either (actually, about Chung: it should be said that she was most the most expert, original-thinking anthropologist among us—and continues to be; her insights about how the art was influencing the co-occurring ethnography were the most acute), but it does represent well that the language and stakes of inquiry were always in a deeply theoretical idiom that in anthropologists' hands always exceeded the narrow reference or else backroom existence of theory work and curiosity among the more pragmatic and technocratic appearances of those varied individuals at the WTO concerned with the business of trade. Such a theory of the case, building it, speaking of it as a core idiom of ethnographic work, was a way to get at the communicative rather than calculative concerns at the WTO (for a shrewd approach of this sort to central bankers, see Holmes 2009).

In the production of a second-act fieldwork experiment with form, "The Theory of the Case" as a polyvalent expression (with an interesting legal doctrinal standing—see, e.g., Wikipedia) of what we were trying to construct during the last weeks of June 2013, first as an expression of the parallel and intersecting work of artists and ethnographers in the same literal as well as project space and then as an expression for symbolic purposes as a presentation to Lamy, is a fascinating exemplar of the arguments of this chapter about how experiments with form settle into fieldwork projects, about the centrality of theory work in their production, and about how they constitute a working programmatic of inquiry—a technology of disciplined question asking.

A Retro/Prospective Note in Conclusion

The programmatics that Faubion wants to restore are consistent with a highly fragmented, lively, and creative realm of contemporary research in anthropology, and that is also consistent with how the individualistic

quest character of the ethnographic fieldwork method depends on instill-
ing discipline—a more systematic collective stake—in that durable quest-
ing modality. His provocation is that such a programmatics cannot arise
from without, from supra-paradigms formulated by the scholarly community itself, but must lie in experimenting with expansive and changing
relational forms (e.g., encounters with diverse kinds of experts at almost
every turn in the pursuit of contemporary fieldwork) already as a potential
within the classic mode and norms of ethnographic inquiry, facing new
contemporary relations and conditions of production. One could say that
much of the attraction of theory and its use by anthropologists in their production of ethnographic projects and its distinctive textual outcomes have
been an effort, by limited means, to make this argument time and again
in ethnographic writing over the past three decades. It has been difficult
to exceed more than a gesture toward a referentialist programmatics in its
tendentialist guise.

As I in this chapter (and Faubion) argue, only a material/pragmatic
interruption in the relation of theory to the production of ethnography
will provide an alternative programmatics—actually the only functioning
one. And this involves a different sense of theory work as an activity at the
core of the experience of fieldwork research, with a recognition of different participants, different roles, different circulations, different account-
abilities, and receptions—for which new forms of production are needed
in retaining the durable ethnographic paradigm as the emblematic core
of anthropological inquiry. As outlined here, these are already being attempted in experiments with new technologies of making research that
emphasize the accessibility of raw, prototypical forms of knowledge that
are the essence of theory making and concept work in anthropology today,
continually unsettled in the making and remaking of questions as a driver
of where ethnographic inquiry as fieldwork literally goes.[8]

Without new forms of theory work, professionally sanctioned and
implemented in pedagogy, and especially "method," the difference that
Faubion (and I) have been trying to delineate could easily be assimilated
to the habits of the ghosts of referentialist programmatics that still haunt
anthropology and the hopes of some of its practitioners.

4

Theorizing the Present Ethnographically

Andreas Glaeser

Social theory is still taught mostly in a rather conventional history-of-ideas fashion. As such, it is presented as a rather peculiar kind of genealogy in which not only are theories identified with their authors but both love and hate between authors are seen as equally generative of further theory/ author offspring. Thus, we learn that Marxism is the rebellious child of Hegelianism or that Lévi-Straussian structuralism issues from a union between the Durkheimian sociology of religion and Saussurian linguistics. To be sure, many teachers of social theory pepper their courses with psychoanalytically and sociology-of-knowledge-inspired excursions, but these remain mostly ivy crawling around the branches of the genealogical tree of theories/authors. The more trivial problem with treating theory development as largely independent from the political and economic bread-and-butter issues of its time lies in merely misunderstanding authors and discourses. The more profound problem is that in failing to reflect on this connection the practices of theory development are performatively cut off from what has been historically their animating center. After all, it is the relationship between theories and politics, however tenuous, real, or imagined, that has historically endowed it with its particular significance. Cut loose from this animus, theory development as a conversation among theorists is in danger of becoming an academic parlor game.

Any effort to rethink social theory for our time must therefore begin by reconsidering its investments in matters political. In this respect, it is important to note that over the centuries the relationship between theory development and politics has changed considerably. I thus begin this chapter with a very brief and unavoidably schematic and teleological reconsideration of the relation of the *political* history of social theory to the present.[1] I also briefly point to the fact that each phase or style in the political history of social theory was characterized by a particular truth regime (Foucault 1976). The main point of this brief historical overview is to recover the likely reasons why much of social theory lost its once so obvious link to politics. In the second section of this chapter, I wonder about possible contemporary criteria for the evaluation of theory for our time that can serve both as tools of critique and as signposts for where we might want to go with our theoretical practices. These criteria build on and in some ways reinterpret the call to reflexive theoretical practices that began with the work of the Frankfurt School. In the third and main part of this paper, I propose one possible modality of theorizing that appears fruitful in light of the criteria I propose. I do so by rethinking the relationship between ethnography and social theory in terms of narratives and their emplotment, which, on the one hand, builds on Aristotle's *Poetics* to grapple with contextually sensitive processes of signification and, on the other, relies on a social ontology that I have elsewhere called consequent processualism (Glaeser 2005, 2011, 2014). I especially argue that, given the checkered career of practices aiming to conceptualize social life, ethnography is for a number of reasons a promising medium in which to pursue the theoretization of the social. I also argue that the practice of a reflexive ethnography is vitally dependent on explicit theoretization of its ethnographic material.

Social Theory in Historical Perspective

There are at least two commonplace modern attitudes to social theory and its practitioners. The first sees efforts to theorize social life as a creative response to an acute social and political crisis.[2] Apprehended with modern eyes, that is to say seen retrospectively, the bursts of political philosophizing in the wake of major social crisis since antiquity seem to support such a connection.[3] The link in question is also taken to characterize the emergence of the social sciences in the late-eighteenth, nineteenth, and early-twentieth centuries, when the perception of crisis became almost permanent, a condition of the modern, which it has been, with short interruptions, ever since.[4] As a putative answer to crisis, theory rhetorically carries an accent of existential urgency. It points to the hope that, at its very best, theory provides the conceptual machinery for an adequate interpretation of social life. Theory in this sense is credited with the power to provide orientation. It promises understanding of what has happened, how social life hangs together, and how it might develop in the future. Theory thus also promises a greater degree of freedom resulting from higher levels of self-consciousness and the possibility of planning. Successful social theorists are seen in this perspective as particular kinds of modern heroes or, if seen as detractors, also antiheroes. Karl Marx and Friedrich Hayek are cases in point.

The second attitude sheds a cynical light on social theory and its producers. Modern critics have seen clearly that theoreticians have learned to use the diagnosis of crisis to justify their work and to draw attention to it. Thus social theory has been repeatedly accused of nervous crisis-mongering undertaken for rather selfish claims making in the perennial vanity fair of public intellectual life. The restless and often abstract and self-absorbed conceptualization of social life is seen from this perspective more as a symptom of, than as a serious attempt to, offer solutions to any real crisis. Seen in this light, social theorists appear as charlatans, not so different from other confidence men and impostors.

Both these attitudes have a relatively precise historical origin and can be traced back to the aftermath of the French Revolution. Especially the reception of Georg Friedrich Wilhlem Hegel's oeuvre (with Jean-Jacques Rousseau's as an interesting precursor) galvanizes both attitudes to social concept formation. It is important in this context to remember that Hegel still saw himself as a worker in the vineyard of a universal, collective, and unitary philosophical project dedicated to truth. In other words, he saw himself much in the same way as individual natural scientists still see their work today. By contrast, his students became acolytes, refashioning their master into an *individual* hero-creator,[5] while his detractors fashioned him into the arch-symbol of the theorizing charlatan (e.g., Schnädelbach [1999] 2011). Hence, fourth philosophy became pluralized as a *set* of *Weltanschauungen*, that is, as a set of heterogeneous and often incompatible approaches to the world. Outwardly this was made visible by prefacing the term *philosophy* with the names of its putative creators as "Kantian," "Hegelian," "Marxian," and so on, using name designators in a fashion reminiscent of the way the names of great artists since the Renaissance were deployed as markers of style. That this *weltanschaulicher* character of conceptualizations of the social world is with us to this day and is visible in the continuing use of personal name-labels to designate theories (as Parsonian, Foucauldian, etc.), suggesting that embracing a particular social theory is ultimately a matter of personal preference.

It has been commonly understood since then that the classification of theorists as heroes and charlatans is driven by academic or political partisanship. Yet simple partisanship is not what is historically new about this distinction. Long before the French Revolution, political philosophers were seen and treated as political fellow travelers of parties that were constituted by ambitious leaders. Occasionally such philosophers were taken to speak for themselves, but even more typically they were taken as speaking for their party. They were rarely perceived as speaking for some abstract ideal or ideology independent of concrete political actors.[6] Accordingly, exile and publication or distribution restrictions were common fates among them.[7] Yet such dangers issued primarily from their *personal* connections (presumed or real) to the men of power whom they served or aspired to serve as educators and advisors. It issued much less from the content of their writing, other than those parts that could be construed as taking sides in an ongoing conflict between contenders for power.

Religious heresy was partially an exception to this rule. It is important to recall that, from the time of the Church fathers to the Enlightenment, theology assumed absolute intellectual primacy in the western European world. The task of social thought under the dominion of theology was for centuries to come prefigured by Augustine's model of the two "cities."[8] Augustine juxtaposes his city of God as the true community of destination for the Christian pilgrim selected by divine grace to the worldly city as a sinful, merely transitional phase of human existence. The task of Christian political philosophy was to illuminate the moral inferiority of the worldly city and to make proposals how best to lead one's life within it in view of the thereafter. Truth for Christian political philosophy remained the agreement with scripture.[9] Accordingly, the accusation of heresy was the means par excellence to discredit a political philosopher and by implication the party with which he was associated. Nobody would then have seen political philosophers' work as heroic for providing intellectual orientation or as charlatanistic for failing to do so. Religion and theology alone could do so.

The reasons for the changing valence of conceptualizations of social life are manifold. There is the revaluation of the here and now, of everyday life, which began with the Protestant Reformation (e.g., Taylor 1989) and which gathered steam with accelerating economic growth. There is also, in part triggered by the success of the natural sciences, the increasing independence of political philosophy from theology. This autonomization of theorizing social life was greatly facilitated by the relative indeterminacy, nay the studied disinterest, of the New Testament with regards to thinking macropolitical orders, which opened a gap that could at least in part be filled by Greek and Roman political philosophy.

The most important reason for the increasing importance of systematic reflections on social life was that the scale, scope, and intentionality of politics had started to change dramatically since the Renaissance (Glaeser 2013). The bread-and-butter business of Medieval politics, the stabilization and promotion of dynastic power through tactics and strategies of territorial gain and control, developed through early modernity into a politics of institutional design bringing an increasing range of human activities under governmental control. These efforts ballooned to bring into view the possibility of choosing among and instituting radically different social orders. Once more, the Protestant Reformation hastened this development by facing ruling bodies with the possibility of choosing their religious affiliation, a move with dramatic consequences for interstate, statewide, and local social organization. The successes of the English, the American, and, above all, the French Revolution appeared to validate the understanding that humans are capable of remaking the social world in which they live according to their own image. Undoubtedly, political philosophy itself, notably the intentional framework developed by contract theory, had its share in this transformation of the political by fuelling the political imagination with the idea of a human rather than divinely created social order.[10] Once this ambition had taken hold in the minds of people while becoming validated as feasible through successful revolutionary practice, politics also grew dependent on conceptual work that could develop and flesh out its intentions, and help it to concretize its imagination of scope and scale. It was thus that political philosophers could acquire heroic stature as the ones who could help humans realize their dreams. Thus, the French revolutionaries went to the barricades with Rousseau in hand, as it were (e.g., Edelstein 2009). Hegel's *Philosophy of Right* is the point of reference for the idea that self-consciousness, that ideas (and a fortiori, their bearers) form one of the two axes around which the dialectics of history unfold. Hegel put intellectuals on the map as necessary agents of a historical process (cf. Boyer 2005). Thinking the social thus became as honorable as before it had been to think the divine. The meaning bestowed by religious practices came to be supplemented and subsequently supplanted by the participation in political projects.

The flip side of this way of understanding history was that social theorists could attract blame for leading humans astray by suggesting false goals, by devising unsuitable means, or by misunderstanding the conditions of political possibility. The biblical distinction between true and false prophets acquired a new meaning in this context. The pluralization and politicization of political philosophy therefore raised the question of its validity in a new and much more urgent way. At issue was no longer the invitation of divine benevolence or wrath but the production of worldly success or failure. Indeed, after the French Revolution social knowledge became as existentially relevant as in centuries past only central religious knowledge had been. Questions of a just social and political order became as vital as Trinitarian theology had been; the issue of economic growth became as central as that of divine grace once was.

The amazing success of the natural sciences suggested that the way out of controversy could lie in rigorous empirical work, thus setting the stage for a new truth regime emphasizing the correspondence of the theory with the world. This proved a further motivation for the development of the social sciences (the other being the practical needs of rulers; e.g., Scott 1998; Fourcade 2009). Hence, the labor of conceptualizing social life gradually fragmented and drifted apart in a number of different directions with three principal tendencies. First, more encompassing social theories emerged that were developed in more or less rigorous dialogues with empirical research of various kinds. They geared themselves toward the explanation of a wide-ranging set of phenomena in the social world as it existed between interpersonal transactions and world historical transformations. The exemplar for this strand of theorizing is Marx's oeuvre.

Second, in contrast to social theories that tried to formulate more encompassing perspectives but also in more or less rigorous dialogue with empirical material, a host of subject-hyphenated theories emerged with self-consciously limited domains. Theories of "gift exchange," "business cycles," and "social stratification" may serve to illustrate this group. At the far end of specialization, such efforts at concept formation fragment into the articulation of single hypotheses that are supposedly "testable" using statistical or other empirical methods.[11] The extremely narrow conceptual base of such work, typically bare of any effort to integrate phenomena across various domains of social life, stretches the notion of theory to its very limit. Both of these strands were eager to shed or hide their link to philosophy, if not always in practice then with determination in name, precisely because they were eager to shed its *Weltanschaulichkeit*. Both strands aspired to be scientific by making universalist claims. Whereas the more encompassing efforts of the first kind continued to cultivate close ties to politics, the subject-hyphenated theories tried to hide these.

Third, one strand remained focused on reason as the principal source of insight but geared it increasingly toward purely normative ends—that is modern political philosophy (in the Anglophone world, also a part of political theory).[12] Fourth, and finally, there emerged an increasing split between conceptual formulation and practical application in administration and politics, not least because of the institutional divide between research practiced at universities and bureaucratic practices. In sum, the validity crisis of social-concept formation in conjunction with professional specialization led to a split into "positive," "normative," and "applied" theories and to increasingly constrictive efforts to define the domain for which a particular theory was supposedly valid in conjunction with empirical research meant to validate the theory.

During the short twentieth century, the heroization and demonization of social theory reached a feverish pitch. Social theories became compacted and simplified into fighting ideologies, their universal claim to truth and appeal to scientificity notwithstanding; their producers were transmogrified into modern-day prophets. This is true to such an extent that liberalism, socialism, and fascism came to be taken as totalizing accounts of and for social life, even though each was built around a "fatal conceit" easily discernible from the perspective of the opposing camps.[13] Accordingly, twentieth-century history can be told as a stepwise battle in which socialism and fascism first challenged and then defeated liberalism in parts of the world, only to see their own subsequent reach for world dominance crushed. Fascism exhausted itself militarily against the joint opposition of socialism and liberalism. And socialism, in turn, imploded, so that liberalism, finally standing without opponents, could radicalize itself once more, in many ways picking up the thread of self-radicalization where it had been forced to leave it off with the advent of the welfare state.[14] The consequences of the totalization of social theories into self-radicalizing ideologies were, and in the case of liberalism continue to be, catastrophic. Volk-centric (i.e., pseudo-)Darwinism (aka fascism) led to terror, mass murder, and all-out global war; nomological historicism (aka socialism) likewise led to mass murder and massive levels of suppression. Mechanistic ontological individualism (aka liberalism) has led to the objectification of humans as profit centers and to massive environmental degradation.

Given these consequences, it is not surprising that a small minority of theorists began to realize with horror how theory was implicated in the ideologization of the world while the vast majority was basking in the glories of political relevance. The dissenters reacted as good intellectuals in similar situations always have: with skepticism, turning it against all those theories, theorems, certainties, and hidden assumptions that seemed to have a share in murder, war, suppression, the objectification of human beings, and the degradation of their natural environment. The first effort in this direction was called critical theory (Horkheimer [1937] 1992; Horkheimer and Adorno [1944] 1988). Its hallmark, the re-appropriation of Kantian, Hegelian, and Marxian techniques of critique to turn them against highly fragmented, historically nonspecific social concept formation, which its practitioners associated with epistemological positivism and political liberalism. They also made an effort to rid increasingly ossified Marxism of some of its metaphysical presuppositions (its economism and historical determinism), which to many intellectuals no longer appeared tenable in the 1920s and 1930s.[15]

A second wave of skepticism, aptly called deconstruction (Derrida [1967] 1976), made its appearance in the late 1960s. It become the methodological core of postmodernism, the essential tool behind the critique of metanarratives (Lyotard [1979] 1984) as the totalizing schemes of social life. Notably in anthropology, deconstruction has been applied to both theory formation and empirical research practices (Clifford and Marcus 1986; Marcus and Fisher 1986; Clifford 1988). It constituted the new discipline of cultural studies and had a profound impact on the humanities, feminism, political philosophy, and critical legal studies.[16] Deconstruction has yielded ample evidence for the deep misogyny, ethnocentrism, racism, and sexism of celebrated texts and theoretical models. Deconstruction has also pushed theorists to see the world from the perspective of people marginalized in various kinds of power struggles.

It is not surprising that both critical theorists and deconstructionists were cast once more as heroes and charlatans, by themselves, by acolytes, and by detractors. The heroization and vilification of the Frankfurt school was supported by the fact that its practitioners refused cooptation with any of the three leading twentieth-century ideologies. Beyond that, their members were authenticated as independent intellectuals by actual life-threatening persecution. The celebration and rejection of deconstruction was, in turn, greatly facilitated by its link to emancipatory political movements, the 1968 students' movement, the women's movement, and various alternative sexuality and gender movements (gay, lesbian, transgender, and queer).

Yet, as modalities of skepticism, both critical theory and deconstruction have been better at highlighting the trappings of problematic modalities of theorizing than at stimulating alternative efforts at constructing social theories adequate for our time. Worse perhaps, precisely because their critiques of theory were so trenchant, they have produced in their wake a great hesitation to produce more comprehensive efforts to theorize social life. The consequences were particularly dramatic for what I have just called more comprehensive theories, which as "grand narratives" were simply swept away by the critique. The intellectual kinds of theorists who used to develop them had turned into critics, and so they stood more or less without institutionalized defense. Subject-hyphenated theories were likewise criticized but were too deeply grounded institutionally to suffer a major blow from the critique. Worse, the deconstructivist attack led them to further entrench themselves, thus widening the rift between the various modalities of crafting theories. Within a subject-hyphenated theory world, more ethnographers have remained open to both comprehensive theorizing and postmodern critique. Yet they have also grown the strange habit of having to theorize *with* someone else. It has become standing practice to seek refuge and theoretical legitimacy by appropriating the concepts of theorists with a reputation as critics who have as such acquired heroic status. By comparison, theoretization from one's own ethnographic data takes second place at best because it seems to fall under the suspicion of doing symbolic violence to the intricate complexities and particularities of people and their lives.

The result is that, in spite there being no lack of critiques of liberalism, there is, intellectually speaking, no social theorizing that could credibly underwrite alternative imaginaries. It is worth noting that, for the first time since the seventeenth century, the hegemonic social order is not confronted with a critical alternative. Absolutism based on ideas of divine grace found its critical alternative in contract theory; classical liberalism found its critical alternative in socialism and communism. Only contemporary neoliberalism stands unchallenged. The need, however, for adequate interpretations of social life offering orientation in a world characterized by growing complexity has not diminished. Our desires to live in a world that affords a higher quality of life for more people has not cooled; and we have not come up with any better way for making it happen than politics. But that is to say that we need theory more than ever. Yet we need better theory and better practices of theoretization situated in more critically effective environments of semi-autonomous institutional domains—including an effort to think without heroes and charlatans in mind. To achieve this, we might have to expect less from individual theoretical contributions and more from the institutional environment in which theory formation takes place.

Adequacy Criteria for Social Scientific Theoretizations

If it is still the task of theory to produce conceptual frameworks for the interpretation of social life, it is important to consider possible criteria that help us to craft theories that are adequate to the task. These criteria should also help us to adjudicate the adequacy of extant theoretical frameworks. In lieu of an exalted but practically irredeemable notion of truth, but also beyond an encompassing skepticism, I propose two levels—a metatheoretical and a substantive one—at which to lodge a number of adequacy criteria. Together they reinterpret and develop what since the 1980s has been called a reflexive approach to social scientific inquiry.[17]

From Truth Seeking to Metaphorical Exploration

The political history of social theory that I have outlined in the last section as well as the experiences gathered with the uses and abuses of theory during the last two hundred years suggest a few metatheoretical criteria for improved theorizing. A great many of the abuses of theory were facilitated by two interacting kinds of reification characterizing naïve scientism,[18] which have been ruthlessly deconstructed by postmodern critics (e.g., Rorty 1979).

The first of these reifications concerns the way in which the objects of social scientific inquiry are imagined. In other words, it concerns matters of ontology, or the ways in which the social world is thought of as composed of differentiable component types and their integration into some kind of structured whole. Above all, there has been a tendency to reify processes by making thing-like—that is, clearly bounded and self-contained—what would be better understood as fluid and constituted in contextual interaction among humans, as well as with artificial objects and the natural environment.[19] Reification in this sense pertains to both components and their relations. Liberalism and fascism, for example, work with reified notions of human beings, their fundamental motives and capacities, and their relations to each other. Among scholars, such assumptions have rightly been criticized as ahistorical. Yet some of the very same scholars who have advanced these criticisms most forcefully, socialists of various stripes among them, have themselves worked with a reified notion of historical development and its telos. Epistemologically speaking, ontological reifications are problematic because both the mundane experiences of social life in increasingly more parts of the world and the historical, ethnographical, and statistical analyses of social life have attested to its enormous plasticity, dynamism, and variability within human time horizons. Even aspects of what has been taken for nature and thus outside of human influence—the global climate being the most prominent example—have more recently become acknowledged as being fundamentally shaped by human action.

The second form of reification characterizing naïve scientism concerns the manners in which the objects of investigation are approached, that is, its epistemology, both in theory and practice. At the core of its epistemic reifications lies a naïve scientistic understanding of what language is and how it is used. In its extreme form, its linguistic ideology (Silverstein 1979) is based in the idea that science can produce some absolute form of truth because—to paraphrase Galilei's famous dictum—the "book of nature" (and by implication that of social life) is written in some language humans can decipher truthfully, either by the grace of God or more generally by methexis in some universe-governing power (such as reason; e.g., Blumenberg 1979). If that is taken to be true, it is conversely not implausible that the correct signs find their equivalent in nature. The result is what is more commonly known as hypostatization, that is, the assumption that words have their equivalent in the world of objects.[20] In naïve scientism, this is most clearly visible in the treatment of "facts" or "data" as immediate properties of the world rather than as other, if "thin" (as opposed to "thick," more abstract, and conceptually integrated; Reed 2011), kinds of signs. Even when less extreme versions of epistemic reification take leave of the idea that the world can be identified with a governing and humanly decipherable generative code, that is, where the awareness has spread that language in whatever form is but a medium, the assumption of the transparency of language (a formal one, such as mathematics included) still often prevails. The problem with this linguistic ideology is, above, all the false certainty it conveys by suggesting the possibility of truth as a possession.[21]

Linguistic and ontological reification support each other (Whorf [1939] 1956). Ontological reification distorts the world in a particular way, and linguistic reification makes these distortions invisible by naturalizing them. Thus reification becomes self-reinforcing, and science becomes self-mythologizing (Horkheimer and Adorno [1944] 1988). The problems with reification do not remain at the epistemological level alone, however. It is commonplace that reification can have serious ethical consequences by objectifying and thus dehumanizing people.[22] And finally and arguably most important, reification limits the possibility for reformist politics by bracketing aspects of the world as being off limits for human intervention, by misrecognizing apt means for political goals, and by disempowering agents with concomitant consequences for epistemic and ethical practices (Glaeser 2011, 2013). In other words, reifications severely curtail the social imagination. In this respect, Margret Thatcher's famous phrase "there is no alternative" (commonly referred to as TINA) is as politically deadening as the insistence by really existing socialism on the inevitable course of socialism to communism.

Even if this notion of double reification identifies some of problems with "traditional" theory (Horkheimer [1937] 1992) in a useful manner, it is less clear how best to proceed from here. Notoriously, the positive theory-developing aspects of critical theory have been rather vague. All warnings against reification notwithstanding, it would clearly require super-human skills to theorize a complex world in which all components move at once. Every recognizable analytical structuring presupposes that some components are held constant, thus providing a scaffolding for the rest. The question is, then, not how we could do without any constants but only how to look at these scaffoldings in a nonreifying way such that the scaffolding remains in view, arguable, and changeable. What we need is a rigorous yet playful attitude toward the conceptual apparatuses that allow us to compare and develop insight. To start with, we might benefit from a term that captures this attitude well, something far removed from the trappings of the absolute that is inherent, for example, in a notion such as "law," with its word-of-God resonances, or such as "nature," with its cosmological echoes of eternal universality.

It would be as step forward if we became ethically cognizant and practically comfortable with the regulative idea that the conceptual apparatuses we construct stand at best in an insight-generating metaphorical relationship to the world.[23] Metaphors can and, if adequate, do afford insights into the process of bringing to bear a differentiated and integrated structure as a "source" on parts of the world as its "target" (Whorf [1939] 1956; Lakoff 1993). Theory at its very best is such an insight-generating source, part of a metaphorical mapping. The world explored by applying differentiations and integrations of the source in a stepwise manner to the target will, at least at first, not be more complex than the sources themselves. If the sources are hierarchical, only super- and subordinated aspects of the world will light up in the process of transposing; if the sources differentiate only few qualities, they cannot illuminate more in the target either. The metaphoric quality of theory-to-world mappings implies that conceptual frameworks rich in modalities of distinguishing and integrating may be preferable in situations that aim at exploring complexities. Conversely a conceptual framework offering modalities of identification bringing many phenomena under unifying rubrics is preferable when simplification is of the essence.

If the conceptual structure of theory can serve as a source for the metaphoric exploration of the world, then the thin semiotic precipitate of experiences in the world, commonly referred to as facts or data, can also become the source for the metaphorical development of theory. Of course, this process of reverse transposition can work only if data are differentiated and integrated in discernible ways. And that typically happens through some systematic way first of generating or encoding the world and then of using pattern-search techniques, both of which commonly travel under the rubric of "method." In the end, we have a two-way metaphoric relationship that remains productive precisely as long as the metaphoric predication remains "alive" or "impertinent" (Ricoeur [1975] 1977), that is, not collapsible and, indeed, other. There is merit, then, in allowing theory some play of free speculation skating on nothing but the logic and/or the aesthetics of concepts to think of new figures of synthesized analysis. Theories as sources can become richer in this way, even though there is no guarantee of relevance for what is in essence a kind of playing. And there is merit in the hamster-like, nose- to-the-ground gathering of seemingly arbitrary facts as well as in the self-consciously mechanistic exploration of patterns in the data. It is potentially useful to engage in the autistic solipsism of both these activities precisely to the degree that eventually they come face to face with being a nuisance for each other. It is too bad, then, that most hamsters do not enjoy skating and that most skaters are averse to dirt.

Theorizing the world as a metaphorical operation works precisely because concepts are different from what they try to illuminate. But this is to postulate the alterity of theory as a precondition for insight. Theories as spitting images of the world would be totally useless because they could in their completion no longer support the processes of discovery. This also means that the use of any structured source as tool of discovery for a target will necessarily break down at some point because similarities only ever go so far before they become unhelpful because their further pursuit leads to absurdities.[24] This means that we should expect even the best of theories to offer only limited insights of varying degrees, even for the domains for which they explicitly make claims of applicability. And we should also expect much of the world to escape the harness of the metaphor, even as we may hope to have discovered aspects and relations that matter. Consequently, we should always be ready to embrace a plurality of conceptualizations for the exploration of the world. We should never expect to have a single unified theory of everything social life can be. Clearly a single metaphor, or integrated set of metaphors, ceases to function properly as such if it does not have to face alternatives. This also implies that rather than looking at individual theoretical offerings as more or less adequate, we need to look toward a whole field of theories to accomplish this task.

None of this implies that metaphors could not be better or worse as guides to discovery and, in this sense, more or less true. But conceptual worlds as sources have goodness neither in themselves nor for the world but only for particular people wrapped up in certain kinds of concrete practical pursuits in the world.

Six Dimensions of Relevance

A substantial perspective is required, therefore, to give direction to the process of theorizing, of choosing among various possibilities to craft a set of conceptual differentiations and integrations as a source domain for the metaphorical exploration of some aspect of the world.[25] Without such a substantive perspective, theory is in constant danger of being simply irrelevant. Articulating the interpretative needs of people in a particular historical situation for particular kinds of political projects provides such a perspective. Yet the articulation of interpretive needs is clearly contingent on available concepts and emotive understandings. It is useful, therefore, to think of the articulation of interpretive needs, of practices of theoretization, and of the metaphorical illumination of the world as entangled in a hermeneutic circle. Within it, theories that meet interpretive needs can be called substantively adequate.

Thematically, interpretative needs vary with the interests that people pursue in the world. Therefore, a politics of attention that is typically played out in several overlapping institutional domains (including material support, professional fields, and various kinds of publics) nearly inevitably accompanies all projects of theoretization. Particular historical situations also bring with them, however, widely shared interpretative needs. If civil war becomes all-encompassing, peace becomes a central issue. The advent of the anthropocene has arguably for the first time in history created a situation with a universal interpretative need. There has also been a large degree of historical variation. Whereas the ancient Greeks were deeply concerned with the question of a good life in the here and now enabled by supportive institutional arrangements, medieval Christians were chiefly worried about the consequences of worldly involvement for the afterlife; and whereas the early moderns were interested in the conditions supportive to lasting peace, moderns are driven by questions of economic growth, its distribution, and the freedom to pursue individual interests, whatever these may be.

Substantive interests for theory development can be thought of, heuristically, as falling into six categories along two dimensions. The first of these differentiates among concerns about *actuality* (the world as it is), *potentiality* (the world as it could be), and *instrumentality* (possibilities for intervention). The second dimension acknowledges that each of these concerns can be articulated in either a more subjective mode expressing desires or in a more reality-oriented, objective mode. Subjective actuality questions orient us to what we *want* to know about the world as it is. Objective actuality questions ask of social arrangements *what* they are; *how* they operate; and *whence* they came, given our curiosity and epistemic abilities. Subjective potentiality questions wonder what a good life in a good society should be; objective potentiality questions inquire into what they *could* be, given what we know about social life. And, finally, there are questions of *instrumentality*. Subjective instrumentality puzzles over what means we want to use to *improve* the workings of social arrangements, for example, how to govern more justly, how to produce more efficiently, or how to break a political stalemate. Objective instrumentality asks about the means that can be used to achieve certain ends effectively. According to this heuristic, theories can now be substantively adequate or inadequate in six different ways.

Existentially speaking (and from a sociology-of-knowledge perspective too) questions of actuality, potentiality, and instrumentality are interdependent, even co-constitutive. Questions about the what, how, and whence of social arrangements need focus, a meaningful selection criterion that often comes from people's interest in transforming the same or other social arrangements, that is, from a political interest. Successful transformation, in turn, requires keen attention to questions of actuality because success in politics is crucially dependent on useful knowledge (e.g., Scott 19989; Glaeser 2011). This is the ultimate reason why theories need to aspire to some form of objectivity. One could also say that theory, in spite of its alterity, in spite of merely being the source end in metaphoric processes of discovery, must strive for a particular kind of realism in the *process* of discovery rather than in a *structure* of correspondences, even though the latter may be a precondition for the former. The ideas for the directions in which people would want to transform social arrangements are derived from our imaginaries about a better society (e.g., Taylor 2003). These concerns with potentiality, however, are at least in part cultivated by our knowledge of alternative actualities. The exploration of the full breadth of what it can mean to be human has been, after all, one dominant reason for doing history or ethnography in the first place (Benedict [1934] 1989; Kluckhohn 1959).

The fragmentation of inquiries into social life of which I have spoken in the last section very much follows the dividing lines between inquires of the actual, the potential, and the instrumental. All of them have, in their self-understanding as sciences, specialized in objective kinds of inquiry, typically disregarding or even suppressing the subjective orientations of their work. The subject-hyphenated theories have concentrated on actuality. Although empirically typically solid, this work often uses concepts in isolation and can be outright antitheoretical in its refusal to grasp wider social contexts conceptually. At the same time, its adherence to positivism makes it deeply unreflexive. Political and social philosophy, as well as some work done in the humanities, has specialized in potentiality. This work is mostly nonempirical, but it addresses important questions of more comprehensive scope while indulging in historically uprooted, merely speculative concept formation, which seems to describe the everywhere and nowhere. Policy studies have specialized in instrumentality. Institutionally sequestered into special schools or disciplines with an even greater aversion to more comprehensive theorizing, they are typically (even more than subject-hyphenated projects) dedicated to descriptivism.

What we have in the division of labor between people pursuing questions of actuality, potentiality, and instrumentality in isolation from each other is therefore a performative instantiation of a higher-order version of the historical split between empiricism and rationalism. Kant has famously critiqued pure empiricism as blind and pure rationalism as hollow because knowledge presupposes the dynamic interplay of conception and perception. Without recognizing the co-constitution of issues of actuality, potentiality, and instrumentality in both an objective and a subjective register, we end up with a positive science that is as soundly rigorous as it is pointless; we get normative scholarship that is as elegant as it is unrealistic; and we get politics that is as clever about power maintenance as it is devoid of meaningful vision.

The question that is now posed is, how we can reform the research and writing practices in the social sciences to form concepts and theories that are empirically grounded and socially relevant because they speak to the concerns of our time? What can we do to keep them translatable into plans for action; to remain oriented toward developing our human potential for leading meaningful lives; to keep them attuned to potential futures; to make them more encompassing again, showing interdependencies among the various domains of social life; and to keep them from falling into the traps of reification? In what follows, I argue that ethnography is well placed to contribute to such an undertaking because, unlike other methods, it can attend to decisive moments of social processes and because it remains in touch with lived lives in both its subjective and objectives dimensions. But I also argue that ethnography can redeem this promise only if we manage to reform some our ingrained habits of doing ethnography. I begin this task by calling into question the notion that ethnography (and I may throw history into the mix as well) is ultimately about telling the lives of people in different times and places.

Accounting for Processes and the Limits of Narrative

The classical questions asked in the social sciences since the nineteenth century have been of a processual nature such as, What is the specific dynamic of economic development in a particular epoch? How do some countries get onto a trajectory of self-reinforcing economic growth? How did growth become the penultimate concern of politics? How did the nation-state form emerge, and why did it become the dominant form of large-scale political organization in the world? How do selves come about in interaction? In general, one could say: How do institutions emerge, how are they maintained to stay self-similar (if they do) over the course of time, and how do they change?

There are a number of modes of symbolic production available to capture processes. There are serial pictures, such as film, animated film, serial photography, graphic novels, and other time-sequence graphics (e.g., the successions of maps depicting the same terrain that we find in historical atlases); there are mathematical functions in which time is one of the independent variables, whole systems of such equations, and their graphical representation; there are iterative numerical modeling techniques (computer simulations) and iterative game-theoretical models. Most important, however, there is narrative. As a mode of symbolic production, narrative is easily the most widely used in everyday life. But its special position in social life is derived not only from the fact that it is the quantitatively prevalent form of accounting for happenings in time; the other modalities appear to be derivative of narrative, in the sense that they are either direct translations from narrative into a medium other than ordinary language while preserving the structuring dimensions of narrative or that they are interpretable only through the good offices of narrative. Precisely because social scientists are interested in giving accounts of processes, the end of their endeavor often is narrative, for example, by telling people's lives over a day, a week, a year, the whole of the life of a person, family, or clan; by telling the history of a place, an object, or an institution; or by telling the emergence, the unfolding, or the entailments of an event. For some social scientists, this import of narrative in putatively scientific accounts has been a source of discomfort precisely because narrative is shared not only with everyday pursuits but also with the arts. For other social scientists, this continuity among aesthetic, everyday, and scientific practices has been a source comfort and inspiration. They argue that narrative allows them to remain close to the subjective interpretative needs of real people in the world, that it is a source of pleasure and pride due to the fact that telling a good tale well is an acknowledged high art sure to garner an audience, and finally that keeping to narrative is also a matter of the utmost ontological importance because human life in the context of others is constituted narratively.

For all these reasons, seasoned practitioners of both ethnography and historiography have rejected explicit theoretization as part of their accounts. Theory, they insist, needs to remain submerged, implicit in the text so as not to jar its readability. Many feel that theory gets in the way of properly reporting the facts, and that in the end, it is the facts that matter. Another group, consisting mostly of anthropologists working among rural and low-income urban populations in or from the places beyond the North Atlantic wealth belt make another, related argument against theory in their narrative accounts. They feel that theory historically developed and cultivated in the North Atlantic wealth belt imposes categories that must inevitably misrecognize the people they study, thus ultimately becoming involved in acts of what Pierre Bourdieu (1991) has called symbolic violence. I argue that the first of these two arguments is fundamentally flawed even when it points to legitimate concerns with "overtheoretization" and that the second produces an important insight but draws the wrong conclusions from it.

Before proceeding any further, it is useful to introduce a definition of *narrative* as a symbolic form. Paul Ricoeur, prompted by his own monumental three-volume effort to compare fictional and historical narratives ([1983–1985] 1984–1986), defines narrative as a "synthesis of the heterogeneous" (1991, 21). According to him, narrative manages to weave representations of different people—their actions, relationships, feelings, and ideas—as well as their material and spatial conditions into a coherent whole. For Ricoeur ([1983–1985] 1984–1986, 43–45), it is, above all, the temporal structuration of components into a string of actions, plot, that allows synthesis to take effect.

On the basis of this plot-centric understanding of narrative, we can now wonder what, if anything, distinguishes social scientific narratives from artistic ones.[26] At first, one might want to surmise that the former orient themselves to the real world whereas the latter deal in fiction. That such a distinction misses the point is quickly demonstrated by art forms that understand themselves as realist (e.g., Auerbach [1946] 1994). Realist art has always aimed to make fiction to better comprehend the very world in which we live. Indeed, Aristotle in the *Poetics* ([322 BCE] 1970) depicts the craft of composing tragedies, comedies, and epics (then the sum total of what we would call "fictional" today) as *mimēsis praxeos*, an imitation of action in the world.[27] The realism of certain art forms is also the reason why social scientists can stand in awe before certain kinds of literary writing, not as works of art alone but as enterprises directly competing with ethnographic and/or historical efforts at symbolizing the social world. As Aristotle and, after him, romanticist aesthetic philosophers have pointed out, fiction can, with its enormous power to allegorize the general in the particular, easily compete, if not in certain ways outcompete, with ethnography or historiography in its depiction of social reality.

In fact, serious ethnographers or historians have often had intense longings to produce a fictional account of some process to be all the more truthful to fact. On the one hand, this is the case because much fiction is indeed realist and typically reaches, to the envy of the social scientist, a much larger audience. On the other hand, the desire to fictionalize emerges because the empirical record is always spotty, often lacking density precisely where one wishes to have it. Thus social scientific and literary narratives can both be realistic even though their realism is achieved by rather different means. They are different genres characterized by a different poetics. One important difference has emerged, however, from this exploration. Whereas fictional narratives may choose to be realistic, social scientific narratives must not be. What supposedly ascertains realism in social scientific writing is the call to weave narratives from evidence found through research practices currently deemed defensible by a scientific community. Because this is, rarely enough, to tell realistic tales, social scientists regularly supplement evidence with imagination; they engage in fictional extensions of their findings, which, so conventions suggest, should be marked as conjectures but rarely systematically are.

A second distinction that sees social science narratives as explanatory and literary ones as abstaining from explanation is equally misleading. In a certain sense, all narrative has explanatory power by virtue of performing certain selections and ordered associations of Ricoeur's array of heterogeneous narrative elements at the expense of other possibilities. Some of these suggest causality. Still, these explanations are indirect. They work by creating spatio-temporal metonymies and a host of allusions built on formal devices, including tropes, meter, rhyme, and repetition. As a symbolic form, however, narratives do not explicitly reflect on how this interweaving takes place. They do not traditionally attempt to explain how one action gives rise to another; they just let them follow. They do not explain how spaces shape identities; they just let actors pass through them. Nobody has made this point clearer than Walter Benjamin, who says, "Actually, it is half the art of storytelling to keep a story free from explanation as one relates it." And further, illuminating why storytelling must refrain from explanation: "A completely explained story . . . a story which leaves nothing to be desired, nothing to be questioned, loses its personal resonance and disappears from memory because no interpretative work would keep it there" ([1936] 1977, 391). In other words, good stories need to be open gestalts (Iser 1976); they need to be completed by the listeners, who have to come up with their own explanations as they hear the tale.

Aristotle ([322 BCE] 1970) makes a related point. He argues that the connections between the various elements of poetic forms have to be "necessary" or at least "likely." By that he means that the progression of the tale as told by the poet, the mythos, has to appear logical or at least plausible to the audience. What Aristotle seems to have had in mind here is, for example, that in any plot actions and reactions need to follow each other in such a way that readers will find the connections persuasive given what they assume to be true about life in society. Characters, for example, need to be presented in typical places: women as mothers at home, men as citizens in the agora or as heroes on the battlefield. In cases when such regularities are violated—let us say by heroes cutting onions or women giving moving funeral orations—a form of accounting is in place that renders atypicality comprehensible on the basis of other typicalities (or generalities—for example, by placing the female warrior in Sparta or among the Amazons). Aristotle sees such accounting for atypicalities as the characteristic problem of historiography, which he deems for this very reason morally and aesthetically inferior to poetry, which he deems dedicated to general truths. Only then can tales, in his opinion, have the desired effect on the audience, which for him is the prompting of the catharsis that alone allows a kind of moral learning from the play. So, he too, much like Benjamin, makes the active synthesizing activity of the audience central to telling stories.

From the perspective of the two sets of adequacy criteria I presented in the last section, narrative accounts devoid of explicit theorizing are a rather mixed blessing. Substantively, they furnish many tools that prove adequate in many circumstances. Precisely because narratives are used in everyday language, they are a fine medium to convey concerns of subjective actuality, potentiality, and instrumentality. Yet a more fine-grained analysis of the shaping of desire, for example, may quickly make psychoanalytic or other psychological reasoning important. Long practices of objectivizing accounting in a wide range of social domains (law, politics, economic planning, administrative reporting, and history) have also made narratives into formidable tools to take care of objective interests across all three substantive domains. Yet, again, a more complex analysis of flows of money, goods, resources, and ideas of integrative institutions such as markets or bureaucracies will benefit from recourse to systematic theoretization.

The defenders of theory-free narrative could argue against the added caveats that whenever concepts prove really useful they quickly find their way into general narrative practices. Freudian notions of the unconscious or Weberian ideas about bureaucracy can be assumed as general possessions of the listener or reader of narrative and will be mobilized by him or her without the author even mentioning the concept explicitly. Yet this narrative presupposition of theory, of commonly understood manners of linking its sundry elements, poses a serious problem. Any of the many conceptual dichotomies that postmodern theorists took such great pleasure in deconstructing as ideological devices have furnished and continue to furnish narrative dynamics in certain contexts. This is metatheoretically inadequate because these commonsense frameworks may engage in any number of reifications, overblown generalizations that fail to be objectively false when it matters to provide guidance for political interventions that stand a chance to further emancipatory political projects. In fact, demanding that theoretization remain implicit in the narratives told, as many professional historians and ethnographers are prompted to do, uncritically perpetuates potentially problematic storytelling practices.

Consequent Processualism as Metatheoretical Framework

In the preceding section, I have shown that narratives can only at the peril of exploding their genre make explanations explicit, that is, by directly talking about the *principles* they use to interweave their elements. This, however, is precisely what the social sciences must do because they cannot satisfy themselves with indexing commonplace forms of making connections between people, their actions, and their contexts. Instead, the commonplace forms of interweaving must be the starting point for critical reflections. They are merely data for a social scientific analysis of how Ricoeur's array of heterogeneous elements needs to be harmonized and melodized in the process of providing a persuasive social scientific account. Moreover, the social sciences need to deepen this reflection into an analysis of the patterns of the temporal flow of actions, that is, the very principles of processual dynamics. And this is the work of social theory par excellence. Social science must, therefore, not in all of its exemplars but certainly collectively, move beyond narrative to explicit theoretization.

The insights won in theoretization need to be, in turn, used as effective emplotment strategies to weave a story propelled by theoretical logics. Doing so will allow it to bump into data that either resist or support the theoretically emplotted story. On the one hand, this may reflect critically on theory, but on the other, it may also inform further data-gathering efforts. And thus we can move forward and backward, telling theoretically emplotted tales while formulating and reformulating principles of processual dynamics and improving both until we have found a convincing fit between them and the data we have retrieved on the way. In the end, we are left with two formally equal kinds of results—a story and a theory—both presupposing one another, no story without theory and no theory without story. Whereas fiction, at least as we understand it today, must not sociologize or psychologize, the social sciences must not fail to theorize. And theory must be made explicit, not only to ourselves but, in the interests of reflexivity, to our fellow social scientists to assist each other in telling better tales.

If an analysis of process is so central to our undertaking and if we want to theorize its dynamic, we should make a decisive effort to understand it. The examples of processes that I have mentioned—the formation of capitalism, the nation-state, and the self—indicate already that we think of processes in terms of changes to objects. It is precisely here that metaphors can be misleading if the term *object* is taken too literally and analysis becomes limited to a comparative statics of objects at various times. For clearly, the objects in question here are, ontologically speaking, peculiar. They come into being exclusively as the effects of somehow interconnected human activity. Even more precisely, they exist only in these linked activities; they are maintained through repeated and often widely distributed activities, and they change with the character of activities and the connections between actors involved. In other words, the peculiar objects of social processes are *social formations,* and we know them under the name of institutions.

There is nothing new about this insight. Nevertheless, network theory and other forms of social scientific structuralism, systems theory included, have often occluded this fact by treating social structures as given. In fact, the insight that the objects of the social world, that is, institutions, are in fact *continuously* made and remade in socially distributed and coordinated activities is at least as old as Hegel's *Phenomenology*, where it was worked out paradigmatically for the modern social sciences.[28] I am less interested here in the contradiction inherent in the master-slave dialectic than in Hegel's insight that the identity of both can exist only in the interplay between the identification of the one and its recognition by the other. Alexandre Kojève has succinctly summarized the central insight of the *Phenomenology*: "Man is what he is only to the extent that he becomes what he is; his true Being (Sein) is Becoming (Werden), Time, History; and he becomes, he is History only in and by Action that negates the given, the Action of Fighting and of Work" ([1947] 1980, 38). Ever since this theme of social creation, the bringing into existence of institutions in linked activities has been a recurrent theme in the social sciences. It is central to Marx's analysis of commodities and capital. With some success, Max Weber (1922) tries to base the edifice of his mature theory on what he calls "social action," that is, action that is ultimately attuned to the actions of others. He is most explicit about the process of social formation in his analysis of power as a relational characteristic, including his ideal-typical analysis of legitimate domination.

To me, two scholars in particular have contributed most significantly to our understanding of processes of social formation: George Herbert Mead with his analysis of the formation of the self in the internalization of communication and Ludwig Wittgenstein with his analysis of rule-following. They are interesting precisely because they expand the Hegelian notion of the fundamental and irreducible sociality of human beings. Mead (together with Vygotsky [1934] 1986) adds to Hegel's explication of the genesis of self-consciousness as the result of desire directed toward a desiring other, that our very reflexivity and, consequently, our intelligence are institutions achieved through the internalization of dialogue. Wittgenstein ([1957] 1984) digs still deeper by arguing that all human regularities are based in habits, that all regularities in thinking and feeling are in fact the result of ongoing interactions within social communities and consequently institutions. The speech act theorists have contributed to this an intriguing analysis of the dialectic between an act as intended and an act as taken up by another, thus shedding critical light on the very moment when the institutions see the light of day.

As I see it, the careful investigation of the dynamics of the process of social formation is the very linchpin of building social theory. The notion of activity-generated institutions is the right starting point because it can, unlike the notion of structure, adequately connect concerns of actuality, potentiality, and instrumentality in its subjective and objective inflections while offering chances to steer clear of reification. Of course, the question we then must pose is, What activity concept should we choose to guide our inquiry? In a series of publications (Glaeser 2005, 2011, 2014), I have argued that we can develop a promising insight-generating metatheoretical framework by beginning to effect a subtle shift in the activity metaphors we use. Georg Simmel's (1908/1992) concept of interaction, the conceptual backbone of much ethnographic work in the Chicago tradition (Fine 1995), is problematic because it locks researchers in an imaginary of face-to-face mutuality in which they think of activities as looping back and forth among a small set of people. This is the case, however, for only a tiny fraction of activities we undertake within mass-mediated, global market megapolities. And even though "practice" has become the activity concept du jour, and even though it has proven its usefulness in many contexts, practices are themselves already far too aggregated as forms of institutions to make the term useful in understanding the processes of institutionalization, including their own.[29]

I have therefore proposed the admittedly inelegant notion of webbed action-reaction effect flows, which preserves at once the social character of activities while enabling the consideration of a wide variety of effect-flow patterns.[30] The point of the notion of action-reaction effect flows is to understand how persons in a particular space-time node react to the actions of others. It is useful to consider that reactions typically answer to a multiplicity of actions of a multiplicity of actors distributed over different times and different places, to whom the person reacting has qualitatively distinct kinds of relations. It does not matter whether these acts of others lie in the past or are anticipated at some point in the future, whether they are real or imagined, whether these acts were directed at the reacting person qua individual, whether they were directed at the reacting person qua membership in a category, or were directed at others while the reacting person thought they were directed at her. What matters is that by reacting to this mélange of fantasy and experience, thought and feeling, direct and indirect address, the actor gives this multiplicity a common thrust, a common effect. Thus the nonsimultaneous is copresented, the translocal is colocalized, and the perceived and the imagined are co-realized.[31]

Using the notion of webbed action-reaction effect flows as a guiding metaphor in this way immediately draws attention to the import of socio-technological means of projectively articulating action effects across time and space. This includes social and technological means of remembering and forgetting (from commemorative events to legally required file deletion) as well as social and technological means of imagining (from the cultivation of emplotment structures in narrative practices and the ritualistic incantation of threat scenarios to movies and financial modeling with net present value calculations). Analyzing the situation in terms of what is in it and far beyond, the here and the there, the now and the then, the personal and the categorical, the actual and the possible in the moment of reaction forcefully raises for the researcher questions of relevant contexts way beyond the ethnographic present.

Extending the metaphor of action-reaction effect flows illuminates that, in reacting, an actor might be better understood not so much as an originator as much more a collector and recombinant incubator. In reacting, the actor *is* passively mobilized by and actively mobilizes social relationships, understandings (discursive, emotive, visual, auditory, and kinesthetic), the built environment (the material resources he draws on, including food, shelter, and technology), and him- or herself and others as individuals with a particular biography.

All four of these elements, including persons, can be usefully seen as institutions, that is, as owing their existence to the repetition of webbed self-similar action-reaction effect flows. And, as such, they are all dependent on each other for their existence. Persons can be understood as institutions in the sense that as actors they are constituted by the discursive, emotive, and sensate understandings that reliably guide their reactions to the actions of others. Stable reaction patterns, however, depend on stable understandings. If we take heed of Wittgentein's (1946) "private language argument," these can be thought of as coming about only through processes of validation in encounters with others who recognize them in response to an action's success or failure that corroborates them and in resonances with existing memories (Glaeser 2011). Stability and change in understandings are thus linked to stability and change in validations, which issue from more or less stable institutional contexts: environments, and cultural and personal memories. What shines up in this way are series of co-constituting chains of institution-forming deferments. I propose calling these deferment processes institutiosis in analogy to Charles Peirce's (1998) notion of semiosis (Glaeser 2014).

I have called this way of looking at social life consequent processualism precisely because all components of this ontology are seen as more or less stabilized processes whose shape is altered at different speeds, thus making some of them appear more structural than others. I propose to use it as a metatheory, a framework for hypothesis formulation, fact searches, and integration within which one can develop more local theories. On the basis of consequent processualism, analysis can proceed mostly in two different directions. We can begin with observed action-reaction sequences as we encounter them in ethnography and "work forward," as it were, to wonder what social formations they bring about, maintain, or alter.[32] What we need for this is a synthetic ethnographic imagination that can integrate various localities, various actors, and various times into an interconnected social whole.

Alternatively, we can begin with a particular kind of institution and "work backward," as it were, to puzzle over which action-reaction sequences, at which temporal and local nodes, are central for its constitution. What we need in this direction is an analytic ethnographic imagination that can imagine institutions as abstract as international law or only seemingly simple as the papacy as existing in a wide variety of ongoing interconnected action-reaction sequences. In practice, we typically oscillate between these two perspectives, mimicking the old hermeneutic movement from parts to wholes and back.

Let me illustrate my point with an empirical case. It is culled from my book *Political Epistemics: The Secret Police, the Opposition and the End of East German Socialism* (2011). This book is a historical ethnography of the efforts of the Stasi, the secret police of the former German Democratic Republic (GDR; East Germany), to control the peace and civil rights movements in East Berlin during the 1980s. This particular social arena opens a window onto a set of interesting historical puzzles: How did a dedicated group of state and party cadres come to think that suppressing civil society was necessary, good, and right? But also, why did these very same officers fail to shed their own blood—as they had sworn they would in their oath of office—once their beloved socialist fatherland came to be threatened? And then, how did the members of the opposition, who often enough started their lives as enthusiastic members of the communist youth movement, eventually turn their backs on the socialist cause? There are some more layers to this project; my point here is that I understand state socialism in the GDR, its organizational basis as well as its ideology, as a complex of institutions. Because it is constituted by continuous interconnected action-reaction sequences and these actions are shaped by the ways in which people understand their social world cognitively, emotionally, and kinesthetically, I look at how the officers and the opposition members form their understanding of this complex of institutions. I thus try to contribute to the formation of political knowledge and, through it, to the dynamics of political institutions.

Here is a simple concrete example. Stasi officers regularly claimed in their reports that the members of the opposition in the GDR were in fact agents of western secret service organizations, especially of the West German Bundesnachrichtendienst (BND) and the U.S. Central Intelligence Agency (CIA). From today's perspective, these claims may appear quite ludicrous, and many commentators have therefore suggested that such claims were little more than superfluous and disingenuous bureaucratic rituals in which nobody placed any credence. This, however, would be to seriously misunderstand what had been going on in the secret police. Let me apply the analytic lens of consequent processualism to this particular kind of action. The questions to ask are these: First, what antecedent actions were the officers reacting to when they made a claim about members of the GDR opposition being CIA or BND agents, and second, what are the institutions that were maintained (or altered) in such actions as reactions?

Some background is necessary to appreciate the meaning of this claim. Socialist parties in Eastern Europe took it to be one of their most formidable tasks to determine the stage of historical development of their countries. Nobody thought that the assumption of power by a socialist party alone would bring about a socialist or even a communist society. Because the socialists thought they knew the laws of social development, however, stage localization was in fact the primary framework for policy planning. The GDR moved from stages officially labeled "antifascist-democratic reconstruction" over the "construction of the foundations of socialism" to the "comprehensive construction of socialism." In 1971, the ruling party of the GDR proclaimed that a "developed socialist society" had been attained. What is relevant about this construct for my current purposes is that it entailed the understanding that there were no longer any *internal* class enemies in the GDR. It was declared that the class enemy had become entirely external. Accordingly, people fighting the socialist regime on the inside of the GDR could be understood only as agents of external agencies; they could not possibly be seen as acting on their own account.

Now it would be highly implausible to assume that an officer claiming in 1983 that a particular opposition member was in fact a western agent would, in the moment that he acted (that is, wrote down his claim) remember what the party secretary had said in 1971, declaring the GDR to have attained socialism. It would be highly unlikely, that is, if that 1971 message had not somehow been kept alive and continuously made relevant to the work environment of the officers. And this was the case in that the idea of the wholly external class enemy was repeated time and again in party documents, in mandatory party meetings, and in Stasi training materials.

Knowing this is, of course, still far from enough to substantiate the claim that identifying an opposition member as a foreign secret service agent was a reaction to these ideological positions. This becomes plausible only if it is understood at the same time that party members were sworn (as Weber would have called it) to rationalize their entire lives in view of the latest party doctrine and to routinize this as habitus. Moreover, one has to understand that demonstrating this rationalization was universally seen as the most important indicator for the worth of a person in terms of the socialist cause. Socialism propagated what I call an ethics of absolute finality. The argument becomes yet more persuasive if one can show how this ethics was institutionalized in conduct. Indeed, officers, like party members elsewhere, were systematically evaluated and received systematic feedback on their demonstrated ability to align their lives to the needs of the party. One way to perform self-alignment was to make systematic use of the party lingo in bureaucratic documents.

Yet this is still not the whole story. The espionage claim resonated deeply with the Stasi as an organization. It also resonated personally with many officers. Founded in 1950, Stasi started first and foremost as an espionage and anti-espionage bureaucracy. After the failed uprising of 1953, there was in fact little by way of organized political resistance to the socialist government. There was, however, a considerable degree of espionage activity. Not surprisingly, many officers were personally involved in spy-catching activities. This situation was because of the open borders; people disaffected with their lives in East Germany could and did leave, and in addition, spies could come in easily. After the erection of the Berlin Wall in 1961, however, this situation was completely reversed: spying ground down to very low levels, and conversely, political disaffection slowly but surely lost its previous outlet. The irony is that this reversal happened precisely at the moment when the party efforts at developmental-stage localization suggested there could no longer be any internal opposition. Consequently, understanding the opposition as spies was in tune with the personal and organizational identity of the officers and, for many, consistent with their work experience.

In any given case in which an officer actually made a concrete claim that a particular person was a western agent, there were typically several antecedent actions that played a role in articulating this claim. There was either a direct order or a standing order to write this particular report. The report was typically written in response to a meeting with a secret informant who had divulged new information about the opposition member in question. And such meetings were conducted in accordance with a barrage of regulations and local office culture. And then there were other issues of a seemingly unrelated nature. For example, the officer might have been caught driving under the influence, prompting a reprimand from a superior suspecting an unclear class position. This in turn may have prompted the officer to perform a firm class standpoint by subsequently writing reports in a particularly sharp tone. There might have been transferences at work in the officer's making the accusation; that is, the officer might have felt an intense personal dislike for the opposition member he labeled a "western influence agent" because that person reminded him of an old high school foe. In the moral world of socialist secret police officers, there was nothing more vile than an agent of a bourgeois secret service, especially after he or she had supposedly enjoyed the fruits of socialism. Therefore, labeling the opposition member a "western agent" might also have been a way of obtaining catharsis. Analytically speaking, the art of sorting through these antecedent actions is to differentiate what is accidental from what is systematic, that is, what is specific to only this one case from what is a component of many, perhaps even most, cases. Transference and catharsis can be accidental in this sense. But they need not be; they can be the result of systematic emotive understandings cultivated by propaganda, fictional or real hero and villain figures, or something else.

I hope it is clear from this account how various institutions—that is, (1) understandings (here, the ethics of absolute finality and the emotional understanding of the hatred of the class enemy), (2) social relationships (here, between the officer and his superior, his party secretary, and his party group peers), and (3) his own personhood (here, his professional identity as a spy-catcher and his political identity as vigilant member of a Leninist vanguard party)—were mobilized in casting the officer's reaction.

What was the effect, then, of the claim that a particular person was a western agent as a reaction to these antecedent actions? On the most fundamental level, if the social environment reacted as expected to the officer's claim, if the action was a successful performance, if therefore the action-reaction sequencing was spun further, the action reproduced the institutions mobilized in casting it; thus, they were maintained in continuous action-reaction sequences. What was maintained here, too, was the verity of the particular interpretation of oppositional activity, the authority of the party, its ability to divine the exigencies of history, and its right to rule the country and, thus, the socialist system.

Let me draw two important points from this small example. Consider first that the antecedent actions in the example have taken place at different times and in different places and were performed by a set of different actors in different places who have lived and acted in different times. To become effective, these antecedent actions needed to become *projectively articulated* into the presence of the actor. This projective articulation of antecedent actions involves memory practices, disciplinary practices, and so on within organizational contexts; it also involves symbolic mediation articulating actions performed then and there in the here and now through mass communication; and I should hasten to add beyond the example that it involves the mass transportation of material goods. In other words, in most contemporary contexts very little of what is available at one site in terms of cultural forms, material goods, and social relations is a product of it and can exist institutionally only through multiply mediated links to often far away places and times. The relevance of this for fieldwork is as plain as it is consequential for ethnographic practice: it is by no means clear anymore what the relevant context of an action is. Ethnography, therefore, must learn to problematize much more so than it has done so far the kind of sites it has privileged for so long: the neighborhood, the community, the village, and more generally the *immediate* physical and social context as the primary source of explaining actions. Multi-sited ethnographies are only a first step in this direction. In addition ethnography must pay sustained attention to what I have called here techniques of projective articulations, their institutionalization, organization, and politics. This necessarily involves a much more vigorous integration of historical work where history will also mean attention to cumulative data storage and algorithmic forms of analysis relevant through such institutions as credit reports, internet transaction traces, and security agency data files. It requires acute attention to people's integration into translocal flows of understandings; their validation, that is, technically and organizationally mediated communication; and memory practices including the instant access to years' worth of e-mail communications and family photos. This might also mean that it is high time that we begin to recover our long lost connection to psychoanalysis because it provides important means to think about the emotional presence of past experience. Here then is another point where ethnography desperately needs social theory, which allows an ethnographer to unfold a multiplicity of possibly relevant contexts that could then partially be explored empirically to decide, in a back and forth between conceptualization and fieldwork, which of those matter for the case and the particular research interests at hand.

Second, this example makes clear that the maintenance of any particular institution is contingent on the maintenance of other institutions to which they are connected through the kinds of processes I have further above called institutiosis. That is to say, institutions come in structured sets not only of the same kind but also of very different kinds. We should not, therefore, be surprised if we find the kind of catastrophic reproductive failure we saw in 1989 during the so-called velvet revolutions. The action-reaction webs constituting an institution may also not contribute to it in equal measure, which means that some are more central than others. Revolutionary change offers an excellent window into the organization of structured sets of institutions. Sorting through what is systematic from what is accidental, what is central from what is peripheral, necessitates theory. We therefore need to develop the tales we tell and the theories that explain their effective emplotment in a dialectical fashion. The point is not just to get the story right but to know *why* a particular story gets it right and another does not. In the end, ethnographic work must lead to both a theory and a story, and each supposes the other and therefore they should not be presented as if they were independent of each other.

So what about my theoretization of the Stasi case? So far, I have talked mostly about metatheory, a framework for thinking and making theory, not about theory proper. Listening to the officers' tales of their lives and their careers, it began to dawn on me why in 1989 they did not exchange their plain clothes for battle fatigues to halt the velvet revolution with an iron fist to "defend their socialist fatherland to the last drop of their blood," as they had once sworn proudly to do. I learned how radically different the officers' understanding of the developments in the "hot fall" of 1989 was from the "warm" spring and "scalding" summer of 1968 in Prague. In 1968, none of the officers I had a chance to interview had the least doubt that they were facing a fascist counter-revolution that needed to be suppressed with the force of arms, even at the expense of great bloodshed. They firmly believed that the defense of the achievements of socialism by all means outweighed the cost of any regrettable collateral damage. But, in 1989, there was no such clarity of understanding. The officers, too, believed that change was necessary; they, too, saw that the country was in a deep crisis. Indeed, they were thirsting for the party leadership to get the country out of all too apparent stagnation. But the party was exhausted, literally devoid of any ideas. Ironically, that exhaustion of ideas had much to do with the ideologies and practices that had made the secret police big in the first place. What became apparent to my theoretical self ethnographically studying the macro-historical event called the end of socialism is the importance of discursive, emotive, and kinesthetic political understandings for the maintenance of the very institutions that make up a political order.

Therefore, I focused my investigations on the issue of how political understandings stabilize and destabilize over the course of time. That is, I needed to see understandings as institutions. This means I needed to find the action-reaction sequences that produced, reproduced, and altered understandings. And I needed a method to do so in the "muck" from which institutions crystallize, from the action-reaction effect flows of real people caught in fears, inspired by hopes, and entangled in careers, that is, in the sweat of people's lives. I needed to find a way to study the link between understandings and other institutions ethnographically. Thus I began to reconstruct people's understandings of the party, the state, and socialism, both with the help of the texts they had written at various times and through in-depth interviews (reaching with some interviewees a total length of 40 hours), in which I used documents as conversation props and memory aides. Comparing the development of several people participating in the same social arena from various vantage points, I started to see how understandings are shaped through encounters with the world that validate or invalidate understandings. In a process of moving back and forth between eliciting Stasi officers' and opposition members' stories, retelling them in answer to my question, and formulating the dynamics driving their plot, I settled on the analytical distinction among three forms of validation dynamics. They, in turn, enabled me to analyze circular processes of knowledge-making. I call this theory, which I cannot explore here, a sociology of understanding, which also aspires to revive the old Vico-Herder-Weber tradition of studying institutions hermeneutically (see also Glaeser 2014). And built on this edifice I then crafted a more concrete epistemic theory of why socialism failed that is very different from prevalent economic and political accounts.

Conclusion

I began this chapter with an effort to circumscribe the contemporary moment in the development of social theory historically. In Western Europe from the end of the Roman Empire to the eighteenth century, the efforts to theorize human beings' lives in each other's company was subsidiary to, and ultimately licensed by, theology. In the wake of the French Revolution the role of social theorizing changed fundamentally in response to two developments. First, efforts to grasp social life conceptually became decoupled from their authorizing source. The consequence was deep uncertainty about those efforts' validity. At the same time, theoretizations of social life assumed a new stature by their newly assumed power to provide orientation for grand political projects of social transformation. Both of these developments together led on the one hand to what was perceived as the ideologization of politics apexing in the ideological battles of the short twentieth century, which ultimately underwrote mass persecution, mass murder, globalized total warfare, the objectification of human beings, and environmental degradation. On the other hand, this also led to the emergence of the empirical social sciences, which precisely to escape ideology formulated their theories in ever shorter sound bites. This led to fragmentation into countless domain-specific theories of positivistic hypothesis testing. Against ideologization and positivism, reflexive theoretical practices emerged, first critical theory and then deconstruction. These critical modalities of theorizing have done much to reveal the hidden assumptions of "traditional" theoretical efforts, many of which have suppressive political implications. Yet, this rigorous critique has also led to a great hesitation to formulate more comprehensive, synthetically more ambitious social theories.

The only theory tradition that has remained relatively unscathed from these developments is liberalism in its economistic-utilitarian form.[33] As the ideology underwriting the capitalist project of social transformation, and as the only survivor of the twentieth-century battle of ideologies, it has largely proven impervious to critical intervention. Thus not only sheltered from the very critiques that have fragmented Marxism, varieties of structuralism, and cultural-hermeneutic approaches to social life, it also remains the only one of the big eighteenth- and nineteenth-century social imaginaries that still unabashedly offers a comprehensive model of social life. Economistic liberalism has become hegemonic because all previously worked-out alternatives have lost their credibility as alternatives. This situation is highly problematic for a number of reasons. First, no theoretical hegemony can ever be metatheoretically adequate because it tends towards reification. Moreover, economistic liberalism has profound substantive adequacy problems. Its real strength is limited to particular problems of instrumental problems. It is that characteristic that has made it a favorite of stockholders, their supposed agents (managers),[34] and policy wonks. In the actuality dimension economistic liberalism tends to be adequate only where its instrumental use has become pervasive through performative self-realization (e.g. Mackenzie 2008). In its potentiality, economistic liberalism works well for certain types of objective problems but fails entirely to give any meaningful answers to questions posed in a subjective mode.

It is old hat by now that ethnographers have, much more than users of other methods, contributed to what hopefully will last and continue to spread as a reflexive turn. Because of this, ethnographers have done more to think of metatheoretical adequacy than have others. The chance that ethnographers will continue to provide impulses in this direction is rising with the proliferation of the means that informants have at their disposal to contest what ethnographers make of their observations. What may still be news, however, is that ethnographers are also uniquely equipped to provide substantively adequate theoretizations. This is so because providing an understanding of the processes that lead to the formation of the social world is central to rendering theoretical efforts substantively relevant. If everything social can come into existence exclusively through the action-reaction effect sequences of real people in real places and times, then a method is need that can observe this very process of formation. Of all the methods available to us, ethnography is by far the closest to such an undertaking. Reflexive theorizing thus needs ethnography as its empirical partner in dialogue to remain substantively adequate. Indeed, in the long run, theory needs to develop a vivid ethnographic imagination that is prone to translate conceptual distinctions and integrations into scenes of people acting and reacting to each other. Such an imagination would greatly facilitate the metaphorical dialogue between theory and world.

Ethnography has to shed or thoroughly reform some of its prevalent self-understandings to become theoretically more fecund, however. First, narration will always be an important part of ethnography—but it cannot be all of it. Ethnography has to comprehend itself as centrally concerned with the development of new theory, understood as an integrated set of metaphors adequate for interpreting the social world. This has consequences for the kind of work that should be undertaken and for the kinds of places in which one would want to undertake it. Ethnographic projects should be evaluated for the kind of theory-generating potential they have, and field sites should be self-consciously chosen according to the observational opportunities they present for building theory.

Second, given the current needs for new concepts and theories, this also means that ethnography should move massively into new subject areas. Ethnography for a democratic public needs to be critical ethnography of the most relevant social phenomena, including environmental degradation, the dynamics of capitalism, and the frightening corruption of parliamentarian democracy. We need more ethnography of policymaking, locally, nationally, and even internationally. We have far too little in terms of ethnographies of voting and the ways in which citizens make sense of politics. Where are the ethnographies of political campaign management? It is an excellent thing to have ethnographies of exploitation as far as the documentation of suffering is concerned. Solidarity with the downtrodden is commendable; analyzing in detail how inequalities are produced and reproduced is better. That is to say, it is necessary to track the conditions for the possibilities of the exploitation where they occur. This means in all likelihood moving the ethnographic gaze from the neighborhoods in which the poor live to the places where decisions are made that have the consequence of leaving the poor poor. Markets may be currently more important to understand than the shop floor or other sites of production. We need ethnographies of resource use, energy consumption, and waste production at all levels.

Third, with such projects ethnographers might not be able to continue operating in their time-honored artisanal mode of production because they need to address themselves forcefully to the intercontextuality of actions, which means that they need to address the phenomenon of projective articulation much more systematically. This means, for example, that they no longer treat the mass media or bureaucratic organizations only as objects of study in their own right but as means to articulate action effects across time and space. There is not only a need for a structural or rhetorical analysis of news shows but for an analysis of news shows in the context of electoral politics, crisis management, and warfare.

Fourth, knowledge that can link actions to the formation of institutions identifies possibilities for intervention. Politics as an intentional effort to shape institutions is in urgent need of such knowledge. Economists and their clients know this. The appeal of economistic liberal analysis for policymakers lies precisely in its focus on action and its motivation. Economists always have a recommendation about where and how to intervene to shape people's actions. Of course, their recommendations are simple at heart because human beings are no riddle for them and do not need to be observed to be understood. Their story is inevitably one of getting the incentives right. For much of human life (but of course not all), this is an absurd understanding of the social world, leading to a systematic misrecognition of society and its possibilities. I would be very surprised if one could not be much more successful with more *realistic* knowledge about why people do what they do in the contexts in which they live. Ethnography in the key of consequent processualism offers the prospect of sealing the rift between questions of actuality and instrumentality while overcoming the unproductive division of labor that results from the fact-value distinction.

And fifth, somehow I am hopeful that more realistic knowledge about the link among actions, understandings, and institutions will also end up transforming what we label normative theory today. Deliberations of potentiality need to work from actual possibility. This is also an excellent vantage point from which to effectively criticize certain normative ideas, for example, about what democracy ought to be and how it ought to work.

I have high hopes that ethnography, simply because it is the method best suited for studying processes of social formation, will provide the much needed impulses for a revival of social theory and that the social theory that will emerge will have much more obvious linkages to questions of potentiality and instrumentality—for dreaming up better social worlds and better ways to get there while remaining cognizant of the lessons learned from the disasters of the previous century. So, if we want ethnography to be more relevant—for this is what I think lies at the heart of the now so-often-heard call to go "public"—then we should conduct ethnography with an interest in the development of useful concepts in response to the big questions of our time. Ethnography could be the means to write poetry of the social—if we only put our minds and hearts to it.

5

Trans-formations of Biology
and of Theory

Kaushik Sunder Rajan

There are many different guises and registers to theory in anthropology. Pedagogically, it tends to consolidate as a canon. In this guise, theory serves as an intellectual entry point into the field and as a vehicle for socialization and professionalization. My own interest in theory is less canonical. I am interested instead in processes of elucidation—in *theorization*, and its active relationship to the empirical matter that is being elucidated. At a conference I had organized at Irvine in 2004 called "Lively Capital: Biotechnologies, Ethics and Governance in Global Markets," Donna Haraway insisted that what she was most interested in was not how this conversation fit into discourses of political economy or science studies but rather how it helped to make sense of "the stuff of the world under question."[1] That insistence, which has animated Haraway's teaching and writing, has remained vital in orienting my own investments toward theory as always being a process of figuring things out, where the things being figured out matter.

In this more humble guise, theory is less the definitive explanatory statement that can be canonized and more a series of probes. It becomes polymorphic, operating at multiple scales and registers, and always plural, theories. Further, I am interested in theory as *critique*. By critique, I do not mean criti*cism* necessarily but, rather, critique in a Hegelian sense: probing at the limits of a concept or practice. This is related to the idea of theory as *praxis*.

This is not a call for an "activist" theory in any simple sense. Rather, it poses the question of theory as praxeology, as articulated in Marx's famous XIth Thesis on Feuerbach—that, although philosophers have merely described the world, "the point is to change it."[2] This apparently straightforward call to action, in fact, is anything but.[3] Marx, in making such a call, is, I suggest, doing three things. First, he is animating the relationship between the empirical and the philosophical. If theory involves making sense of the "stuff of the world," then Marx's suggestion is that this stuff is not merely inert matter that is processed elsewhere, in the intellect of the philosopher. Rather, there is always a potentially dialogic relationship between the "stuff of the world" and our philosophies that attempt to make sense of it. Second, this implies that theory lies not simply in the abstractions of philosophical work (i.e., not simply at the level of "making sense") but in the active relationships between philosophical abstraction and empirical materiality. Marx's historicist inversion of the Hegelian dialectic is precisely the activation of a different kind of relationship between the "stuff of the world" and the stuff of abstract philosophy, one that refuses to let theory rest, as Hegel does (and even more, as the Young Hegelians, who are the target of Marx's attack in the Theses on Feuerbach, do) at the level of ideas, ideals, and abstraction. And third, the work of theory is always promissory; it always lies in the realm of potential—a potential whose realization is, perhaps always, deferred but that provides the horizon of the ethical and the political. This is the substance of Jacques Derrida's reading of Marx's philosophy in *Specters of Marx*, in which Derrida insists that there is a future orientation to Marx's theory-as-praxis but that it is not a teleological or determined future. Rather, it is, suggests Derrida, *l'avenir*, the future that is to come (rather than the future that will be), a future anterior without which there will be "neither history, nor event, nor promise of justice" (Derrida 1994, 170).

I will elaborate on my investments in theory in this processual, empiricist, and critical sense by discussing ethnography I conducted between 2008 and 2011, but that I have not yet published. This ethnography followed the establishment of the Translational Health Science and Technology Institute of India (THSTI), the first translational research institute established in India. Translational research, in its simplest guise, is biological research that can be "translated" into health outcomes and impact. What any of this means—biological research, translation, health, and outcomes and impact—is intensely at stake in the practices of translational researchers. But at the very least, translational research, in Anglo-American biomedical practice over the past decade, has become an important mantra through which new kinds of audit culture metrics and practices have come to be established. Some elements of this project might serve as an empiric that opens up certain questions of theory that are of relevance to this volume.

Translational Research as an Ethnographic and Theoretical Object

Translational research has become a ubiquitous category in western biomedicine, certainly in its audit cultures, over the past decade. Under the rubric of a formulation that suggests its being a practice that takes biomedical research from bench to bedside, there are some comfortably assumed definitions of what constitutes translational research. One working definition is that translational research is basic research that can lead to therapeutic applications. This definition often operates in university settings—an implicit idea that basic research quite often focuses too much on esoteric aspects of biological mechanism and ends up becoming too divorced from actually advancing human health. Generally, this idea of translational research has its origin story in cancer research, which is a field where mechanistic understandings of how cells proliferate, aggregate, or die has had direct implications for the development of new anticancer therapeutics.[4] A second working definition of translational research, one that clinicians often concern themselves with, begins not with the moving downstream (or outward) of basic research but, rather, with the incorporation of a research sensibility and ethos into clinical practice. Both of these working definitions are institutionally enshrined in funding programs for translational research, such as, in the United States, through the National Institutes of Health (NIH).

An imagination of translational research as bench to bedside presumes it to be linear and unidirectional (beginning in a laboratory and flowing into the world). But, in fact, translational research, far from being a singular idea or process, is polyvalent; far from being unidirectional, is relational in all sorts of ways; and far from being simply about the flow of information and knowledge is, to paraphrase Andrew Pickering, a mangle of practices but also of discourses, ideologies, beliefs, investments, and ideas about biomedicine, about cells, about organisms, and about the world.[5]

I am not just interested in how translational research is complicated. An empirical unpacking of the microsociological intricacy of translational research is undeniably valuable; but it does not necessarily allow us to understand the larger structures and contexts within which various research enterprises unfold under the sign of translational research. For this, I want to also look at how translational research is an unsettled category. It is not just *polyvalent* (involving many different kinds of practices within its purview) but also, I argue, *polymorphic*. In other words, what translational research actually means for different actors is entirely unsettled and varies greatly depending on whom one talks to. These variations occur on professional lines (basic researchers versus clinicians, for instance) and also on disciplinary and institutional lines. (For instance, at a historically entrepreneurial university such as the Massachusetts Institute of Technology [MIT], ideas of translational research are deeply coupled to an ethos of commercialization. This may not be the case, to the same extent, elsewhere). Additional variability is introduced when a concept such as this is ported to different national contexts with different institutional histories and social realities. Yet what makes translational research such an interesting ethnographic concept is not just that its meaning is variable but also that most translational researchers tend to act *as if* its meaning is constant. Hence, there are layers of assumptions, naturalizations, and variations in the meaning and practice of translational research as it becomes instantiated institutionally.

The stakes of translational research are different for its various actors. These stakes are not necessarily about setting a definition of translational research as a field of knowledge. Some of these stakes predate the history of translational research itself as a category. For instance, there are the stakes of biologists, who have, with the increase in the amount of information and knowledge in the life sciences of the past half-century, been contending with increased specializations and subspecializations, exacerbated by the predominantly disciplinary structures of universities, recognizing that understanding biology involves moving across disciplines. These are stakes having to do with multidisciplinarity, stakes that can be made congruent with a concern with translational research, which is also necessarily a form of research practice that often needs to transcend individual disciplines but that is not about the ultimate resolution of something novel and unsettled into the contours of a new field. Or there are the stakes of clinicians, who recognize the need to converse with basic biology researchers or with the communities that they intend to serve and need to figure out the institutional mechanisms as well as the epistemic and discursive means to do so. "Translational research" as a category provides a rubric under which this can be described, but what is at stake, again, is not the formation or stabilization of a field. What is at stake, ethnographically, is not the definition of a new field of knowledge as much as it is the tracing of individual, disciplinary, and institutional trajectories that happen to come together under a rubric that allows the articulation of disparate concerns under a single umbrella. In this regard, translational research functions as, in Susan Leigh Star and James Griesemer's (1989) terms, a boundary object.

My empirical and conceptual interests therefore lie less in settling what translational research "really" is and more in exploring its polyvalence and polymorphism as something ethnographically interesting. Translational research, almost by definition, involves the co-production of the epistemic and the institutional.[6] Because of this, translational researchers necessarily have a sociological imaginary. I am interested in tracing the macrosociological imaginaries within which the polymorphic instantiations of translational research get located in particular places and times.[7]

Within arenas of translational research (however defined), which locate themselves across institutional spaces such as academe and industry, laboratory and clinic, it is impossible to even think of science as operating outside of a larger social domain. At least some, but not all, of this has to do with trajectories of commercialization of the life sciences over the last four decades, in which life scientists immediately see themselves as operating within market logics of various sorts. And some of it has to do with the interaction of laboratory scientists with clinicians, who are always encountering "the social" in its everyday messiness in their relationships with patients and disease. The globalization of the life sciences, which occurs both through diasporic scientists from around the world working in

Euro-American settings and through the emergence of new nodes and centers of life science research outside of Europe and the United States, also forces a broader, less secluded realization of the social and the sociological on many scientists, regardless of their own location or background.

The Translational Health Science and Technology Institute of India as an Object of Ethnographic Study

The empirical focus of my project is the establishment of the first Indian translational research institute, THSTI. This was conceptualized in 2006 and established over the next three to four years, partly in collaboration with the Health, Science and Technology (HST) Division of the Massachusetts Institute of Technology (MIT). HST is a joint program between MIT and Harvard University. Set up in 1971, its aim is to bridge the engineering capabilities of MIT with the clinical capacities of Harvard and create a multidisciplinary pedagogical and research program that will span the two. Students include MDs from Harvard Medical School who, if they choose the HST track, are exposed to laboratory research, and PhD students from MIT who are exposed to clinical rotations.[8]

This means that, while my project is a study of translational research, it is also the study of the development of a particular institution. Just as translational research is not a straightforward "thing" in itself, the evolution of THSTI is not straightforward either. Part of the theoretical question at stake concerns the nature of the ethnographic object itself. What is (are) translational research? What is (are) THSTI? Is this project a study of the former or the latter? Of neither or of both? How do the stakes of various actors involved in THSTI, and my own analytical stakes, come to impact the answers to these questions? How do the relationships that emerge between various actors and myself—relationships that open up the potential for para-ethnographic engagements of various sorts—play a role in answering these questions? These are some of the questions I wish to answer in the remainder of this chapter. Here, I introduce THSTI as a complex institution by describing my own encounter with THSTI, which provides me with a set of multiple partial perspectives (Haraway 1991). Through such partiality, I resist any claims, or aims, of having an objective view of THSTI. Crucially, I insist that none of the actors I study in this project has an objective perspective either.

I encountered THSTI serendipitously in 2008. While I was in India researching another project, an old college acquaintance from the All India Institute of Medical Sciences (AIIMS), in New Delhi, Shiladitya Sengupta, mentioned THSTI to me.[9] Sengupta had always been invested in building institutional capacity for the life sciences in India and, to this end, had developed good personal relationships with a number of its science policy leaders. This included Maharaj K. Bhan, then secretary of the Indian Department of Biotechnology (DBT). The DBT was set up in 1986 as a funding body to facilitate research in the life sciences and the commercial development of biotechnology. Bhan's appointment as DBT secretary in 2004 was an important event in the history of the organization because, as a pediatrician at AIIMS, he was the first clinician appointed as its head. This opened up the possibility of institutional development across basic and clinical research interfaces, something that in India had been almost entirely lacking, except at the initiative of a few isolated individuals and departments.[10]

Bhan entered the science policy environment at a time of serious prioritization on the part on the Indian government to invest in science and technology, and especially in the life sciences. This was in keeping with a larger ideological investment in becoming a global player and the sense that investment in the knowledge economy was an essential component to realize this ambition. This investment primarily took the form of opening new research institutions. The idea of having an institution focused on translational research was central to the road map that Bhan had laid out. Bhan's investment in translational research was, in part, an investment in bridging the acute gap that existed between researchers and clinicians. It was also recognition that his own position of authority provided an unusual window of opportunity for such interactions across the lab-clinic divide to be fostered. In many ways, this imagined institution—which later took shape as THSTI—would be Bhan's legacy institution.

In 2006, Bhan went to the United States to explore the possibility of institutional collaborations that would facilitate the new wave of institutional development in the life sciences in India. The Boston-Cambridge area was one of the places he visited. Sengupta had recently been hired onto the HST faculty, and for him, HST represented the kind of institutional structure that needed to be replicated in an Indian context. Elements of this institutional structure included multidisciplinarity, an accent on commercialization, and a problem-focused approach to research questions. These contrasted with the traditional model of Indian (and, in some ways, even U.S.) research structures, which tended to be embedded in disciplinary structures, often (in India more than the United States) eschewed commercialization as antithetical to the ethos of the research university, and were topic-focused.

In Boston, in part through Sengupta's mediation, Bhan met with Martha Gray, who had been co-director of the HST program since 1995.[11] Her initial training was as an electrical engineer, and she had herself received her PhD in HST, which enabled her encounter with the biological sciences, and had taught all her career at HST. Hence, her biographical trajectory spanned nearly three decades across the history of HST. Bhan and Gray saw mutual benefit in interacting with each other. For Bhan, what Gray had done with HST was consonant with the imagination that he had for THSTI, if not in every detail, then at least in its structure and ethos. Meanwhile, for Gray, the possibility that HST, which had a structure that she believed in greatly, could serve as a model for an initiative in another country was extremely appealing. HST had produced many leading scientists who were internationally recognized.[12] Yet Gray's perception was that HST had remained a relatively marginal presence within MIT, which was still dominated by the more traditional disciplines.

There are a number of important things to emphasize in terms of the development of THSTI circa 2006 (when it was not even called THSTI and was merely an idea). One is that what I have just narrated is one trajectory for the development of this institution. Because of my own entry into studying this institution through Sengupta, this was the trajectory that I was immediately confronted with and had access to. What I saw and the kinds of initial conversations I was drawn into were consequent to the contingency of my earlier acquaintance with Sengupta but also to the contingency of my having earned my PhD at MIT. I had, for instance, taken a class offered through HST, cotaught by Michael Fischer, Byron Good, and Mary-Jo Good, and I recognized the challenges Gray faced in instantiating a multidisciplinary research environment at MIT as similar in certain ways to those that Fischer had faced in attempting to do so as chair of the Science, Technology and Society (STS) Program (where I had received my PhD) in the late 1990s and early 2000s.[13] In other words, my enrollment in studying THSTI was a function of my own biographical trajectory. I mention this not simply as an access story but as something that situates my own perspective, which started off being very close to Gray's and broadened (and in some ways diverged) only after spending more than a year in India in 2009–2010. My own initial understanding of what THSTI was, therefore, was quite similar to that of people who were involved in this initiative from HST. Other people in India had other, in some cases radically different, initial understandings about the nature and ethos of the institution they were building and about the importance or relevance of HST in its establishment.

My fieldwork, initially, involved sitting in on planning meetings for THSTI, starting in summer 2008. Over the next three years, I interviewed most of the people involved in the establishment of THSTI, on tape whenever they were comfortable with it or else informally and conversationally. I also sat in on as many planning meetings as I could. In 2009–2010, I spent thirteen months doing continuous fieldwork in Delhi. This was the time when THSTI moved from being an idea to actually materializing as an institution. There were two ways in which this materialization occurred. The first was physical, through the establishment of interim laboratory facilities in Gurgaon, just outside Delhi. Labs were built and set up; the first staff scientists, administrators, and PhD students moved in to the facilities; and research projects began. This happened almost entirely independently of MIT involvement or direction. The second was in terms of human resource development, as a search for founding faculty was conducted. HST was responsible for planning, conducting, and managing the search, and so this was the site of its most active involvement and contribution. Gray appointed me as a nonvoting member of the search committee. I participated in the meetings of the committee as well as in the interview process, including asking questions of candidates and contributing my thoughts and feedback to the committee during deliberations. During the course of my time in Delhi, the material reality of THSTI diverged in significant ways from the initial ideas that people at MIT had from 2006–2008, just as my own perspectives on THSTI diverged considerably from the HST perspective.

I continued following the institution actively until April 2011, at which point, in a dramatic meeting in Cambridge between some India-based THSTI faculty and HST faculty, it became clear that the divergences were so substantial that the collaboration, for all practical purposes, was dead.

THSTI as an institution, however, lives on, developing in some ways that are similar to, and other ways distinct from, its initial imagination by actors such as Bhan and Gray. The HST collaborative investments also live on in other locales. Over the past five years, Gray has, for instance, been collaborating with the regional government of Madrid in an initiative called M+Vision, which involves capacity building for biomedical imaging in Madrid through the establishment of a fellows program that is located between Madrid and Cambridge. The involvement of HST faculty and the establishment of an HST ethos are active components of this collaboration.

Three Critical Moments of Investment

I next briefly describe three critical moments at which the emergent contours of THSTI came to be at stake. These moments concern situations in which different visions, investments, and sociological imaginaries—of translational research, of THSTI itself, and of institutional development for the life sciences—were articulated. I do not suggest that the outcomes of these moments resulted in the success or failure of institutional development in any simple causal sense—although, of course, the ways in which these moments resolved had consequences for how the institution developed and certainly were elements of the structural and ideational differences that eventually led to the breakdown of the collaboration with HST. These three moments concern, first, the distinct ideas held by key actors in the institution about the configuration of the centers that would constitute THSTI (which were related, also, to ideas about the overall ethos of the institution and the role that HST would play in providing THSTI with its structure and ethos); second, a distinct set of investments and ideas of what constitutes the kind of translational research that needed to happen in the institution, which was broadly articulated as a distinction between a focus on bench-to-market and bench-to-community solutions, on the one hand, and a distinction between translational research activity that focused on artifacts and one that focused on policies, on the other; and third, differences that emerged in the priorities and perceptions of HST- and India-based actors in the process of the HST-run search for founding faculty.

Each of these critical moments is a function of very specific investments on the part of particular individuals involved in the development of THSTI. But those investments, themselves, are reflections of biographies that are institutionally and sociologically embedded. They might be contingent and idiosyncratic investments, but they are not simply "opinions" that are disembedded from where these individuals come from and what positions they represent. The differences here concern the very specific investments that those involved with HST had—especially with multidisciplinarity and a problem-focused research ethos—but also the investments that are embedded in MIT as a private university that has historically been deeply wedded to an entrepreneurial idea of the sciences and that is presently developing into a global corporate university. Equally, they concern investments that scientists in India have that range from neoliberal aspirations of becoming (and being recognized as) "global players" to postcolonial antagonisms against global power hierarchies and differentiations as they manifest in the structure and ethos of institutional development. (In some cases, indeed, neoliberal aspiration and postcolonial antagonism could quite comfortably coexist within the same individual). But the differences also have to do with dynamics and perceptions of race, class, caste, gender, language, accent, and culture. Indeed, one of the clearest things to emerge in these critical moments was that it was not just biomedical translation that was at stake in this initiative but cross-national translation, one whose own explanation—often seen as a challenge of managing power differentials by Indian actors and as a challenge of managing cultural difference by those from HST—acutely indicated the striations at stake in the very structure of the institution. Hence, although the critical moments that I mention are themselves, in some cases, around trivial matters, often voiced simply as opinions in meetings, the stakes that they contained were deeply consequential and concern fundamental questions having to do with global relations of production and sociologies of power, hierarchy, and difference.

In addition to these structural differences, there are two sensibilities that I would like to draw attention to. One is at the ideational level and is what I call the "Alice in Wonderland" sensibility. There are very different ideas and ideals, of translational research, of institutional culture and organization, and of how science is to be performed, that each of the actors involved with THSTI has held. At one level, what is at stake for me in narrating these differences is the quintessentially anthropological project of highlighting multiple situated perspectives to show the intentional or motivational side of social action. But at another level, talking to these people often made me feel a little bit like Alice on her wanderings—meeting a series of quirky, passionate, deeply committed people, each of whom has a very strong perspective on the world and each of whom holds forth on that perspective at great length, in apparent disregard or concern for the fact that other equally strong and rather different perspectives are held by other colleagues. There is a certain farcical quality to this that I want to highlight. But it is a farce that must be taken seriously—not just because it is always worthwhile to remember Marx's (1852) invocation about the deadly seriousness of the farcical but also because, at some level, this was arguably the structuring ethos of THSTI as a complex institution. This narrative is *not* a story of building institutions through the production of consensus but rather, one that traces the contours and consequences of the articulation of radical dissension and the emergent possibilities (and impossibilities) of institutional development that flow from it.[14]

A second ethos is what I call the "Lost in Translation" ethos. This involves noting all the points at which people who are deeply engaged with each other in collegial endeavors fail to understand where the other is coming from. This is not intolerance; it is just a genuine lack of understanding of another's perspective, a function, quite often, of different normative structures and what might, in shorthand, be referred to as cultural constructs, which are entirely naturalized in the normal course but which suddenly get questioned and come to matter in the case of collaborations across sensibilities, disciplines, and borders.

First Critical Moment—the Structure of THSTI

THSTI was conceptualized by M. K. Bhan as, itself, a cluster of institutions and as part of a larger institutional cluster. The two niche institutions that were initially established within THSTI were organized around broad areas of research. One was the Vaccines and Infectious Diseases Research Centre (VIDRC) and the other was the Pediatric Biology Centre (PBC). The larger institutional cluster of which THSTI would become a component was to be located in Faridabad, just outside Delhi. This was one of two clusters being developed by the DBT, the second being located in Bangalore and built on the campus of the already existing National Centre for Biological Sciences (NCBS), arguably the premier Indian basic research institution in the life sciences. The imagination of biotech clusters owes itself in part to the models provided by Silicon Valley, Cambridge (Massachusetts and the United Kingdom), and San Diego as areas that have fostered intense research and commercial activity in the life sciences because of a critical mass of high-quality institutions. But it also owes itself to similar institutional configurations that have developed, or are developing, elsewhere in Asia. One example is Biopolis in Singapore; another is the focus in China on biotech clusters as a mechanism for institutional development.[15] The ambition behind these clusters was that they would foster what Bhan would often refer to as an "ecosystem of innovation." Hence, if a specific motivation for an institution such as THSTI involved bridging gaps between laboratory research and clinical care, then this must also be situated in the context of a larger desire for, and embrace of, "innovation" as a mantra for the life sciences in India. This context cannot be confined to Bhan's aspirations but situates the larger arc of institutional development in the life sciences in India over the past fifteen years.

There are a couple of differences between the structure of THSTI as conceived and those of other life science institutions in India. For one thing, in spite of certain topic-focused niches within the institution (VIDRC and PBC), this was an attempt to establish an institution without determining its overall agenda or focal research area in advance (beyond the overarching and highly polymorphic imperative to do "translational research"). And for another, there was a scale and complexity to the imagination of this institution and its cluster, matched perhaps by that of the parallel Bangalore cluster but, unlike its counterpart in Bangalore, without an already existing and functional research institute around which the cluster would develop. THSTI was imagined as a core institute to the Faridabad cluster in the manner that NCBS would be for the Bangalore cluster; but unlike NCBS, which was established in 1993, THSTI itself had to be established from scratch alongside the larger cluster.

In fact, there was considerable indeterminacy about how THSTI would actually be constituted, both internally in relation to its niche centers and in relation to the larger cluster of which it was part. This indeterminacy was reflected in the positions of three key actors involved in the initial establishment of the institution: Sudhanshu Vrati was the head (and still is) of VIDRC; Satyajit Rath at the time deeply influenced, although never formally headed, PBC; and Martha Gray had the task of providing the institution its HST component, although, again, without any formal institutional authority. How that HST component would materialize in relation to the actual structure of THSTI turned out to be a contentious issue.

Since the very beginning of formal planning for THSTI in 2008, the relationships among these three components remained unclear. For Gray, the entire institute needed to operate under one umbrella, with the "HST ethos" of multidisciplinarity and problem-focused research as its uniting principle. In addition, Gray assumed that the development of institutional infrastructures that would articulate to commercial possibilities, which is central to the functioning of HST in Cambridge, was desirable. There was resistance to such a singular "HST ethos" from Vrati and Rath, to different degrees and for different reasons. Vrati's ideas of translational research were coupled to commercialization but also to an idea of focus—topic-focused, agenda-driven, and top-down. Rath's ideas were driven by commitments to social justice and a hope for a research university that could be relevant to a country where 30 percent of the population is destitute and, hence, falls out of the market altogether. The HST ethos as articulated by Gray differed substantially from Vrati's disciplinary, topic-focused investments as they did from Rath's resistance to market-driven paradigms for biomedical research institutions.

These differences in investments in the ideas and ideals of translational research had consequences for the ways in which each of these foundational figures imagined the relationship between THSTI and its two constituent centers, VIDRC and PBC. Gray would articulate THSTI as one institution, modeled on HST. VIDRC and PBC, in this imagination, would be niche centers within the larger institution, granted a certain level of autonomy to focus on their own specific topic areas; but they would be still be a part of THSTI, which would be unified and defined by the "HST ethos." HST itself has such centers, which are referred to as research nuclei. An example that Gray would often point to as a model was the Wellman Center for Photobiology, located in the Massachusetts General Hospital, which is a large building that has people from fields as diverse as physics (building optical devices) and clinical medicine, united only by the fact that they all in different ways use light to address biomedical research problems.

As far as a number of people in India were concerned, however, THSTI was to be constituted by three relatively autonomous centers: VIDRC, PBC and HST. Neither Vrati nor Rath, for instance, saw a reason to buy into an "HST ethos," although Rath was more willing to build unifying collegial structures across the different components. To this end, Rath agreed to co-chair the search committee for founding faculty that was run out of HST, in spite of his reservations about the "HST ethos." Vrati, on the other hand, refused to have anything to do with the HST-run search and appointed founding faculty to VIDRC independently. This resulted, eventually, in two entirely different processes by which faculty were eventually appointed to the institution—one, a "THSTI" faculty search run out of Boston in collaboration with scientists from around India, and another, a VIDRC faculty search run by Vrati in collaboration with nobody. Once an institution that existed only in name and structure actually came to be peopled by Vrati's separate search for and hiring of founding faculty, a set of practical initial conditions was established that could, from that moment on, never be ignored. However much Gray might have wanted a unifying "HST ethos," the fact that there were three junior faculty members who had been hired through a process that completely disregarded such an ethos, and even disregarded the need for a unified process of faculty hires, meant that such an ethos was never actually going to be instantiated in any way that would be singularly defining of THSTI writ large.

Although Vrati's hiring actions might simply be seen (and, indeed, was seen by many) as a lack of collegiality, they also indicate the very different origin stories that existed for THSTI even in the minds and biographies of those who peopled the institution. Vrati's idea of the genesis of THSTI had nothing to do with the account that I have just provided, which routes through Cambridge and picks up HST en route as a central facet of how the institution is imagined. That account, as I have suggested, closely mirrors the way in which Gray and Sengupta understood the THSTI genesis. As far as Vrati was concerned, the idea of building a new institution that would focus on vaccine development was already in the works; it was decided that it would be folded into a larger structure such as THSTI, both as a matter of convenience and because vaccine development could easily be seen as a translational research activity. If there had to be other components to THSTI that did not focus on vaccine development, so be it; but Vrati was never going to have a situation in which he would allow those other components to impinge on either his ideas of translational research (which closely approximate an older idea of applied research through the commercialization of technologies and artifacts that are developed out of university research environments) or on his autonomy as director of VIDRC.

There was another level of structural indeterminacy, which operated at the level of the relationship between THSTI and the larger biotech cluster of which it is a part. From the HST perspective, THSTI was to be the centerpiece and driver of the entire cluster; even more, there was a sense that THSTI would be a nodal organization for collaborative ventures with institutions around India in ways that would allow the dissemination of an "HST ethos" on a national scale. From the perspective of actors involved in other parts of the cluster, however, THSTI was just one small part of the cluster, and the role of HST was simply to manage and advise on particular aspects of that small component. One person involved in other parts of the cluster told me that I was limiting myself by focusing my research just on THSTI because "what we are building is much bigger than THSTI."

Second Critical Moment—Bench-to-Market versus
Bench-to-Community, Artifacts versus Policies

In an early THSTI planning meeting, in July 2008, Uma Chandra Mouli Natchu, a fellow associated with the PBC, insisted that any translational research mandate at THSTI should encompass both "bench-to-market" and "bench-to-community" foci. This speaks to different rationalities by which translational research is often imagined.

The simplest formula that is used to describe translational research tends to be bench-to-bedside. But there were other sociological imaginaries that structured the bench-to-bedside formulation in the context of imagining and planning THSTI; the dominant one was bench-to-market. Institutions such as technology licensing offices and instruments such as intellectual property are crucial to the materialization of this imagination of translational research, as are incentives for entrepreneurial activity and investment opportunities, including from venture capitalists. At a place such as MIT, which is historically one of the most entrepreneurial universities in the world and which does not have a medical school, it is normative of think of research as commercializable and to think of translational research as research that can be commercialized. Indeed, one HST faculty member told me in so many words that it is not possible for him to imagine translation without a boardroom.

This imagination of translational research as being a process of taking things from bench to market seamlessly was also present in the Indian context, although not for the same historical reasons that it operated so strongly at MIT. At one level, the emphasis on bench to market was a function of a realization that academic institutions, although generally good at discovery research, tend to be poor at scaling up and manufacturing things that emerge from discoveries, making industry involvement often essential. But at another level, what was operational was a larger ideological imagination of "innovative" science, where innovation gets implicitly and naturally equated with novelty and with the commercial (and commercializable) dissemination of novel products. This intercalates with broader Indian elite desires for India to be a "global player," something that one sees across the board in Indian elite imaginations and that reflects in multiple policy spheres.

The bench-to-market imaginary was dominant in the imagination and establishment of THSTI. It was shared, albeit in different ways and with different resonances, by Vrati, Gray, Sengupta, and Bhan. The counterpoint to this, set up by Natchu, was bench-to-community. This suggested that for THSTI to truly fulfill its transformative potential of thinking of ways to get research to the market represented a limited and impoverished imagination of translational research.

This is not to say that community was not imagined in bench-to-market paradigms. Indeed, in the founding mission of THSTI, there was much bottom-of-the-pyramid rhetoric that was articulated, of the sort that has become seamlessly integrated into many neoliberal market discourses, under the sign of bench-to-market. It is just to say that, in bench-to-market imaginaries, community is imagined as the trickle-down beneficiary of building more and more commercial and entrepreneurial capabilities—as if capacity building simply involved building capacity to stimulate capital flows and access would then take care of itself. In other words, the call for a bench-to-community sensibility, at its most radical, animated ideas of translational research with a sociological imaginary and a value system that went beyond those of capital. At the very least, it was an attempt to inject some of the concerns of public health into an institutionalization of translational research. Within THSTI, the PBC tried to carve out an institutional niche where bench-to-community concerns could drive the imagination of translation. And so, although the only conversations at an event to inaugurate interim lab facilities for THSTI concerned how to build capacity for intellectual property generation and protection, one of the first major decisions taken at PBC regarded what kind of hospital—a primary health center, a district-level local hospital, or a tertiary care hospital—the institution would collaborate with.

In itself, bench-to-community ideas of translational research are neither new nor necessarily radical. In the United States, such ideas are central to the current imagination of translational research of the NIH, and "community outreach" is an integral part of its audit cultures. The different inflections of bench-to-market and bench-to-community are reflected in what is often referred to as T-0 versus T-1 translational modalities, or translational concerns with innovation as opposed to diffusion. Quite often, ideas of community outreach are conscripted into nothing more than blood-sampling exercises in poor or marginal populations to feed into clinical research, and contemporary public health, especially as it expands into its current, capital-intensive avatars of global health, is intensely neoliberalized, full of bottom-of-the-pyramid rhetoric of its own, and increasingly driven by public-private partnerships. The question at stake for THSTI, then, was less a simple binary one of whether "the market" or "the community" (both, themselves, terms requiring much empirical and conceptual unpacking) would be the imagined or real end point of translational research activities and more one of what kinds of norms, value systems, imaginations, and institutional praxis could be enshrined under the rubric of one or the other formulation.

In this regard, it is worth recognizing that *both* bench-to-market and bench-to-community ideas of translational research presume a certain technocratic directionality—as if translational research is about technological production and, then, a subsequent concern with how to disseminate that technology so that it impacts society. The sociological imaginary, here, is of a society that is both outside and comes after technoscience. This is where Rath introduced a further wrinkle, by constantly insisting that "translation is not about artifacts but about policies." In other words, Rath's insistence was that an institutional imagination for translational research cannot afford to confine itself to linear and temporally dislocated ideas of technological development followed by dissemination; rather, there had to be an imagination of how the social and political are imbricated within the very conceptualization of translational research. This opens up praxiological definitions and dimensions of translational research.

An example of a typical, artifact-driven idea of translational research, which Rath once suggested to me, is coming up with a new drug for tuberculosis. (This, in fact, is an active endeavor in Indian biomedicine today, through the Open Source Drug Discovery initiative of the Council for Scientific and Industrial Research). A policy-driven idea would seek to imagine what an adequate policy for tuberculosis prevention and treatment would be. Such an undertaking could undoubtedly include research and development of new diagnostics or therapeutics; however, it would have to be much broader and include social scientific and policy expertise in the very design of institutional capacity (rather than, as is typically the case, an add-on or afterthought after the fact, in the manner of technology assessment). There is a very different, and potentially radical, imagination of the social, the institutional, and the translational in such a conception.

Third Critical Moment—Normative Differences in Faculty Hiring

While these larger ideational questions were sometimes explicitly discussed in the early stages of planning for THSTI, they were replaced in 2009 and 2010 by more practical and immediate ones. The most important of these concerned faculty hiring. HST had the task of running a search for founding faculty for THSTI, a task that was usurped to some extent by Vrati's independent search for and hiring of founding faculty for VIDRC, as already mentioned. The process that Vrati employed was fairly typical for Indian research institutions. It involved his putting out an advertisement, creating a short list of possible candidates, interviewing them, and making appointments. His entire process took a matter of weeks. In contrast, the stakes of hiring founding faculty were much higher for Gray, who felt that identifying the right faculty at the outset would be crucial to the success of the institution. In her opinion, such faculty needed to not simply be scientifically productive but have the "right phenotype"— including factors such as multidisciplinary training, collaborative ability, and leadership and institution-building skills. The HST search was designed to highlight these skills.

What this led to was an elaborate search process, which played out in summer 2010. It involved fifteen faculty members, of whom nine were from HST and based in Boston, and the remaining six were from various scientific institutions around India. It was organized in two cohorts, each a week-long interview of five short-listed candidates in Boston. Potentially, all the short-listed candidates could be hired; so the candidates were not competing against each other but simply for a position. Each week was structured like a reality TV show, as scientific presentations were supplemented by teaching and visioning exercises, as well as by exposure to various aspects of the HST program and to itinerant ethnographers who happened to be present. The entire process, starting with a call for applications, their screening, and the drawing up of short lists, all involving cross-national conference calls with search committee members, took a number of months.

In the very practical founding of THSTI, then, there were different temporalities to faculty-search processes in different parts of the institution. Gray's perception of the VIDRC process was precisely that it was not tailored to identifying faculty for a different kind of institution because it reinforced and took at face value the traditional metrics by which scientists were always evaluated, such as publications. In any case, she felt there was something noncollegial about running a separate process for VIDRC, given that her idea of THSTI was of a single institution, which therefore, she felt, ought to have a single faculty search so that a similar "phenotype" of scientists would be hired across the institution. From Vrati's perspective, the elaborate nature of the MIT-devised search process was simply a waste of time and money, and was holding THSTI back—a point that could be justified by the fact that the third faculty member at VIDRC had been hired by May 2010, at which point the interview rounds had still not been completed for the HST-run search. Vrati's perception was shared by a number of people in India, even as people at HST took great pride in the careful and unique design of the entire process.

Even within the HST-designed search process, however, there were different resonances and pressure points. For instance, one major difference concerned letters of recommendation. These were in many ways the defining markers of quality for HST-based members of the search committee, especially if the letter was written by someone they knew. For a subjective process where evaluating character attributes was as important as evaluating research productivity, the letters really mattered and were parsed and discussed at great length. Many people in India, however, saw letters of recommendation as simply nepotistic—as a way in which closed networks propagated themselves by pushing their own forward. For them, ultimately, publications were the true measure of a candidates' worth, not because publications were perceived as transparently indicative of scientific quality but because they constituted an objective metric by which different people could be compared. In a country where people in all walks of life are often hired or promoted based on their connections rather than on their ability, there is a huge sensitivity to any kind of evaluation process that might be seen as overly subjective. But at HST, this sensitivity was simply read as conservatism, as a narrow and short-sighted way of evaluating candidates simply on the basis of how much they had produced.

Indeed, more generally, committee members from HST were willing to do that typically American (and MIT) thing—betting on potential. Those in India were generally more reluctant to do so and wanted to see a proven track record—not simply because potential was risky or subjective but because betting on potential presumes having the infrastructure that allows the realization of that potential. Hiring someone to build something out of nothing meant that it was not just the institution that was being put at risk from a poor hire; individual careers were also being put at risk if the institution failed.

The way in which people at MIT felt such risk to the individual could be mitigated was by mentoring—by having in place a network of senior faculty members already on the ground in India, who would care for and protect these young faculty members who had been hired. But *mentoring* was a word that often had different connotations in India, where senior faculty often "care for" junior faculty by promoting them as their protégés. In other words, mentoring in the Indian context has often taken the form of feudal patronage. Hence, there were some in India who were actively allergic to the idea of mentoring junior faculty. But this allergy could never be understood by those in Boston, who tended to see this as, simply, an unwillingness to support younger faculty.

In addition to these different sensibilities in evaluating candidates—differences that did, nonetheless, allow enough of a consensus to emerge that three candidates were selected through the search process—there were differences in ideas about how those candidates should then be recruited. Those at HST felt strongly that recruiting should be similar to how it tends to be done in the United States, where candidates are feted, cajoled, and made to feel welcome. Gray, for instance, felt that at the very least candidates should be flown out to India and, ideally, should be introduced to key scientists around India, not just at THSTI, so they could get a broader sense of what was happening in the life sciences in India writ large. This was perceived as essential to recruiting the best candidates. These candidates were all Indians who had gone to the United States or the United Kingdom to study for PhDs or on postdoctoral fellowships, and who were wary of going back to a scientific culture that they knew of as often stifling and hierarchical. Gray felt that a recruiting exercise would show them otherwise, in terms of what they saw on the ground, and that just the fact that so much care was being taken to recruit them would indicate to them how much they would be valued and supported should they take the position. In contrast, many in India wondered at the utility of this. Partly, this was because such elaborate recruiting hardly happens in India—usually, candidates have to fly to India at their own expense to be interviewed and are not flown in. So the elaborate recruitment was seen as an unprecedented and unnecessary expense. But even more than that, there were equity and organizational culture questions at stake, given that three faculty members had already been hired at VIDRC without such fanfare, even though all three had returned to India from postdoctoral positions in the United States. There was a sentiment that creating a song and dance about recruiting three faculty members when three others had not been similarly feted would set dynamics of hierarchy and resentment among the new faculty across the different parts of the institution. But, again, often these sensitivities were not easily picked up on, and the perception on the HST side was that the Indians were unwilling to go the extra yard to make junior faculty feel supported.

At stake in all these differences are not just differences of opinion but the ways in which those differences of opinion are animated by, and layered into, complicated affective registers. Yet what is surprising here is not that there were differences of opinion in the hiring process but, rather, that in spite of a process that was so spread out across space, ideas, and ideals decisions could be made in a mutually respectful manner. This opens up questions of collegiality—where does it come from, and what does it entail? What kinds of affective sensibilities does it come with? How do people who come from, and operate in, different environments learn to work together even when they know they disagree? What do people come to respect about each other, and what does respect even mean in these contexts? Which groups of people have to consistently make compromises for such agreements to be reached? I emphasize here that agreement did not necessarily translate into consensus; it often suggested the conditions under which institutional development could move forward in spite of continued dissension. There are questions here about individual subjectivities and sensibilities but also about the ways in which relationalities are forged, imagined, activated, and constrained. This is not simply a contest of different opinions or of strategic and pragmatic compromises, although certainly all those elements exist. It is a story of individuals and their modes of knowing and relating to worlds around them in ways that cannot be reduced either to simply character attributes or to cultural ways of doing things. Yet both individual biographies and cultural contexts matter immensely.

Structure and Its Counterparts: Agency, Contingency, Peopling

The theoretical challenge that I face in writing up this project concerns, at its most fundamental, the relationship among *structural elements* of a political economy, constituted by global aspirations on the side of Indian science policymakers as well as U.S. scientific institution-builders and marked by power hierarchies, different sociological imaginaries of translational research, and distinct ideas about what an ideal institutional culture is and how one goes about instituting it; the ways in which these aspirations, hierarchies, and imaginaries actually materialize on the ground in *institutional form*, which are always a function of both individual investments and preexisting structural constraints (on the Indian side, the bureaucratic constraints imposed by the DBT, which is a public funding body answerable to the Indian Parliament and, therefore, eager to show tangible and measurable success in the building of THSTI; on the U.S. side, the constraints imposed by the interests of MIT as an increasingly global corporate university that is investing its brand in capacity building for life sciences around the world); and the ways in which these structural relations and institutional structures are created, enabled, and constrained by the very specific investments of, and affective relations between, those who *people* THSTI. At stake here is a conceptualization of how relationships between global macrostructures—which involve states, corporate universities, and capital flows—intercalate with the micro-intimacies of individuals and their aspirations and commitments. The meso-scale of analysis here is the institutional.[16]

This is a project that throws up questions relating to structure and agency, structure and contingency, and scales of analysis (macro and micro). These are not new questions but a reiteration of some of the oldest dilemmas in the human and social sciences. My story of THSTI, when written, will be one of a very small, elite, and highly networked group of people who become institutional founders and leaders. Yet stories such as this—having to do with the globalization and recalibration of contemporary biomedicine—must aspire to illustrate something beyond the particular investments and idiosyncrasies of such specific individuals and networks. How can we reconcile this fundamental contradiction, of the absolute particularity of the aspirations and commitments of certain individuals and their relationships, which contributed to the establishment of THSTI (the kind of particularity whose elucidation is indeed the function and value of ethnography), with the more general historical, structural, and conceptual currents in relation to which they must be located, which constitutes the potential for theory?

There are several structural contexts at stake in this project, layered onto various agential ones. The *structural contexts*—having to do with the laboratory-clinic interface, on the one hand, and the idea of innovation, speaking to questions of commercialization and the academic-industrial interface, on the other—speak to two common registers within which the problematic of translational research is posed. But there is also the context of globalization and the particular ways in which the U.S. university comes into contact with Indian efforts at institution building through particular imaginations of a "global" biomedicine, imaginations that are often incongruent, and sometimes incommensurable, across various elements of the collaboration. The *agential contexts* speak to the stories, trajectories, and investments of the various people involved with THSTI. These operate at the level of psychobiography (ambitions, desires, ideological, and political commitments), of sociobiography (the social contexts out of which actors come but also their explicit and implicit sociological imaginaries), and of relationality (questions of trust, collegiality, and friendship but also, in various ways and at various stages, of pedagogy, mentoring, patronage, mistrust, and betrayal).

Structure and agency, structure and contingency, macro and micro: none of these is a simple binary. They are layered, striated. The work of theory here is not to arbitrate the binary or to find some adequate point (such as the institutional) at which explanations can rest but, rather, to work the striations, to elucidate the topologies that constitute something like THSTI, something like translational research, and something like a contemporary global biomedicine that is being built through highly capitalized and highly affective institutional and individual investments. This is, in part, a mapping project. But this mapping must always be contextualized and can never be done simply from the outside; the nature of the ethnographic entanglement that emerges in the process of such mapping is also consequential. In the remainder of this section, I elaborate on the relationship between conceptualization and contextualization, which, I suggest, is precisely a problem of conjunctural attentiveness. In the next section, I open up questions of ethnographic entanglement by discussing the para-ethnographic and the praxiological as constitutive to the very process of theoretical elucidation.

The story of THSTI has to situate accounts of the actions and perspectives of a handful of lead players who were involved in its conceptualization in relation to the larger contexts and trajectories, within which these lead players came to be significant actors at all and within which their operations were enabled or constrained in various ways. It is this *situation* that I have referred to, earlier in this essay, as attentiveness to *conjuncture*. I want to insist that the particular ways in which THSTI emerged—indeed, the very emergence of this institution as THSTI—was a function of the particular group of people who were responsible for its constitution. Furthermore, this was not a random group of people who happened to come together—they were already deeply networked. It is important to note how an institution that has set itself up in such ambitious, historical, and national terms was in fact forged by a very few people who in several cases were a part of preexisting networks.

For instance, as I mentioned, my own entry into following this institution was a function of the fact that Shiladitya Sengupta and I were both undergraduates at AIIMS, New Delhi. When I attended my first THSTI planning meeting in Delhi in July 2008, at Sengupta's invitation, I walked into a room that contained ten people, including myself. Of these ten, five of us had links, current or past, to AIIMS. Indeed, four of us had been in college at the same time. One of us (myself) was now an anthropologist taking notes of the meeting (with an STS PhD from MIT, postdoc at Harvard, and a master's in biochemistry from Oxford). A second (Sengupta) was a biomedical scientist with dual appointments at Harvard and MIT researching nanotechnology-based drug delivery systems (with a postdoc from MIT and PhD from Cambridge). And a third (Natchu, quoted earlier in relation to bench-to-community emphases) is one of my best friends from college, who at the time was finishing his PhD in public health at Harvard. Five people also had current or past links to Harvard and/or MIT. Of course, this networking speaks to only one trajectory of the origin of THSTI, the one that I had most immediate access to, but it was a consequential trajectory. Perhaps a reason why someone such as Vrati never bought into this trajectory was a function of different ideas and ideals of translational research, different personal and institutional ambitions, and less generous investments in collegiality than some others involved with the development of THSTI. But it was probably also a function of the fact that these were not his networks and did not represent his biographical trajectories.

Individual investments and biographical trajectories are deeply significant to the story of THSTI. At the same time, it would be too simple (and simply wrong) to suggest that the emergence of THSTI is just a function of these very particular investments and trajectories. Thus, I am wrestling with the conceptualization of a very particular, contingent story having to do with certain people and events that have the consequence of building institutional structures with the potential to be significant nodes in the global reconfiguration of biomedical imagination and practice. But I do not wish to imply a straightforward linear relationship between those contingencies and their larger institutional, structural, and historical outcomes.

In the context of THSTI, the question that arises is, Had this particular configuration of people not happened to get together at a particular moment in time, would others have taken their place? The answer has to be yes and no. There is no question that science policy leaders such as Bhan (and his contemporaries and successors, such as Ramesh Mashelkar and Samir Brahmachari, directors-general of the Indian Council for Scientific and Industrial Research through the 2000s, or K. Vijayraghavan, the current secretary of DBT) have had, or will have, an enormous hand in shaping the direction of the institutionalization of Indian science. These are charismatic, visionary leaders with transformative agendas that they have not been shy to articulate. It is unlikely that a translational research institute would have been imagined as a nodal institution in developing biomedical capacity by another secretary of the DBT who did not have a similar interest in bridging research and the clinic, and who did not have a research trajectory that crossed those boundaries. Bhan's own appointment and continuation as DBT secretary were themselves contingent events. Indeed, in 2009, there was considerable anxiety among a number of people involved with THSTI regarding the outcome of the Indian Parliamentary elections because it was assumed that, if the Congress government were replaced by one led by the opposition Bharatiya Janata Party (BJP), then Bhan's tenure as secretary of DBT, which was due to end that year, would not be extended. Yet the ascensions to power of figures such as Bhan are not entirely accidental events and are themselves a function of broader historical trajectories in India over the past two decades, such as a political embrace of global neoliberal capitalist trajectories that sees an investment in the knowledge economy and in science and technology as desirable and an embrace of U.S. technoscientific and institutional models as those to imitate to become a "global player," which creates a valence for concepts such as translational research in the first place.[17]

Similarly, there is no questioning the uniqueness of HST as a model to base an imagination of a translational research institution on, and it is likely that, had it not been for the contingent networks that brought Bhan into contact with HST, different imaginations of this institution might have emerged. Yet, at some level, there is a template to the relationship between HST and THSTI that is not entirely unique. For instance, the basic elements of this relationship—as involving an elite U.S. university, which was involved primarily in hiring and training fellows or faculty who will initiate projects in India—can also be seen in a parallel initiative with Stanford University, called the Stanford-India Biodesign Centre. In addition, from the perspective of MIT the pattern of its relationship with the Indian government in building life science institutions in other parts of the world is also not unique; as mentioned, HST itself has subsequently become involved in a similar collaboration, M+Vision, with the regional government of Madrid. And MIT as a global corporate university is involved in multimillion-dollar collaborations for scientific partnership and institutional capacity building with the governments of Singapore and Russia. Structurally, these are stories of global capital, imperialist relations of production, and the neoliberal corporatization of the research university.

At stake then are enduring histories of global, capitalist, and imperialist relations of production that animate the structuring of an institution such as THSTI; also at stake are the sensibilities, motivations, desires, and aspirations of individuals who people it. How, for instance, does one understand Gray's motivations for getting involved with a country that she had no prior context for, animated by fierce commitments to and ideals about how research should be institutionalized—commitments that come from her own pedagogical formations, legacy desires, and also what can only be called an ethics and politics? Or the fact that Rath, intellectually and politically opposed to a simple incorporation of an "HST ethos" across THSTI, co-chaired a search process designed by HST, an enormous commitment of time and energy? Or the intellectual and indeed emotional labor of the search-committee members from HST, none of whom are formally involved in THSTI, some but not all of whom have connections to India of varying degrees of depth, and all of whom undertook the process of sifting through four hundred applications for faculty positions over and above all their teaching, research, and service commitments in their "everyday" jobs at MIT? Or, indeed, the straightforward self-confidence of Vrati, who succeeded in getting faculty hired, and labs up and running, faster than anyone else, with a go-it-alone attitude that speaks to a very different concern for and imagination of collegiality than that held by many others in the initiative? Or the hubris of Sengupta, younger than most of the other key actors yet believing that he could remake Indian science in an image of his own making? These are the animating factors behind THSTI, and the animations are deeply striated at the level of global structures and of individual affect.

Marx is a critical inspiration for providing a method for the situated unfolding of structural logics and processes; specifically his attempt, in *The Eighteenth Brumaire of Louis Bonaparte* ([1852] 1977), to empirically situate and conceptualize a contemporary moment in the context of an event that was contingent and counterintuitive (the ascension to power of Louis Bonaparte, the counterrevolutionary, in France on the backs of peasants whose economic interests would in fact be compromised by his rule). Marx manages a simultaneous attentiveness to the absolute particularities of history and event in France, specifically during the period from 1848 to 1852, while situating those in the context of structural, historical, and sociological relationships of various sorts. In the process, the importance of agency and contingency is not lost; *The Eighteenth Brumaire* is, ultimately, the story of Louis Bonaparte, and it would not have been the same story regardless of the personage who assumed power in France. But agency and contingency are always situated and contextualized. This is the attentiveness to conjuncture that allows the structural and the contingent, the agential and the biographical, to be thought together.

There are more recent examples of methodological moves to theorize structure and agency together from within the past three decades of science and technology studies (STS) and the anthropology of science. For instance, Michael Fischer's (2012) attempts to think through the relationships between structure and peopling in contemporary life sciences at a moment of its globalization, which is a development and realization of a promissory call made with George Marcus in *Anthropology as Cultural Critique* that posed questions of the representation of the political economic and the psychobiographical as central ones for anthropology to contend with in its "experimental moment" of the mid-1980s (Marcus and Fischer 1986). Or Sheila Jasanoff's (2005) insistence on the *content* of institutions, not just on their forms and connections, as natural and social orders are co-produced in different ways in different locales, even within advanced liberal structures of governance. Or Donna Haraway's (1991, 1997) constant concern with *worlding,* how objects contain imploded worlds, histories, and practices of world-making within them.

All these scholars are concerned with theorization that takes difference seriously. My investment in the structural, as a counterpart and counterpoint to the agential, the contingent, and the biographical, is not simply an attempt to provide a larger canvas of abstraction against which the empirical can be rendered sensible. That would be a move to Theory, with a capital T, as the act of distant intellectual and philosophical abstraction away from the empirical. It is, rather, that attentiveness to structure renders difference *visible* without resorting to relativist essentialism. Structure is not determinate; it is what elucidates relationships, across place (concerns with location, geography, and globalization) and time (concerns with history).

I hope that it is evident from my account so far that one of the things most at stake in this project concerns the elucidation of the nature of emergent global relationships in institution building for biomedical research. On the one hand, these relationships, as they are forged between actors in India and at HST, are marked by different perspectives on the part of particular individuals; an institution that gets built through these differences is marked by hybrid investments. On the other hand, these hybridities never play out in a nonhierarchical manner. Although the power differentials at stake are complicated, some elements can be discerned. For instance, ideals of translational research that seek to go beyond the market, beyond appropriation by the logics of capital, are in this initiative significant but always minor relative to those that valorize translational research as, always already, an enterprise that is tied in to market structures and logics. Or someone such as Vrati, who is located in Delhi, on the ground, had the power to make his ideas of translational research practical in a way that the more distant actors at HST, in spite of a far more elaborate theorization of institutional ideals, did not, a power that was made more tangible precisely because it was enacted in a noncollegial manner that did not wait for collaborative authorization. Or however powerless the HST actors might have been in rendering their ethos as structuring THSTI, there was still a normative valence to their imaginations of institution building, one that allowed them, constantly, to render the resistance on the part of Indians to their initiatives in terms of cultural backwardness (explanations such as "bureaucratic red-tape" and "hierarchical institutional cultures" would often be used to describe Indian positions and actions).

Perhaps the most fundamental difference between India- and HST-based actors, however, was this: whereas the Indians had to act diasporic, those at MIT did not. By this, I mean that, for conversations to occur across the collaborating entities, the Indians had to constantly recognize where HST actors, literally and figuratively, were coming from. They had to understand a normative structure of "global" science that was being instituted as if it were placeless but that was, in fact, deeply inscribed not just by American value systems but also MIT and HST value systems (commercialization; multidisciplinarity; problem-focused research; collaborative, nonhierarchical work environments; and betting on potential). Actors at HST, most notably Gray, constantly attempted to understand and negotiate Indian sensibilities on their own terms, but such sensibilities were often coded by them in terms of cultural difference. This had practical consequences. One was the construction of a faculty-search process that involved nine faculty members from HST, of whom only Gray and Sengupta ever visited India as part of the search. Although some of the others did have an acquaintance with India, and a couple were diasporic Indians themselves, it was believed that one could search for faculty members of "the right phenotype" simply by having the context of HST and without ever encountering THSTI on the ground in India.

Another, related, consequence was the ability on the part of HST actors to assume *terra nullius*—the Indian institutional landscape as a blank slate that could be mapped, inhabited, and normed in the image of HST. That Indians might express different value systems and ideals of institutional development, scientific investments, or translational research consequent to cultural difference was accepted. Gray even came to understand that different sociological contexts might render different meanings of translational research desirable or operable (e.g., a more limited value to purely market-based approaches than at MIT). But there was never an appreciation, either in my conversations with HST faculty or in any of the meetings I attended that included them, of the fact that Indian life sciences already had a deeply striated institutional landscape that had developed over half-a-century of postindependence history and that the positions of actors in India were at least in some measure a function of their locations within, and biographical trajectories out of, such a landscape. *Terra nullius*, of course, is the most foundational of colonial imaginaries. Even if, as individuals, actors at HST generally exhibited a progressive liberal sentiment about building global scientific capacity and often interacted with Indian actors with a great degree of personal humility and respect, the fundamental structural, and structuring, aspect of the collaboration was one in which it was always possible—even easy—for HST actors to imagine India as a clean slate that could be written on, an imagination that is precisely one that constructs the world as flat, that constructs collaborations as simply the articulation of networks, that evacuates from itself the need for the recognition of structure, history, or conjuncture.

Such an imagination afforded the Indians, structurally, with more or less three choices: a willingness to be reinscribed through an intensely located imaginary of "the global" that comes out of a very particular institutional environment but has the power to act as if placeless; reluctant, resistant collegiality; or, simply, opposition and disengagement. Sengupta epitomized the first position. Without a doubt, he was a strong believer in the "HST ethos"; but then he was an HST faculty member himself. Rath epitomized the second; it meant that he remained, constantly, both the constructive presence and the contrary voice in the initiative—but it was a contrary voice that could always be heard with respect and then discounted. And Vrati epitomized the third; his was a disengagement that was undoubtedly obstructionist but that could only be coded and understood as recalcitrant, noncollegial, and backward-thinking by those at HST. That it might have also been the acting out of certain constrained structural subject positions that were always already unequal was never contemplated. After all, let us remember that we live in a world where it is *impossible* to imagine a situation in which Indian scientists, however accomplished at institution building, could imagine MIT as a blank slate to inscribe their imaginaries on. That is the terrain of global inequality on which such collaborations, structurally, play out.

This has consequences at the level of peopling as well. I have talked about the imaginary of translation at play in the biomedical notion of translational research and suggested that, layered onto that, is the constant importance of cross-national translation in collaborations such as that of THSTI with HST. If the former represents an institutional and epistemic mobilization of the notion of translation, then the latter represents its sociological mobilization in (depending on one's location) either cultural or postcolonial terms. But there is also the "translation" that is at stake in terms of individual biographies. The story of contemporary institution building in the Indian life sciences involves that of people who have themselves lived diasporic trajectories, whose biographies have invariably entailed significant spells of study or research outside the country, usually in the United States or the United Kingdom (or, in Vrati's case, Australia). In this regard, virtually every Indian scientist involved in the THSTI initiative is, to use Salman Rushdie's autobiographical phrase, a "translated man" (or woman) (Rushdie [1983] 1995). This is the biographical counterpart to the structural inequity that I have just pointed to; whereas virtually every Indian involved with THSTI has experienced "global" science in Anglo-American institutional environments as part of their own formation as scientists, most HST faculty rarely, if ever, experienced Indian institutional environments even as part of their active involvement in the faculty search for THSTI. They just did not have to translate themselves in the same ways as the Indians did.

Rushdie provides a counterpart to Marx, Fischer, Jasanoff, Haraway, and others for thinking about the striated relationship between the structural and its agential/contingent/biographical others.[18] In *Midnight's*

Children, Rushdie asks a foundational question that links, as the entire premise of the book, the biographical to the structural: What might it mean to think of an individual's destiny as entwined with that of a nation? The story of the protagonist Saleem Sinai, and his doppelganger Shiva, both born at exactly the stroke of midnight on August 15, 1947, as India acquired freedom from British rule, highlights this question through a magical realist mode of extreme caricature. But it is a serious question, having to do with the role of the Indian elite as custodians of a nation in formation; the ways in which individuals shape nations and nations shape individuals (the cracks appearing in Saleem's life mirroring the cracks appearing in the foundational dreams of the Indian nation at Independence); the contingencies of fate that create differences in the biographical trajectories of those who inhabit the nation (the switching at birth of Saleem and Shiva by the nurse Mary, allowing Saleem to grow up as the son of the rich Sinai household and condemning Shiva to a life of poverty); the ironies of those trajectories as, possibly, always materializing in contingent and unexpected ways (Shiva emerging as the hero of the 1971 Indo-Pakistan war while Saleem's life has been torn apart); the constant questions of paternity and inheritance (Who is Saleem's father?: a question that, even when answered, has no easy answer, and speaks not just to questions of familial kinship but also to cultural and diasporic inheritance, the postcolonial elite Indian as always, inescapably, in some measure a British creation); the dream of the nation—and the individual—as, ultimately, inscribed in a dream of a radical democratic cosmopolitanism (the image of Bombay as, constantly, the image of the ideal nation of midnight's varied children, in stark contrast to conservative authoritarian Pakistan); and, perhaps most important, the story of the imbrication of biography and nation as being a particularly generational story.

There is something that Rushdie is portraying that is important to understand in relation to the contemporary moment of institution building in Indian science and that speaks to a foundational conceptual striation in the understanding of the relationship between individuals and institutions as perceived by the Indian actors and those at HST in the building of THSTI. This is, at some level, a function of the fact that whereas the HST actors can imagine a "global" biomedicine that does not have to transit through an explicitly nationalist sentiment (a function, in part, of the way in which an institutional context such as at MIT can, in spite of its absolute particularity, self-render itself as if placeless), there is necessarily always some kind of nationalist animation at the heart of the actions and hopes of the Indian actors (a function, in turn, of occupying an emergent and aspirational but nonetheless undoubtedly minor location in the institutional, financial, and reputational hierarchies of global biomedicine). This is a nationalism that can manifest in many forms, ranging from the desire to be a global player to a desire to shun the global and focus on national self-reliance. It is not an exclusionary nationalism, but, in varying degrees and different ways, it is a diasporic, cosmopolitan, and postcolonial one, seeking to engage the (especially Anglo-American) "global" world, although often in terms different from those that have been set for it.

But there is something more than nationalism that is at stake here. There is a sense of the possibility of national destiny that can be shaped by individual biography. However significant Martha Gray might think the "HST ethos" is, there is just no way in which she can imagine her role as a co-director of the program for thirteen years as shaping U.S. national destiny (even just at a scientific, institutional level) in the same way. Gray's stakes are high, and she certainly is invested in HST as a model for a better way to teach, do, and institutionalize the life sciences. But her stakes are not articulated to the nation in any explicit way. When she saw THSTI as a nodal organization that would reshape the landscape of biomedical research and institutionalization in India, what she hoped for was a reshaping of *biomedical research* through the norms and forms that HST would provide. When Indian actors see such a role for THSTI, what they hope for, alongside, is a reshaping, in some way or another, of the *nation*.

There is, in addition, a generational story at stake here. The current generation of scientific institutional leaders in India—many of whom are in their fifties—came of age as scientists and citizens between the mid-1980s and 1990s. They were in the main trained in the United States or the United Kingdom and are for the most part invested in a less hierarchical and gerontocratic institutional mind-set than was prevalent in the generations that preceded them. But their coming of age also happened in a politically tumultuous time—marked by the rise of radical right-wing Hindu fundamentalist and nationalist politics; the mobilization of caste politics of both progressive and reactionary varieties; the establishment of a serious feminist politics that would influence legislation and social activism; the growth of a certain kind of grassroots civil society advocacy marked by events such as the Bhopal gas disaster; and India's transition, very rapidly, to a neoliberal economy from a state socialist one. The consequences of these changes are not discernible in any simple pattern across the various Indian scientists involved in this (and other) institutional initiatives in the life sciences, but it creates a generational ethos of its own, marked not just by different conceptions of institutional hierarchy from the past but also by an absence of a sense of neoliberal entitlement that one sees in many younger Indian diasporic biologists.

I once asked Satyajit Rath about this in regards to his own investments in THSTI. I asked him why, given his criticisms of the dominant rationales under which translational research and institutional development were being conceived, given his disagreements with the "HST ethos," given his general or openly articulated sense of despair regarding the establishment and direction of THSTI, he gives so much of his time and energy to the institution. His response: "I am an upper class, upper caste male in a casteist, patriarchal society. Guilt, of course." I think responses like that serve as starting points in thinking about what theory, critique, and praxis might mean in projects such as this.

Para-Ethnography and the Praxiological

I wish in this concluding section to think about the relationship of theory to ethnography and to praxis. There is an affinity in these two relationships, given that ethnography and praxis are both modes of critical engagement with the "stuff of the world" in ways that are ethical and political. I give expression to this affinity through the notion of stakes. By stakes, I am not suggesting a straightforward notion of significance or impact. Rather, I am invoking an active and continual conceptualization of one's relationship to the "stuff of the world" that one is studying. This ties into George Marcus's accentuation, in his thinking about and teaching of fieldwork across his career, on metamethod—pushing to the forefront how one even thinks about the mundane everyday activities that we perform before, within, or after fieldwork to imagine our projects, conceptualize what we see, and narrate our stuff and our concepts.[19] Metamethod is precisely *not* about telling people what to do or how to do it. It is, rather, about creating the conditions of possibility for imagining ourselves as ethnographers, as colleagues, as scholars, and as interlocutors with the present. I wish to suggest here an active relationship among metamethod (the reflexive conceptualization of our relationship as ethnographers to the "stuff of the world" that we are critically engaged with), method (the more formal articulation of how one does ethnography), and theory (an abstraction that serves some purpose of clarification through, in the case of ethnographic work, the narration of fieldwork but in ways that always aspire to exceed simply the archiving or documentation of that which is encountered in and through fieldwork).

The idea that these linkages and imbrications do not just have to be "found" in a field that is "out there" (which comes out of a certain Malinowskian inheritance of the ideology of fieldwork) but can also be actively staged in ways that have the potential for reshaping fieldwork and opening up theoretical possibilities, animates the conceptualization of what Marcus (2000) has termed a "para-site." This is a conversation involving key informants that attempts to stage certain debates in a manner that is unfamiliar and, it is hoped, generative, both to the ethnographer who is hoping to gain certain insights into the way actors are thinking about a problem and to the actors themselves, who ideally will be confronted by new modalities of problematizing familiar debates.[20]

I organized a para-site myself as part of my research. This was set up as an anthropological experiment to stage and elaborate the debate between bench-to-market and bench-to-community ideas of translational research by porting the various debates occurring around THSTI into a more general conversation around capacity building for translational research. This was held at MIT in November 2009 and brought together various people who could contribute to this conversation. Participants were invited from the United States, the United Kingdom, Canada, and India. Some, but not all, were involved with THSTI. The participants included basic scientists; people in industry (researchers and managers); a number of people from, or affiliated in some way with, the HST program as examples of researchers who worked at the basic research-industry interface; people working in public health and community health; and social scientists who had expertise in organizational issues in the life sciences.[21] Polymorphic ideas and ideals of translational research were articulated (and disarticulated) in this simulated setting, and these opened up certain conversations having to do with institution building for THSTI.

My stakes in the para-site were twofold. First, this was a staged field site, bringing key informants into a room to engage in a dialogue, including informants who might not normally encounter each other in the course of their everyday lives. For example, a senior executive at Johnson & Johnson, and a physician and community health activist from Dharwad, Karnataka, are not two people who might ever meet. Yet both, in different ways, were engaged in projects of relevance to the conceptualization of translational research, and in the para-site they had the opportunity to converse with each other. The fact that they utterly failed to do so was itself a telling insight into the limits of conversation across disparate sociological imaginaries, one deeply concerned with community health and global inequity, and another with multinational corporate-driven innovation. Second, this was also an attempt to bring certain otherwise marginal positions into a conversation about capacity building for translational research, which, both at MIT and in India, tends to be dominated by imaginaries that are market-driven and technocratic. Although oppositional positions to such market-driven technocracy are strongly articulated by some in India, they represent a minor thread in institution building for biomedicine, even at THSTI (where, as I have mentioned, they have tended to materialize most strongly in the PBC). Part of what the staging of the para-site allowed was a simulation of epistemic equivalence among the different invited actors, where a community health activist from Northern Karnataka would actually get as much space, and equal time, to air his views about what translational research might mean as an executive from a big pharmaceutical company in an institutional setting such as MIT, where such views are rarely aired (even though, ultimately, he ended up being largely ignored). The first stake speaks to an ethnographic conceptualization of the para-site; the second speaks to its praxiological conceptualization.

But from the perspectives of some of my key informants, the stakes of the para-site were different. The actors at THSTI were involved not just in building an institution but in themselves conceptualizing notions such as translational research. If I as an ethnographer was engaged with them in a project of para-ethnography, then they, in turn, were perhaps engaged with me in para-theory. The para-site became a para-ethnographic field site for me, but I was not the only one who was engaged in generating concepts or theory out of that site. So too were my informants. And "conceptualization," for them, was not a theoretical abstraction but concerned the actual ways and means by which institutional structures and ethos could be materialized. At the same time, this materialization required the abstract conceptualization of a host of terms, including but not restricted to translation itself. Gray herself was especially invested in the notion of *culture*. She cared about this both at the level of institutional culture—the patterns of interaction that needed to exist within institutional spaces for them to establish certain kinds of ethos—and at the level of national culture as she grappled with what she saw as cultural differences between HST and Indians in how they imagined the ideal conduct of science and the building of scientific institutions as challenges to be confronted in the establishment of THSTI. These are conceptualizations for which these actors could potentially turn to anthropologists and for which Gray often did. Here, for instance, is how she explained the importance of the para-site to the conceptualization of THSTI to a potential funder:

> To a large extent, any effort to build a translational research effort must involve a change in (or building of) culture. Some may argue this point, but one can easily see that if the present academic culture were sufficient, then there would be much more translation (however defined). Now many more people call their work translational, but one could argue that some of this is a re-branding, and not a change. Put simply, changing culture is hard! (And, I say this backed by my 13+ year experience trying to sustain and grow culture change within well-established institutions.) Having begun to work with Kaushik, I have immediately come to appreciate the enormous value of bringing an anthropological perspective to these discussions. With the framework and perspective he and his profession provide, I believe that we have a much higher likelihood of developing and executing on strategies to build institutions and programs in India (THSTI) and around the world. This won't all happen in this workshop, but the workshop is a critical first step.[22]

Gray saw the para-site as providing the potential for reflexivity, especially cultural reflexivity. These were not the same stakes, necessarily, that others in the room (or others involved in THSTI who were not at the para-site) had; as I have suggested, for a number of the Indians involved in the collaboration with HST the real challenge was not a difference of *culture* as much as a difference of *power* that existed between a global corporate university such as MIT and a "developing" nation trying to establish institutional capacity. The para-site allowed for a mapping and articulation of some of these stakes, but it did not necessarily lead to tangible consequences or impact. THSTI did not suddenly become a culturally reflexive organization, whatever that might mean, just because I had organized a para-site. There were attempts to at least create potentially useful documents out of the para-site, such as a white paper that I drafted and sent to Bhan at the DBT. To the best of my knowledge, the white paper itself, even if read, was of absolutely no consequence to anyone or anything. In that regard, the ethnographic value of staging an anthropological experiment that allowed me to note the dialogic articulation of different perspectives that would otherwise have only been garnered in isolation across space and time far exceeded its praxiological value of actually impacting institutional development in any direct way; para-ethnography for me was served more tangibly than was para-theory for my informants. Gray herself, after the staging of the para-site, became invested in this as a model for future dialogues that could potentially feed into institution building; however, that was never realized within the context of THSTI because the collaboration with HST progressively unraveled.

But then, as I have insisted, praxis can never be translated or measured simply by impact. There was another level at which the praxiological was opened up through experiments such as the para-site, in terms of the ways in which it allowed an explicit articulation of my investments, beyond being an observer, documenter, and narrator of institutional development, to some of my informants and, indeed, to myself as I attempted to think through my own stakes in this project. This speaks directly to the tensions that emerge from a project of critical engagement with an institution such as THSTI, and I turn to this as a final set of reflections in this chapter.

I first wrote up some aspects of the THSTI project as an imagined book introduction in late 2011, shortly after the dissolution of the collaboration with HST, which I regarded as a convenient end point to my fieldwork. This attempted to situate some of the multiple perspectives at play in the initiative, including through what I hoped was a fair and balanced portrayal of some of the significant differences in the conceptualization of the institution, through ideas of institutional structure, ideals of translational research, and mechanisms of faculty hiring and recruitment. Those are perspectives and differences that I have reproduced as the empirical core of this essay. I shared the draft introduction with Satyajit Rath, who by this time had developed into not just a key informant but also a critical interlocutor. He responded by asking, Isn't this account both relativist and dishonest?

This was not a hostile question. Rath is attuned to some of the complexities of social scientific research and is, himself, one of the most sociologically reflexive of the actors involved with THSTI. He is also someone who is well acquainted with the larger trajectory of my work, having read a number of things I have written on clinical trials and access to medicines. He has explicit leftist background and affiliations, including to people's science and health movements. And both of us have been involved in activist interlocution on some of the issues that have arisen in those arenas, a quite different modality of para-ethnographic engagement than I have engaged in with THSTI. What Rath was pointing to in his critique, then, was a different ethnographic modality that he saw in my writing on THSTI compared to that on clinical trials and access to medicines, where the political emerges quite clearly as interventionist. This latter register of the political is not an attempt to "change the world" or tell activists what to do or rescue the voice of the victim but to operate a modality of critique that explicitly points to crisis, contradiction, exploitation, and alienation and that tries to make sense of that through structural and historical analysis. The THSTI work, however, shows a stronger residue of another ethnographic ethos and sensibility. This is one that focuses on unpacking the intentional or motivational side of social action, on understanding how certain imaginaries operate and where they come from. These are two ethnographic modalities that, in my own mind, sit sometimes uneasily together.

Some of the unease comes from the politics of representation that are involved. In the clinical trials and access to medicines project, it is clear where my affinities lie: toward a politics that resists the appropriation of health by capital and even insists on the necessity of imagining what a socialization of health might look like. In the THSTI project, the binaries are not so easy. Crudely speaking, there are at least three kinds of political sensibilities that are reflected in the THSTI initiative. There are, as mentioned earlier, hypercapitalist, neoliberal sensibilities operating out of many quarters in India, in explicit tension with leftist, postcolonial, public; and community health–driven sensibilities that provide the possibility for alternative imaginaries of translational research to the dominant ones. The liberal positions that come from HST are of a third kind, occupying neither position but occasionally forming affinities with one or the other.

This leads, for me, to the tension of writing something that is faithfully descriptive of all the positions that are on the table while pushing and writing *for* some of the minor, alternative, or nonhegemonic imaginaries that might actually think of translational research in nontechnocratic terms. The tension that is contained here consists, at its heart, of the two meanings of representation, as portraiture and as proxy. In terms of providing an empirically thick, analytically rich description of the terrain that I am studying, drawing as thick a portrait of that terrain, constituted as it is by multiple biographies, stakes, and sociological imaginaries, is essential. In terms of taking a critical stand, pointing out how some of these imaginaries are in fact more sociologically rigorous or progressive than others is essential. But thick portraiture does involve a certain distancing from taking a stance; it does require informants' voices and perspectives to speak for themselves; it involves a privileging of the actors' point of view—it entails a certain degree of relativism as itself a critical modality. And taking a stance does involve privileging certain voices over others, certain positions over others—and that contains within it the seed of betrayal. Hence, Rath's point about relativism and dishonesty points to the double binds within which projects of critique, especially when multisited, comparative, and relational, are located.

This betrayal is particularly tricky in relation to my informants at HST. While I need to be rigorously descriptive of the hypercapitalist positions coming out of India, it is easy for me to also adopt a critical attitude to those positions because my antagonism to those positions is evident (and not particularly threatening) to those informants who adopt them. It is also easy for me to be critical of the left/activist positions at play in India because I have developed enough comradeship with those actors that they know my critiques come largely from a place of solidarity. But HST provides a much more difficult problem. On the one hand, this is a group of deeply imaginative, innovative institution builders committed to fostering multidisciplinary research, open to social science interlocution, capable of imagining a global biomedicine that involves building capacity in other parts of the world. This is not a group that has gone into India telling Indians how to do translational research; Gray, for instance, has always emphasized that the institutional milieu has to be relevant to Indian contexts and has to grow organically out of and in response to those contexts. This is a group that spent an enormous amount of time and energy on THSTI, ultimately without much to show for it in terms of tangible impact on the institution.

On the other hand, this is the story of a global corporate university engaged in a partnership with a developing country to build capacity in a context that the concerned actors at MIT generally know very little about, using public money from that developing country, and often not understanding the historical, sociological, institutional, or cultural nuances that make the collaboration full of friction. The power differentials are stark, as are the capital differentials. The Indian government paid MIT $5 million for this collaboration. From the perspective of Indian bureaucrats justifying this expenditure to Parliament, there is a pressure to constantly show accountability, to show tangible results of particular sorts. From the perspective of MIT, the collaboration from a financial point of view is only as significant as an NIH grant and is miniscule compared to the half-billion-dollar collaboration with the Singapore government.

Similarly, whereas from one perspective there is an enormous amount of material and affective labor, over and above the call of duty, on the part of HST faculty to build capacity in another country for the good of global science, from another perspective there is, as I have described, the imagination of a clean slate full of potential that can be written on by the "HST ethos," inattentive to the actually existing realities and histories within which Indian biomedical imaginaries are being configured on the ground, which has structural resonances with colonial imaginaries of *terra nullius* and elicits, with reason, allergic and antagonistic postcolonial responses on the part of Indian actors. From an HST perspective, what is at stake is the ethical imperative to build global scientific capacity. From an Indian perspective, what is seen are the stark differentials in global power relationships. Foregrounding the former seems like relativism to someone like Rath, who is well aware of my own stance in other intellectual contexts, which insists on highlighting the latter. Foregrounding the latter potentially betrays the relationships that I have developed with my informants at HST, who are well aware of my left-postcolonial sensibilities but who have built affinity with me based on other shared sensibilities, around things such as the marginality and importance of multidisciplinarity in discipline-dominated university structures, and who do not necessarily understand the postcolonial subject positions that are at stake, assuming as they often do that the world of technoscience is flat, even while operating on a terrain that is deeply striated. I have attempted, in this chapter, to actively foreground these striations and inequalities; it remains to be seen how my interlocutors at HST might respond to this.

Even the question of power differentials is vexed. There is the radical inequity between a corporate university with the brand value of MIT and an Indian scientific institution in the very early stages of its existence. But many actors in India, especially of the hypercapitalist ilk, are more than willing to trade in the fungibility of that brand value, not because they share the "HST ethos" but because it is seen as something that can be leveraged to their own ends. And while a more postcolonial, nontechnocratic imaginary of translational research in India does exist as a minor strand in the debates on capacity building, in relation to what is perceived as the hegemonic, market-driven imaginary of HST, actors at HST themselves see their imaginary of biomedical science as a minor discourse, operating at the margins of the still discipline-driven institutional structure of MIT. The spatial structure of this terrain is constituted in such a way that HST is hegemonic in relation to India, yet marginal in relation to MIT; hence, the activation of antihegemonic sentiments on the part of Indians is seen as a further marginalization of well-intentioned sensibilities on the part of actors at HST. The temporal structure of this terrain is constituted in such a way that the emergent forms of life that are stake are always underwritten by questions of what stays still—in this case, the endurance of relational structures that are colonial in effect, if not necessarily in intent. Theory must operate within these structures and will necessarily lead to positions that are critical, at least structurally, of HST positions that in other contexts I have deep affinity and sympathy for.

In conclusion, what I am arguing for here is a praxiological theory that foregrounds, both through conjunctural contextualization and para-ethnographic staging and entanglement, the ways in which different kinds of stakes can be made to implicate each other and the always uncomfortable tensions and double binds that reside within such implications for analysts who seek to combine faithful portraiture with faithful interlocution and intervention. Postcolonial contexts highlight this in particularly sharp and resonant ways; this is the very ground of postcolonial dis-ease. I wish to think about how these stakes have implications for the refunctioning of ethnography and for the conceptualization of a theory that is "more than" what it used to be.

6

Figuring Out Theory

Ethnographic Sketches

Kim Fortun

When I teach ethnographic research design, I often begin by showing students a set of photos of outdoor built structures, asking them what they see. Sometimes they just stare; my favorite instance was when they read the images, with increasing collective momentum, as conveying how the built environment reflects and reinforces race and income inequality. I could not see it, although their narratives were compelling.

I then asked if it helped to know that the images came from a children's book titled *Alphabet City* by Stephen Johnson (1995). Reliably, there are expressions of recognition.

This, I tell them, is one way to think about the work of theory in ethnography. It directs but also delimits what you see. It is productive and constraining.

This can be a good time to read Elizabeth Povinelli's *The Cunning of Recognition* (2002), which powerfully points to the politics of theory and the recognition it produces (and disallows). *The Cunning of Recognition* describes how multiculturalism—a political theory that draws out and

Images courtesy of Stephen T. Johnson, *Alphabet City*,
Viking Children's Books, New York, 1995.

purports to value cultural difference—can actually cut out difference by
codifying in advance what difference consists of and looks like. Indigenous Australians, Povinelli shows, can be seen by the Australian state only
when they embody what the state has deemed authentic traditional culture. Other forms of indigenous practice do not count. One lesson, akin
to that of *Alphabet City*: ethnographers should themselves use theory with
fear and trembling, mindful of how it provides perspective and mindful
also of what theory obscures and discounts.

It also can be a good time to read Gregory Bateson's *Naven* ([1936] 1958), which—through both argument and textual design—also draws attention to the funny roles of theory in ethnography. *Naven* describes an Iatmul (New Guinea) puberty ritual that involved gender-role switching in a performance that Bateson read to invert or relieve the tension that accumulates through daily interaction between women and men—in a

charged interactive loop that Bateson termed "schismogenesis." Schismo-genesis, Bateson argued, is what happens when there are encounters across difference. Schismogensis can be symmetrical or complementary: sym-metrical when two parties are equal (as in a wrestling match, when two athletes matched in size and ability interact); complementary when the two parties are different (because holding unequal authority, as between a parent and child or because different in position or kind, as between

performer and audience). Both forms of schismogenesis, Bateson (1935, 181–82; [1936] 1958, 175–77) argues, are likely to escalate, furthering differentiation through cumulative interaction.

Naven thus illustrates how theory can be *drawn* from ethnographic material, articulating processes or practices that are potentially generalizable, or at least portable (Boyer and Howe, this volume; Boyer and Yurchak 2010). *Naven* also points to the way theory can orient ethnographic work. An ethnographer can look out for schismogenesis in different settings, at different scales, explaining processes as seemingly different as an arms race, class struggle, family, interdisciplinarity, schizophrenia, and creativity (Feld 1995; Hoffman 1981, 37–49; Bateson et al. 1956).

And then there are the *refractive* implications of *Naven*.[1] Extending from Bateson, one can understand encounters between an ethnographer and the world she studies as encounters across difference, as a schismogenic dance wherein the ethnographer and the world she studies accrue identity through increasing differentiation. The ethnographer knows her subject, in a manner increasingly divorced from it; the very quest for deep understanding and thick description produces an imperial stance, a double bind. There is a structural challenge, this suggests, especially with ethnography over the longer term: extended encounters across difference produce stand-offs rather than the immersion so idealized in ethnography. Epistemological humility—awareness of the difference between observer and observed—only exacerbates the divide. A *Naven*-like exercise that vents and shifts escalating differentiation would seem to be in order. What might that be for ethnographers themselves?

Bateson himself is suggestive. *Naven* is about Iatmul social life and ritual. But it is also, in George Marcus's 1985 re-reading, "a judgment about the adequacy of analytic writing and descriptive rhetoric." In Marcus's reading, Bateson was "firm in his construction of data as observed behaviors" (1985, 68), reflecting the habits of British science in which he was raised. He did not question the epistemological dimensions of empiricism. What Bateson did question—with what Marcus refers to as a "highly developed hermeneutic sensibility" (1985, 70)—was the capacity of empiricist modes of writing to capture what he had observed; for Bateson, it was writing that was limited.

Bateson's solution was analytic promiscuity—reliance on multiple analytic frames rather than only one, using theory to offset the limits of representation. Marcus suggests that we imagine the textual design of *Naven* as a target with three concentric circles around a bull's eye. The center is Bateson's ethnographic material. Each circle is a different analytic perspective on the material in the bull's eye.[2] One sees Iatmul social life but also the ways any particular analytic/theoretical framework orients and delimits understanding. Theory is used to produce one of many possible angles on data-as-the-world.

Theory cannot, however, fix the problem of ethnographic writing for Bateson. In Marcus's reading, *Naven* is a failed essay—an essay "gone haywire"—that puts Bateson on the run away from ethnographic writing for the rest of his career. Dialogue becomes Bateson's mode.

Other directions are possible, and I try to draw this out in teaching ethnographic research design—which includes the design of texts to carry ethnographic experiments. There is theory all 'round, at many points in the ethnographic process, carrying out many more kinds of work, than is often acknowledged.

Sketching Research

I have developed the theory and practice of theory that I describe here over years teaching PhD students research design in a Department of Science and Technology Studies (STS) where many, but not all, students head toward ethnographic projects; all, by virtue of being in STS, have to "figure out methods" appropriate to their concerns.[3] My most ambitious goal is to help students build big research imaginations—and supporting skills—that can see them through many projects, always attuned to the entwined scholarly and political calls of their context. Methodological acuity and adeptness is "the deliverable."[4]

Over fifteen weeks, students in "Figuring Out Methods" compose about forty "sketches," each directed by examples and questions that I provide. Each sketch is short—punctuated, in Jacques Lacan's sense[5]—and designed to be replayed, redone. I encourage students to stay with their sketches over time, watching them evolve with their projects. Sketches are meant to be cared for and continually rewritten,[6] providing a space through which shifts in research focus and sensibility can happen as though shifts are *supposed* to happen. The sketches are meant to provide structure without determination.[7]

The research sketches are not intended to add up neatly. As a set, they are something of an end in themselves, a step toward what—via Bateson—we might call an "ecology of research." But they can feed into a formal research proposal, a genre that I insist has analytic purchase (acknowledging, via Maurice Blanchot, that all effort to be comprehensive, all effort to remember, depends on forgetting and "cuts," on writing as/of disaster; Blanchot 1986).

Image courtesy of Stephen T. Johnson, *Alphabet City*, Viking Children's Books, New York, 1995.

The sketches are thus both for and against method, an effort to cultivate what I think of as kaleidoscopic perspective—an ability to see one's world of study through alphabets, numbers, and a multiplicity of other frames (so to speak).

Critical here to articulation of a theory and practice of theory in ethnography is the way a set of structured sketches can lace theory into many moments of the research process in a way that progressively delinates an object of concern and its semiotic field, while—at the same time—multiplying (like Bateson in *Naven*) how the object comes into view.[8]

Theory in Cultural Critique

There are many ways to land on a research topic or question, and the two are not the same. A research *topic* is a domain of interest, almost inevitably shared with others. A research *project* delineates what a particular researcher or research group will do within a domain. Different disciplines, and different traditions within disciplines, undertake this delineation differently. For ethnographers, especially, the effort is paradoxical—a functional double bind: one is educated to wait, to let research questions emerge from within "the field" and associated material so that predictable, culturally charged conceptualizations are not imposed on a project in advance. One is also educated to recognize that value—what seems important and interesting—is always semiotically produced; one thus must be wary of what seems of organic or essential interest, aware that what a researcher sees—as important, as problematic—is always overdetermined. To simply wait on "the field" to structure a project thus also carries high risk of predictable conceptualization. Ethnographic research design happens in the space between—mindful of risks of both overdetermination and naïve confidence that overdetermination can be avoided. Sketching toward research design is a way to turn (theoretical) recognition of this paradox (and possible impasse) into practice.

A sketch that maps a research domain, its contradictions, and potential points of ethnographic entry illustrates the strategy. Drawn from the core argument in Marcus and Fischer's *Anthropology as Cultural Critique* (1986), the sketch suggests how a project can be delineated by asking where the world is out of synch with the way it is conventionally conceived— whether in popular thought or social theory. Marcus and Fischer describe and encourage ethnographic projects designed to unsettle habitual conceptualization (of the way belief or political systems work, for example) as a way to open space for new conceptualization. Ethnography is to lay ground for the experimental.

The first question in the sketch is thus counterintuitive, asking what *cannot* be articulated in dominant idioms—what is glossed over, ignored, even disavowed. In my work, for example, I am particularly concerned with incapacity to articulate environmental problems as problems—scientifically, legally, in the news, in everyday interactions. The second question asks for a mapping—at first preliminary—of the discursive formation that characterizes the domain, indicating how it works and excludes, and what risks it poses. Discursive gaps occur when people encounter a problematic condition for which there is no available idiom, no way of thinking that can grasp what is at hand. Discursive risks emerge from a tendency to rely, nonetheless, on established idioms and ways of thinking.[9]

ETHNOGRAPHIC SKETCH: Theory as Cultural Critique

- From your point of view (experiential, situational, ethnographic, theoretical, political, etc.), what conditions, dynamics, and problems are not adequately recognized in dominant discourses (popular and/or theoretical)?
- What are the discursive habits, gaps, and risks of your domain of interest, and where can they be drawn out?
- What cultural actors are helping articulate the discursive habits, gaps, and risks in your domain of interest, and how can you interact with them?
- How are the questions in your domain of interest social theoretical questions? In other words, how can you conceive of your research questions in a way that can allow your work to be informed by (and contribute to) the work of other scholars?
- What kinds of description, analysis, and representation can draw your concerns into view?
- How can/should you configure the "object" of concern that will center your data collection, analysis, and writing?

The third question takes an emic turn, asking who in the domain of interest is party to the ethnographer's own critique—in some way, shape, or form. This lays ground for ethnographic encounters through which critical understanding of a domain can emerge collaboratively, combining the perspectives of the ethnographer and those she studies.[10] The fourth question asks how the issues and dynamics of a particular domain pose social theoretical questions. This is usually difficult for students to articulate early on; leaving a blank space for later articulation can be an effective way to keep theory in mind, without forcing it. Other sketches, too, will return to the question.[11]

The next question asks for a preliminary (but with time increasingly detailed) description of the *kinds* of description, analysis, and expression one can imagine drawing one's concerns into views. Thinking of oneself as sketching is particularly productive here, licensing the kind of conceptual and creative play called for. The last question also has a sketched quality to it, asking what could and should become figure in one's ethnographic telling. As I have written about previously, play with figure and ground is an important, seemingly interminable dimension of ethnography. It is how and where a research project is literally delineated.

In this sketch, theory operates through a particular conception of how ethnography can be configured for critical effect. It also encourages the ethnographer to really leverage her own situated perspective and expertise; it puts the ethnographer in the game, so to speak. This, too, enacts a particular theory of value and knowledge, lacing ethnography into the complex effort to acknowledge and activate the way observers are part and productive of the systems they study. This sketch (and others) provides space to play out the implications.

Theory in/as Collaboration

There are also other roles and ways to theory in ethnography. In a sketch titled "Abstracting Essays," students write abstracts for three essays or presentations that could come out of their research material. In another sketch, "Abstracting Collections," students write abstracts for conference panels or edited volumes in which their work could appear, as a presentation or essay. For some students, it is easier to first write their own essay or presentation abstracts; for some, it is easier to first write the abstracts for the panels or edited collection. It is a matter of style.[12]

The two sketches imply one another but start from different places. In the first (writing three abstracts for essays or presentation), students metonymize, coming up with different ways of framing and articulating their own research, suggesting how each is part of a larger whole (addressing a question shared among scholars—a theoretical question). In the second sketch, students metaphorize, creating a structure that draws out likeness across different research projects and papers, creating a shared (theoretical) space. The challenge is to think theoretically by thinking collaboratively, to advance theorization of one's own project by articulating its relationship to others.

ETHNOGRAPHIC SKETCH: Abstracting Essays

Late Industrialism: Producing Inequalities

Drawing on long-running anthropological research on the lived experience, science, and politics of toxic chemicals, this presentation will explore the dynamics of today's "late industrialism," a historical period characterized by aging industrial infrastructure, landscapes dotted with toxic-waste ponds, rising incidence of cancer and chronic disease, climate instability, exhausted paradigms and disciplines, and the remarkable imbrication of commercial interests in knowledge production, legal decisions, and politics at all scales. It is a period riven with hazards of many kinds, operating synergistically and cumulatively. The presentation will highlight how late industrialism produces new vulnerabilities and new forms and patterns of inequality. The presentation will also highlight a need for new modes of collaboration to address the problems of late industrialism, drawing together researchers from many fields (including student researchers), other citizens, and activists in legal and political arenas.

Disaster Analytics

How can one think through disaster, and what kind of analytic purchase results? This presentation will revolve around this question, exploring how and why to pursue comparative disaster studies, and why it makes sense to think in terms of both acute catastrophic disaster and chronic slow disaster—drawing together thinking about Fukushima, Bhopal, and deep-water drilling for oil, climate change, the shale gas boom, and the global asthma epidemic. Mindful of discursive and political risks in apocalyptic gestures, I will nonetheless argue for intensified, strategic engagement with disaster analytics, leveraging what postcolonial critic Gayatri Spivak (1987) has called "forced readings." This is especially important in our current historical period, which I think of as "late industrialism." Beginning in the mid-1980s, marked heuristically by the 1984 Bhopal disaster, late industrialism is characterized by both acute and chronic disasters, emergent from tightly coupled, ecological, technological, political, economic, social, and cultural systems, many of which are overextended, fractured by serial retrofitting, and notably difficult to visualize, conceptualize, and coordinate responses to.

Late Industrialism and the Redoubled Double
Binds of Expertise

Expertise is blinding; in honing particular thought styles, analytic capacities and ways of solving problems, experts necessarily discount some types of evidence, analysis, and problem solving. Expertise is thus a double bind—both critically important and, in itself, hazardous. This is especially so in late industrialism, a historical period characterized by remarkable high skill and technical capacity, by a need for extremely complex coordination among different kinds of experts, and by problems that involve coupled technological, ecological, sociocultural and political-economic systems. Late industrialism is also characterized by remarkable commercial pressure on knowledge production and expert action. In this presentation, I will map the highly charged conditions of expertise in late industrialism. I will also describe how environmental health scientists have responded, building new collaborations, data infrastructure, and relationships with policy arenas.

ETHNOGRAPHIC SKETCH: Abstracting Collections

Inequality, 2015

Social inequality is produced and legitimated in different ways in different times and places, calling for continually refreshed and nuanced analyses. Papers in this panel will strive to specify the forms and dynamics of inequality that have characterized the first decades of the twenty-first century in different settings around the world. Presenters will question how established theories of inequality continue to have relevance in contemporary contexts—considering, for example, the continuing operation of a general dynamic such as "intersectionality" (theorized in the late 1980s by Kimberlé Crenshaw [1990, 1991, 2010], legal scholar, to explain how inequality is exacerbated when race, gender, and class combine). Presenters will also consider the evolving effects of market and religious fundamentalisms, environmental degradation, and other phenomena that have shaped life chances and social dynamics since 2000.

From Risk Society to Anthropocenes

Carolyn Merchants' *The Death of Nature* was first published in 1980, a year after the disaster at Three Mile Island. Charles Perrow's *Normal Accidents* was first published in 1984, the same year as the Bhopal disaster. Ulrich Beck's seminal *Risk Society* was first published in German in 1986, just months before the Chernobyl disaster. All these texts (and others of the period) laid the ground for decades of research designed to draw out the technical, environmental, and conceptual risks of high modernity. The frameworks and arguments in these texts remain important today—so much so that changing conditions, and a corollary need for new analytic frameworks, could easily be missed. Presentations on this panel will build on, question, and extend social theory articulated in the 1980s to address environmental threats, considering both new disasters (fast and slow), and more recent theorization (of "vibrant matter" by Jane Bennett [2010], for example, of "modes of existence" by

Bruno Latour [2011], and of "the anthropocene" by a growing body of researchers).

Practices and Politics of Expertise

Expertise is often cast in opposition to lay knowledge and characterized as rule-bound, instrumental, and narrowly technocratic. This generalization misses critical differences in expert practices and culture across disciplines, historical periods, and geographical contexts. Extending rich streams of work in the history, anthropology, and sociology of science, papers on this panel will describe particular formations of expertise, the genealogies from which they emerged, the ideologies they harbor, and the ways they are reproduced—and questioned—in contemporary educational settings.

As examples, I have provided abstracts drawn from my own project designed to bring what I have termed "late industrialism" into view. My concern with late industrialism stems from years of effort to make sense of environmental problems as *cultural* problems—problems that are difficult to make sense of because of dominant ways of thinking about production, pollution, responsibility, and a slew of other concepts that have carried industrial order. In fundamental ways, my effort to make sense of late industrialism extends from my early research focused on the Bhopal disaster, a disaster that rendered the limits of industrial order starkly visible.

Working on the Bhopal case had a forceful impact on the way I think about theory in ethnography. It called on me to attend to the empirical—to let the gross detail of the story speak, underdetermined by theory, saying something other or more that what any theory could cover. Bhopal also, however, made me painfully aware of the limits of representation and need for deeply critical analysis to make sense of the way Bhopal failed to register—legally, politically, culturally—despite the gross detail, clear negligence, and failures of accountability involved. I thus learned early to think with other people's work, always tying it back to "Bhopal" expansively conceived, striving to borrow tricks of analysis and description through which the many tragedies of Bhopal could be addressed. Theory became a driver of ethnographic questions, a way to put my projects in conversation with others.

For many students, too, thinking about conversation and collaboration is easier than thinking about theory directly. Once one discerns a shared thematic, one is on the way to theory, understood here as a way of thinking that creates (rather than assumes) comparative relations and perspective. Meaning is not assumed to reside in one's subject but to be created discursively, through the creation of fields of similarity and difference.[13]

Theory in Research Questions

After sketching abstracts for both one's own essays and for collectivities one can imagine being part of, it is often (somewhat) easier to explicitly articulate one's research question in theoretical terms. Somewhat. In my experience, research questions rarely feel "right," but it is still useful to force them into words. And wording matters. Playing with wording often has considerable import, pointing to different directions of work or to different kinds of material that can be used to address the questions. It is also critical to let research questions iterate over time. Indeed, this could be said to be a signature technique of ethnographic research, wherein empirical material is allowed to really drive a research project. One thus sketches questions rather than trying to nail them down.

A project's research questions can be thought of (and sketched) as a cascade. The top level is a question that is good for your project but also good for others, working with different material. This question is big enough to imply, if not require, a collaborative response and, thus, can be called theoretical. The next level down is a question that one will aspire to answer in the proposed study. The next level down is a place for interview questions.

ETHNOGRAPHIC SKETCH: Cascading Questions

Working title: *Late Industrialism: Making Environmental Sense*
1. What conditions and dynamics in contemporary societies produce hazards and harm?
   1.1 What hazards and harms are drawn into view in conceptualizing the contemporary as "late industrial"?

1.2 What legacies of industrial order—ecological, technological, political, and so on—shape and delimit contemporary conditions?

1.3 What discursive formations characterize late industrialism, what do they problematize, and what do they occlude?

1.4 What forms and patterns of inequality are produced by late industrialism?

2. What initiatives in contemporary societies produce possibilities for well-being and justice in the future—including, but also beyond, what can be presently imagined?

   2.1 What initiatives have been pursued to make (empirical, conceptual, and political) sense of late industrialism, what has motivated them, what are their limits, and how have these limits been recognized and strategized?

      2.1.1 What kinds of studies have been pursued by scientists, activists, and government agencies, and what has motivated them?

      2.1.2 What kinds of organizations and programs have been built (or imagined) to deal with the realities of late industrialism in the near and long term?

      2.1.3 What kinds of pedagogies have been developed (or imagined) to enroll people in late industrial realities and challenges?

3. What pedagogies and politics are implicated in the work of (experimental) ethnography?

   3.1 What pedagogies and politics are implicated in experimental ethnographic work on/in late industrialism?

      3.1.1 What kinds of literacy will help people make sense of late industrialism, and how can ethnographers help cultivate them?

      3.1.2 What kinds of governance are called for by late industrialism, and what kinds of roles can ethnographers play in their operation?

      3.1.3 What kinds of research can help sustain engagement with late industrialism over the *longue durée*?

Together, this cascade weaves the theoretical and empirical together, and sets up a structure that can remain stable while its content shifts. Field experience revealing the special explanatory purchase of a particular interview question, for example, may suggest that the question above it needs to shift or be re-articulated. Or one can become interested (or obsessed) with a new theoretical or political argument, and this can provoke a new cascade of grounding questions. The challenge is to see many different ways into one's world of study, cultivating kaleidoscopic perspective alongside fine-tuned understanding of how every question and perspective cuts some of the world in and some of the world out.

Again, I have provided an example from my own effort to capture late industrialism—ethnographically and theoretically. The questions have been sketched again and again. Even as I work to pull my material and analysis into a book manuscript, they will not settle down. Sketching allows one to live with this, enacting still more theoretical assumptions about the way ethnography works.

Building for Middle Terms

Still another sketch is expressly deconstructive, laying out the binaries that sustain a particular discursive formation and the ways binaries become untethered and shift, producing what Michael Fischer (2003) has called "lively languages." What could be called postmodern ethnography—ethnography attuned to the collapse of metanarratives—listens for these lively languages. And they can be anticipated through discursive mapping done in the process of ethnographic research design.

To imagine this sketch, I point students to Mike Fortun and Herb Bernstein's *Muddling Through: Pursuing Science and Truths in the 21st Century* (1998). Fortun and Bernstein explicate the difference between idealized and actual scientific practice, showing how science-in-practice can best be described with a set of terms that runs down the "muddled middle" of the binaries though which science is often conceived, pitting science against religion, politics, literature, and history. The consequences of dominant ways of conceptualizing science are sobering.

ETHNOGRAPHIC SKETCH: Binaries and Third Terms

Late Industrialism: Making Environmental Sense?

Anterior terms	Middle terms	Posterior terms
Modern	Never subject to law	Never been modern (Latour)
	Soiled states	
Production	Pollution	Consumption
Property	Trespass	
Extraction as value	Ecological as value	Wild as value
Healthy	Chronic, disrupted, body-burdened	Sick, diseased
Native, natural	"Invasive"	Alien
	Crashing pollinators	
Security, control	Normal accidents (Perrow)	
	Compound disaster	
	Intersectionality (Crenshaw 1990, 1991, 2010)	
Science + commercial interests	Science + civic interests	Science versus lay knowledge
Visible	Visualized	Invisible
"Essential, fixed position" (Haraway)	Diffraction, iteration	Refraction, differences
Generalizable	Comparable	Particular
Reductionism	Kaleidoscopic	Situated
Market fundamentalism	Governance, and/as stewardships	State command and control
Expert	Educated, collaborative	

There is no language for a politically responsive science. And no place for uncertainty or ambiguity in what would count as scientific—making it very difficult to deal with the complex causalities of environmental problems, for example. Watched ethnographically, however, science-in-practice operates otherwise and is more aptly described with a set of terms that points to the ways science involves judgment (rather than strict representation set against construction) and is more "charged" than neutral *or* political. Science, in Fortun and Bernstein's rendering, operates more like Peircean Thirdness (a matter of interpretation) rather than like Peircean Secondness (a matter of fact) set against a Peircian Firstness (matters of immediate affect and effect). Science is where Firstness and Secondness are brought, through Thirdness, into relation. Science works through signifying practices.

This kind of sketch can be used to create space for describing phenomena that habitual discourse cannot address (as in Fortun and Bernstein's example). Here, the ethnographer has space to record what *she* observes as difficult to articulate in either analytic or vernacular terms. The same structure can be used to record emergent terms voiced by the ethnographer's interlocutors. The ethnographer records the "lively languages" that often emerge in communities riveted by change, trying to outrun their own habits of articulation. The example I have provided here is a combination, laying out the discursive formation of what I have called "industrial order," which systematically undercuts recognition of pollution and other environmental health problems.

Theory in Teaching Methods

Theory can orient or emerge from ethnographic analysis; theory can also orient the design of ethnographic texts, literally from cover to cover.[14] And theory, as Bateson demonstrated in *Naven,* can be refracting, bringing the research subject/object into view in different ways—offsetting nominalism, animating juxtaposition. Viewed in this way, theory enables *différance* in a Derridean sense (1982).

It thus makes sense to sketch theory, in many different ways, in the process of research design and throughout the research process itself. Collecting sketches enacts a theory of theory akin to a poststructuralist theory of language, privileging the capacity of theory to structure *and* refract, a capacity to settle *and* shift meaning and understanding.

Thinking in these terms can undercut the anxiety that "theory" so often provokes. As Derrida pointed out in his seminal essay "Structure, Sign, and

Play" (1978), the habitual aim of the human sciences is to center meaning and fix it, and thereby reduce anxiety. "The concept of centered structure," Derrida writes, "is based on a fundamental ground, a play which is constituted upon a fundamental immobility and a reassuring certitude, which is itself beyond the reach of play. And on the basis of this certitude anxiety can be mastered, for anxiety is invariably the result of a certain mode of being implicated in the game, of being caught by the game, of being as it were at stake in the game from the outset" (1978, 279). But mastery comes at a price, especially for ethnographers. Mastery and resolution are out of synch with the change the ethnographer inevitably encounters. Mastery also suggests a satisfaction with available modes of analysis; the restless analytic pluralism exhibited by Bateson embodies something different—a stubborn but ever unsatisfied pursuit of understanding that is by definition experimental.

Sketching toward ethnographic research design, practice, and writing thus does many kinds of work. It interweaves theory into ethnographic practice at many junctures. It can animate thinking about the kinds of theory ethnographic projects can produce. And it works affectively and aesthetically. Both the ethnographer as subject and the subject she studies are put into play. Sketching, the ethnographer subject learns not to master anxiety but, instead, to accept and productively play with decentered, underdetermined, repeatedly transmuting subjects of concern. Teaching theory, then, becomes an exercise in subject formation on multiple registers.

Part II

PEDAGOGY, TRAINING, ANALYTICAL METHOD

The second half of this book reframes our conceptual and methodological reflections on theory through the lens of training and pedagogy. Because training and pedagogy intrinsically involve complex relationships across professional generations, we thought it best to design this part of the project as a conversation among advisors (the editors, drawing also on their own experiences as doctoral students at Harvard University; University of California, Berkeley; and the University of Chicago) and six former graduate students representing three further PhD programs (Cornell University, Rice University, and University of California, Irvine). These former advisees, now professionals in their own rights, had all expressed interest in methodological considerations of theory in the past. They thus seemed to us a fruitful group to convene to discuss how students encounter theory in the course of training and how early pedagogical presentations and receptions of theory shape research practice and the professionalization process.

In 2011, to open the exchange, the editors formulated four prompts for general consideration. These prompts asked the former advisees to reflect (in writing) on key questions raised by the volume's project. The prompts and the six response papers are reproduced next. Following the papers (responses) are three extended excerpts (dialogue) from the transcript of a teleconference that took place on February 3, 2012, among all nine participants in this section of the volume. During the teleconference, the conversation moved from reactions to the common themes that arose in the response papers toward thinking about how teaching and training theory could operate differently in anthropology today. A brief afterword follows the dialogue, which highlights key themes and suggests practical techniques for evolving theory teaching and training in anthropology from the conventional "theory course" (which, in its typical spirit and form, we view as highly un-anthropological) and toward a training in "analytical method" that better reflects the distinctive epistemic project of anthropology and that will help to improve our ethics of concept work, both within ethnography and throughout our training and research practices.

Prompts

1. How and when in your training did you first encounter theory as part of anthropology's method? How was "theory" defined for you?
2. What role(s) has theory subsequently played in your professionalization/training process and in your research? What does "theory" mean to you today?
3. Is there anything distinctive about anthropology's epistemic engagement with theory—that is, "anthropological theory talk"—seen from the perspective of the human sciences more broadly?
4. What would you do to change or improve, in terms of pedagogy and training, how anthropology relates to theory?

7

Responses

Theory as Parallax and Provocation

Andrea Ballestero

Theory Then and Theory Now

The prompt to which this short essay responds starts with a question of origin. When and where did I first encounter theory? In the spirit of life histories, of the sort that anthropology finds intriguing, I could answer that I found theory in a graduate seminar. As informants often do, however, I will shift my answer (and hence the question) to say that theory was there before anthropology or the classroom in the United States. Preceding my encounter with anthropology, theory was in the world, in dialectical materialism explaining the coup d'état in Chile and the military junta in Argentina. Under the label of philosophy, theory was also there in high school when I was assigned Freud's "The Ego and the Id" for psychology class. Theory was always a worldly affair.

Life histories are difficult, especially when one is asked to identify beginnings. But, as informants do, I will also entertain the question, and answer that I encountered "theory," as an objectified anthropological entity demanding identification, in graduate school. The memory is vivid. The room had no windows and we sat around the seminar table. The topic was capitalism and life, and during our first meeting, after going through the syllabus, the professor asked for a definition of *theory*. Following a brief yet awkward silence, we were able to craft something of a discussion until the question was returned to the professor who, wittingly, refused to give a definition and instead leaped into the unfolding of the class to say that there, in the duration of our course, we would examine what theory might be.

I withdrew from the class. Maybe a conflict with another required course, a reevaluation of the credit load, or a conflict with teaching obligations forced me to do so. But after all these years, I continue to wonder whether the class spent any time discussing what theory *qua* theory is. I think of this never-heard definition as a symbol of my unruly engagement with theory—a personal relation that has become intellectually productive and slightly risky. Thus, going back to the life history that the prompt invites, I could say that theory became anthropology's not as a list of authors but as a modality of thought always demanding elucidation—not as a generic form of logical argumentation but as a case-specific way of assembling particularity and generality to engage with the world. Theory became a mode of engagement with the ideas of others that went beyond the "application" of concepts to new contexts. Understanding theory as a form of engagement has made me wary of strong and sustained identifications with distinct schools of thought. This does not mean, however, that ideas are individual accomplishments devoid of histories and genealogies. It does imply, though, that to the extent that we can reflexively decide between theoretical orientations, those histories and genealogies are not deterministic. They are open-ended structures with the capacity of being transformed through the questions that we endeavor to ask in a specific inquiry.

My doubts about strong and sustained theoretical identification in ethnographic inquiry can be explained in relation to density. It seems that very strong theoretical identification often saturates ethnographic projects before they unfold. Leaving very little room for surprise or spark, this identification seems to result in a form of theoretical forecasting that is problematic and for which, most of the time, ethnographic engagement is made to appear, if not unnecessary, without theoretical significance beyond the provision of "empirical" illustration. In such cases, it seems that the story to be told is known before the research commences: theoretical saturation at the expense of analytic reconfiguration.

In my work, I try to sidestep this saturated theoretical determinism by paying attention to theory as a particular mode of braiding a question through a research project. Certainly, I am not suggesting one starts anew with every project. One can, however, intentionally bracket comfortable theoretical markers that seem to work too well and whose insights can be anticipated. This would be a tactic of induced discomfort that might, initially, favor inquisitive untidiness over elegant parsimony. A bit unruly, yet far from claiming any anarchist sensibilities, this intellectual attitude toward theory recognizes the genealogies of ideas but is not bound to their kinship maps as guidelines for argumentation or explanation. This modality of theory work keeps space for ethnographic surprise, as theoretical surprise, tactically open.

I trace one of the precursors of this relation with theory to my graduate training. During my first year in the anthropology PhD program at the University of California, Irvine, I enrolled in the required three-quarter proseminar sequence. The class was designed to introduce students to a selection of conceptual and theoretical discussions in anthropology and adjacent fields from the eighteenth century onward. The class was organized as a series of three oscillations. Each quarter circled back and reassessed anthropology, and to some extent the human sciences, by asking questions about society, power, or knowledge. Our seminar was designed to shake up, from the very beginning of our training, assumptions of epistemic hierarchy, linear genealogies, and teleological thinking. Frazer, Leach, Latour, Strathern, Evans-Pritchard, Grosz, and Geertz were all part of the mix, as were Marx, Durkheim, Weber, and others.

I could have inferred from that experience a sense of theory as a system of canonical and interconnected ideas that travel beyond the specific conjunctures from which they were drawn. The cyclical structure of the course, however, enacted a historical sensibility that did not rely on clear lines of authority or evolutionary undertones of knowledge progress.

While introducing us to exciting intellectual traditions, the class valued surprise and recursivity, and disrupted predictable graduate "criticism of everything" by calling our attention to unexpected and disruptive anticipations and survivals. More than anything else, the proseminar series opened our eyes to the deep historicity of knowledge forms, especially of theoretical ideas. I could have taken the proseminar as a rich "knowledge bank" from which to borrow explanations to elucidate the complications of the world. But the very structure of this pedagogical experience took me elsewhere. Instead of thinking of theory as a resource to be extracted and consumed, or assembled and produced, theory, in its thinglike form, appeared to have a certain precariousness—a fragility inflicted by how the proseminar, and other critical theory classes I took, revealed the radical historicity of works and names labeled theoretical. In this line, I could say that my systematic encounter with theory was also a systematic destabilization of any belief in its solidity as a transcendent object.

Looking back to the proseminar, I am not sure whether theory was ever explicitly defined there either. Or perhaps I have forgotten the definition that was given. Regardless, the effect is what is interesting. This lack of definition allowed me to deem works with fundamentally different aesthetics as theoretical. Rather than using a definition to sieve through bodies of thought that deserve the label from others that do not, I came to consider theory as something to be deciphered by what a particular author helps me do, see, or sense. Theory was never a *found object* with self-evident forms and uses. It was always a way to interrogate worlds whose contours were never self-evident. Theory was a collective, historically specific effort to put the words captured by others to work for both understanding their ideas and to help me better craft the questions and ethnographic sensibilities that continue to animate my projects.

It seems to me that this form of theory differs from at least some trends of contemporary anthropology that reduce theory to explanation. The world presents itself in all of its messiness and Tsing, Peirce, or Hegel are invoked to loosen the empirical knot. It is as if authors and their most recognized concepts circulate as tokens of authority, icons of lineages, ingredients to help enrich our writings, and/or genealogies that grant historical depth to one's thinking. The invocation of a theorist or a concept, clearly marked as such, with all the linguistic devices necessary to do so, draws into a text a highly specific rhetorical power. Think, for instance, about the contexts and tones with which David Schneider, Karl Marx, or bell hooks make it into a text to support, challenge, or interrupt an idea. As is probably clear, the use of theory as direct clarification to afford more power to one's words seemed, early on in my training and to this day, somewhat limiting of the creative potential of anthropological intellectual labor.

A key moment in the development of this view came during a seminar discussion of Malinowski's *Coral Gardens and Their Magic* (1935). In the conversation, my own thinking about theory began to fold onto itself, making an already existing discomfort speakable. At the moment, what had been a bodily anxiety for which I did not have a language took the form of an argument. A fellow student offered a critical observation that *Coral Gardens* lacked any theoretical spine. Where is the theory here? he asked. I was perplexed by the contention that there was no theory in the book, and we got into a heated discussion around whether theory needs to be labeled, identified as such, to actually exist. In a way, my friend's critique was that in *Coral Gardens* theory was not lifted from the rest of the text in the shape of citations of others' ideas or as declarative statements that summarized Malinowski's own theorizations.

I can see the pragmatic utility of turning theory into a thing that is textually marked through citation practices and textual differentiation techniques (e.g., parentheses and quotation marks). Theory-as-thing is extremely efficient in establishing glosses that make possible many of the discussions anthropologists are engaged in. Proclaiming and labeling things theoretical, and bounding them into a systematized assemblage of ideas is, has become part and parcel of, what we do. In this form, theory strings observations together and turns them into elegant bodies of interconnected and cohesive concepts. The functionality of theory in this form, and our familiarity with it, makes all the more understandable the presentist request for Malinowski to drop more citations and alerts us more clearly to his theorizations in *Coral Gardens*. The downside of this preference for clearly marked theory is that it justifies what I think of as a form of thin nominalism.

By thin nominalism I refer to what seems to be a perceived need to coin new terms if one is to make a theoretical contribution. In some cases, the proposed terms are in fact new categories of thought, but in others the analytic work sustaining those new names and word combinations is an assemblage of theory as literary references, as bounded explanations, as things. The unfortunate consequence is that ethnography that does not develop beautifully bounded "theoretical" phrases is sometimes taken as nontheoretical. In turn, when clearly marked, these statements become efficient scaffolds for an edifice whose name might be peculiar but whose form can often be anticipated. I find that this type of work seldom provides the insight that anthropology, at least in theory (so to speak), promises.

My ambivalence about becoming complacent with theory by taking it as a thing and by fetishizing its nominalist and rhetorical power opens a good occasion to outline two thought experiments that I use to work with theory in my research and teaching: theory as parallax and theory as provocation. In their use, these artifacts of thought help me frame ethnographic questions, and possibly answers, in ways that cannot be fully anticipated. I have used them not to generate a predetermined type of ethnographic text or a rhetorical strategy but to lay the grounds from which a question or insight can emerge. These are not mechanisms of elucidation. Instead, they help develop questions and worlds that need to be examined because they do not map neatly into theoretical family charts.

Parallax and Provocation as Theory Artifacts

Designing my dissertation research and writing my oral examination documents were two moments of my training when theory as a parallax began to take shape, although at the time I did not use that wording. A parallax alters one's vision of an object as a function of the existence of shifting positions from which said object can be apprehended. By shifting one's perspectives, the object's reference to other elements in the plane of view also shifts, revealing certain relations and obscuring others. This is not mere recognition that there might be multiple perspectives on an object. It is a second-level realization of what becomes comprehensible through the parallax, with its coexisting and multiple lines of view. With the parallax the possibility of multiple angles of observation cannot be ignored to settle into a preferred perspective. Through the parallax, that very possibility becomes the object of theoretical reflection through the particularities of the specific ethnographic project at hand.

The relations between elements made visible through the parallax (e.g., questions, concepts, objects of study, hunches) work as schematics of investigation in which the role of theory is much more than elegant explications of gathered events. Parallax theorizations help assemble spaces of inquiry whose most exciting corners are their blurred spots, those worlds that escape clear articulation and slide off when perspectives shift. With the parallax, the aspiration for a complex enough picture that mirrors the empirical vanishes, because comprehensiveness and complexity are structurally impossible to capture. The parallax is constituted by the fact that there are things that cannot be seen, cannot be known. While the unseeable changes from one moment to the next, it never ceases to exist. Under these circumstances, theory cannot be said to either precede or follow an object of study. Theory as parallax constitutes that object of investigation as something that simultaneously preexists the act of observation and is created by the parallax itself. As a mode of thinking, the parallax is essentially a series of movements, a chain of shifts that transform an ethnographic project into glimpses that are momentarily captured through different texts or other representational devices such as the research proposal, the sound collage, the journal article, the monograph, or the exhibition—none of them fully exhausting the possibilities the parallax opens.

This use of theory is different from saying that a theoretical approach provides a perspective on an issue. This orientation would seem to me more like using a theory, as a bounded thing, to explain a predetermined phenomenon. Conversely, the parallax is useful because it puts theory to work in the creation of a problem space in need of exploration. In thinking with the parallax, the question of what theory is remains bracketed. That taxonomic desire is stopped in its tracks. Here theory is thought about in terms of what it can do. Its definitional fixity melts into action. In the parallax, theory is an artifact in motion that is momentarily positioned at an angle to produce an empirical configuration asking for scrutiny, before being repositioned again. Here, theory helps produce questions whose answers cannot be anticipated because one does not yet know what it is that one wants to know.

The second use of theory that I want to refer to is the deliberate staging of provocation as an epistemic mood. The idea of provocation goes back to my interactions in the field, to a series of instances when my informants probed or educated me on theory. On one occasion, after giving a presentation on my preliminary findings to some of my collaborators in Brazil, one audience member asked whether I had considered how Habermas would explain the public spaces the state had created in Ceará. On another occasion, during a long trip in Costa Rica, a collaborator gave me a lecture on Lacanian psychoanalysis and suggested thinking about desire to understand the lack of any important accomplishments in the Costa Rican public sector. In its thinglike form, as a bounded idea identifiable with an author, theory seemed to always be ahead of me in the field. As many scholars working on expert regimes and technical issues have noted, theory is no longer a valuable resource to distinguish the researcher's insights from the views and explanations of our informants. Considering this, what is left for theory as thing to do? One answer is provocation. By exerting gentle pressure and irritating the comfortable reliance on a particular theoretical tradition, provocation pushes one to constant self-evaluation, in the best style of our neoliberal times. It forces me to constantly revisit that which is left behind or outside the purview of a particular thought tradition. The repressed returns, with a provocative attitude, to ask for justification of its exclusion. What a Habermasian approach for thinking about public hearings in Brazil overlooks, for instance, would have to figure in the explicit crafting of an object of investigation. Its exclusion would demand consideration although not necessarily inclusion as an interview question or field site.

A provocation sets a certain mood, it produces a particular atmosphere for theorizing. In my rendering, it includes a sense of epistemic care for the excluded, for that which ends up being out of theoretical limits, and especially for that which is out of our analytic zones of comfort. As provocation, then, theory incites, irritates, and instigates. Whether provocation works as a productive thinking device is a question in need of disciplined examination and one to be assessed through its specific usages. Provocation is a serious game. Its politics are delicate given that one traverses the murky waters of potentially violent disruption. Its practice is, inevitably, an ethical field that demands epistemic reflexivity beyond positionality. And, importantly, it is not about the fetish of innovation.

Teaching and Learning Theory

What is the route of this form of theory through anthropological writing? With my students, I am doing two things to explore what that route might look like. First, in graduate teaching I have paired "theory" with ethnographies to query where and how authors connect to or depart from one another. I have chosen ethnographies that explicitly claim to use a particular theorist with original texts from those authors. Tracing theory as assumptions, as rhetorical tools, as points of closure, or as gifts that you might pass on has been an extremely instructive exercise. This pedagogical exercise, coupled with more traditional courses on theory, exposes students to the history of ideas, demystifies the cohesiveness of theory, and shows the multiple registers at which theoretical work is ethnographically done. Second, I have designed a research conceptualization class around exercises for which students use textual and nontextual materials to draw their own research schematics. This is not a research design or methods class. It is a studio where readings and exercises are not planned to increase theoretical knowledge but are conceptual iterations of the possible avenues that they can use to arrive at their own analytic puzzles. The exercises include writing assignments as well as experimentation with other media and materials. I think of the exercises, between seven and ten per semester, as processes of theorization in their own right (some of these exercises can be found at www.ethnographystudio.ning.com). They do not rest on the textual cinching together of data and theory, but skip the distinction altogether and push analytic and conceptual experimentation through ethnographic elements that students have gathered in their preliminary investigations of their topics.

These experiments and my own reliance on parallax and provocation as theory artifacts are possible, in part, because of our peculiar historical conjuncture. On the one hand, an important part of cultural anthropology is enthralled by the valuation of multiple forms of knowledge, having for the most part relegated attempts for generality to the colonialist, universalist corner. Somehow, we have all become experts holding different forms of knowledge as technocrats, consultants, traditional knowledge holders, tacit knowledge makers. That epistemic multiplicity is implicitly and explicitly celebrated. On the other hand, anthropologists are embracing the fact that theory as thing is something that they share with their informants and not necessarily something that the researcher brings to that relation. Both of these factors move some to speak of a crisis of anthropological theory. While averse to crisis talk because it often hurries action at the expense of careful analysis, I can see where the concern comes from. There are even calls to stop the kinds of theory work we are doing and replace it with "purely" ethnographic theorizations. But, considering the ways in which theory appears in anthropological works that explore expert regimes, a separation between what we might call ethnographic theorization and theory as thing seems difficult. Emphasizing a separation between these two forms of theory presumes that it is always clear how they differ from each other. Yet, that distinction is difficult for certain ethnographic projects for which theory is itself ethnographic fact—the Brazil and Costa Rica instances I mentioned above are good examples. Thus, instead of cutting out thinglike theory from our accounts, we could be less timid about moving it out of its authoritative explanatory position and into a place where it becomes an ethnographic object in need of investigation. Lacan's invocation during a car ride with a water activist becomes meaningful, not because of how Lacanian psychoanalysis substantively explains desire, but because of my informant's sense that this way of understanding desire says something about the worlds that he works in. In a situation like this, if anthropology stopped thinking with theories that have travelled (embodied by say, Foucault, Kristeva, Viveiros de Castro, Agamben, Lacan, or Latour), it would be cutting off a slice of what for some of us is the field. Alternatively, one could think more about and with theory as thing in its field travels—engage with it more radically, to the point that theory, as ethnographic object, implodes into its own boundaries and, in the process, creates more open and expansive space for anthropology to do what it does best: reveal the unexpected forms the world is constantly taking.

Undisciplined Engagements: Anthropology, Ethnography, Theory

Lisa Breglia

1

I arrived to anthropology late in my education. An English major with several years of graduate school already under my belt—including doctoral work in a cultural studies PhD program—one thing I felt familiar and comfortable with was theory. I was certainly privileged to be fully versed in the provocative thought-exercises of poststructuralism (I took semester-long Derrida seminars as an undergraduate) and the genealogies of postmodernity. Luckily, I emerged quite eager and passionate for intellectual inquiry rather than bored and cynical. But perhaps things were not all good.

Leaving the undisciplined world of cultural studies behind, I entered the discipline of anthropology, especially lured by the promise of a tried and true method: ethnographic fieldwork. "Anthropological theory" for me was a series of terms, models, and historical figures contained in a green textbook imparted to me by a mentor, Jean-Paul Dumont, on my transition to anthropology. Himself a student of Lévi-Strauss, Jean-Paul made an early important contribution to the 1980s reflexive turn in the discipline, *The Headman and I: Ambiguity and Ambivalence in the Fieldwork Experience* (1978). Over his long career, Jean-Paul had seen theory in anthropology at its most structured and participated in its fracturing. As my professor in a critical ethnography course while I was a cultural studies student, he (among others) inspired my disciplinary move to anthropology. Knowing that I was going directly to the PhD without the foundational experience of a single anthropology course, he was (conservatively) anxious that I was not properly disciplined. I tried to prepare myself for my doctoral work, but I found no inspiration within the covers of that book. I put it aside. The gesture was not, however, a rejection of theory. Instead, it was part of my deepening commitment to theory—undisciplined theory.

During my doctoral coursework in anthropology, I spent a great deal of time in the classroom studying social and cultural theory. My commitment to theory was manifest in an intensive study of rhetoric and hermeneutics, discourse analysis, social space, memory, and practice. Theory was activated and energized as I began to concentrate my attention specifically on the ethnographic object of study. Outside of the classroom and one on one with faculty members, I began to shape a research project that, although admittedly revealing my interdisciplinary background, took disciplinary anthropology, and especially the changing modes and models of ethnographic engagement, quite seriously. My theory-heavy background and poststructuralist pedigree placed me among my cohort as one highly interested in "experimental ethnography"—which was true. Yet what I learned from an interdisciplinary engagement with theory at the crossroads of anthropology is that fieldwork is always, in a sense, experimental. Thus, I purposefully conducted fieldwork in a "traditional" or Malinowskian mise-en-scène of fieldwork. The outcome proved decidedly hybrid—an interdisciplinary, theoretically innovative "traditional" fieldwork-based ethnography.

My undisciplined engagement with theory continued throughout my apprenticeship research and into the writing of my first book. An anonymous reviewer of my manuscript for the University of Texas Press wrote, "I can picture the author riding her bike through the village thinking about Deleuze and Guattari." The funny thing is that it was true! Not only did I spend an inordinate amount of time tacking back and forth between two villages on a borrowed pedal-less, child-size bicycle, but also I did indeed think through theory, through the field.

I did not consult the green theory textbook in the field, writing my dissertation, or the manuscript for my first book. But as an assistant professor in my first post, I pulled out that textbook to teach a course, Contemporary Anthropological Theory, to undergraduates. The goal of the course was to give background and context leading up to the 1980s theoretical turns in the discipline and, moving on from there, to describe the proliferation of trends in the discipline. I knew that, for me, theory in anthropology was most salient when put in the context of ethnography. How, I wondered (textbook in hand), am I going to bring this to life for my students when what I really wanted to do was introduce theory as organically connected to the experience of fieldwork? So, on the first day of class I left the textbook behind. Instead, I brought along to class *The Headman and I.* I photocopied for each student a single page that displayed a photograph of a Panare child looking back at the camera in a delightful parody of the ethnographer himself—in the boy's affected gesture of holding a cigarette and his thin legs in oversized boots. Using that photo as an evocative textual launching point, we had a rich discussion introducing the themes of 1980s writing culture moment: the crisis of representation, reflexivity, and the spatial and temporal dimensions of creating an ethnographic object of study.

Given the choice of the two pedagogical artifacts—the photo or the textbook—the former much more perfectly represents my own engagement with theory in anthropology than the latter. Evocative of an active mise-en-scène of an already-theorized field, Jean Paul's picture of the Panare boy at once contains traces of my own pedagogical genealogy as well as that of the discipline itself. Perhaps he knew all along that he was giving me—the undisciplined student of theory—a true lesson on the place of theory in anthropology.

2

As I moved from my first project to my second project, I would say that the role of theory matured and, in effect, settled into a deeper layer of not only my thinking but my writing, too. My research in new sites and on new topics tends toward the same theoretical inspirations, even as the object of study reformulates itself. The effect of the maturation is a transition from "theories" as apparent in my research and writing to a much more baked-in "theorization." The practical effect of this is quite apparent: in my second book project, there are very few citations of theorists per se, whereas my first book is littered with such mentions.

There is a second role played by theory in my professional life. What drew me from a theory-heavy interdisciplinary background into anthropology was a desire and commitment to conduct field research, and my research interests increasingly became shaped around the theorization of ethnography rather than anthropology per se. I came into the disciplinary study of anthropology as an interdisciplinary scholar with an extensive training in theory. I have subsequently moved back into interdisciplinary work as I direct a large graduate and undergraduate global studies program. Situating myself as both a researcher and an administrator with a vision for building an interdisciplinary curriculum, I have come to define myself as an "interdisciplinary ethnographer," which frees me to engage with a range of theory while maintaining what I have come to think of as a lifeline to anthropology via ethnography.

3

Theory can help anthropology maintain its relevance in terms of the distinctive contributions it makes to the human sciences. The distinctive nature of the epistemic engagement of anthropology with theory, however, is that the engagement, which is ostensibly "theoretical," is in fact disguising a host of multiple commitments: the desire to produce nuanced ethnography, the need to produce generalizable results that can be used in comparative contexts, and a politicized desire to produce research in the public interest. These multiple commitments often get bundled together, tacked onto interpretive models, and subsumed under "theory."

Theory has an important role in maintaining the currency of anthropology in a continually (politically and economically) transforming world. What counts as theory in anthropology is increasingly shared across many disciplines. This is a good thing. It brings the discipline into broader conversations that cut across the human sciences. Cross-disciplinary theoretical approaches and innovations may also contribute to more robust and mobile circuits of anthropological knowledge outside of academia.

At the same time, the explosion of interdisciplinary work in the human sciences threatens the relevance of anthropology. But we can cite a specific weakness shared by the interdisciplinary niches that have grown in popularity—a lack of both theoretical and, in turn, methodological distinction (if not rigor). I feel this especially acutely in my own interdisciplinary location of global studies, where qualitative and quantitative approaches vie for prominence and visibility. In this particular case, anthropology will maintain it relevance through unique contributions to theorizing global processes and problems specifically attainable through ethnographic research.

4

Contemporary pedagogy and training in anthropology programs must respond to the changing intellectual and institutional contexts reshaping the disciplines. This means that attention must specifically be paid to the role of theory as it intersects with the practice of ethnography—if anthropology hopes to maintain a disciplinary identity in the face of various challenges and demands. Theory (in a broad anthropological sense) can be summoned to make anthropological work increasingly flexible, nuanced, sophisticated, and complicated yet translatable and mobile. At the same time, theory can continually be brought to bear on the ethnographic endeavor.

Anthropology students should attend specifically to the role of theory in ethnography because perhaps anthropology departments are training *ethnographers* as much as they are training *anthropologists*. This has particular currency outside the walls of the university in that "doing ethnography" has increasing value to a wider, nonacademic community (Marcus 2008). In collaborative modes, "theory" cannot divide interlocutors, allied audiences, or partners from stakeholders in research. Theory should not be alienated from the work of fieldwork—in other words, from the labor of ethnographic knowledge production, which—in the experimental mise-en-scène of fieldwork—is, at its core, collaborative.

This means foregrounding the organic relationship shared between theory and fieldwork. Pedagogically, this requires a reframing our approach to the usual temporal (and spatial) logics of "reasoning" the relationship between theory and fieldwork away from deductive versus inductive (or the "middle road"). Emphasis should be placed on crafting objects of study that account for the already-theorized nature of the field.

Theory Making: From the Raw to the Cooked

Jessica Marie Falcone

Anthropology's Own Myth

As an undergraduate at New College of Florida, I had my first real taste of theory in a course called "Myth and Ritual." It was my very first anthropology course, and I had enrolled with visions of mythology dancing in my head. I wanted pure, unadulterated Mayan creation myths. I wanted a straight narration of divination in Madagascar. I wanted a world of stories. Although I enjoyed the readings, I was initially frustrated that the authors' theoretical stylings seemed to persistently eclipse the actual myth and ritual. The lack of "primary" material was truly vexing at the time. In my literature classes, we read novels and handled the stories and poems directly. In my Buddhism class, we were mostly reading primary texts in translation. So, why was my anthropology professor, the wise and wonderful Maria Vesperi, focused like a laser on what other anthropologists had to say about myth and ritual? Edmund Leach, Victor Turner, Mary Douglas, Claude Lévi-Strauss . . . ! I was perplexed about why anthropology tended to channel its primary data to readers through a narrow frame called "theory." Maria did not explicitly address or define "theory," but my peers and

I puzzled over it in private; in that class, the theories usually worked to expose a human experience that extended beyond the case studies at hand. Our syllabus was a parade of theories, and because we soon learned that many of these framings were already deemed unfashionable, I did not understand why on earth I should care about them. Nearly three-quarters of my way through the course, while sitting in the library fishing desperately for a coherent myth in my required reading for the week, it dawned on me that theory *is* anthropology's myth. The mythology I was learning the most about in that class was our own.

Theory was alienating at first. I had felt like a stranger walking through an unfamiliar neighborhood at night; each house had a lit-up room or two that I could see only through a window with the curtains partially drawn, so there was more obscured and hidden than there was exposed. As I passed the houses in the chilly dark of night, I wanted nothing more than to be inside where it was warm, bright, and clear. As I began to pay attention to anthropological writing, however, it became apparent that the walls and windows keeping me separated from the bright and unobscured view of the actual myth and ritual was actually the analytical scaffolding of the discipline. It is only through the windows of theoretical engagement that our data are shared with readers. If I wanted to handle the solidity, the primacy, of pure data, I realized, then I would have to go out and do fieldwork myself; and then, I would have to decide for myself what to expose and what to leave unseen, and how to frame it all through theoretical window-dressing.

I may have been ambivalent about the significance of theory at the outset, but I did learn enough in that class to know that Lévi-Strauss might have suggested that what I was craving was too raw—undigested data, fieldnotes, field summaries, journals, and such. In the social milieu of anthropology, we needed to cook (prepare) our raw data before serving them up for consumption. Our various theories, then, could be seen as disparate recipes for cooking the unadulterated data we elicit.

"Amazonian Doom!"

As an anthropology graduate student at Cornell University, theory took on a new valence that was part professionalization and part sport. In our pro-seminar (pro-sem) courses—we took one in each of our two first

semesters—we got an inside look at how professors represented the theoretical world of anthropology through syllabi that featured the significant
hits (and sometimes misses) of social theory. We learned "distinction" in
Bourdieu-ian terms, but we were learning "taste" in a theoretical rather
than aesthetic milieu. In the process, some of us were being educated out
of some the academic crushes on theories that we had come across before.
Some of my cohort mourned this re-education and worked hard to hold on
to certain metanarratives that we were being taught that were now hope-
lessly passé. Some of our mentors, and some of us, tried to rescue pieces of
formerly popular theories, but those still clinging firmly to absolutes and
totalities were often dismissed as irrevocably old school. I remember a conversation on the quad when one of my cohort plied me with theoretical
questions to discern whether I was "hard core" or not. (I was not, alas.) I
also remember one friend who confessed that she had begun to keep her
love for Weber under wraps—hidden and secret; Weber had become her
guilty pleasure.

Others gleefully critiqued *everything* that had come before, in effect
embracing a kind of uber-destructive deconstruction in which no one was
left standing. Pro-sem had us all dutifully questioning metanarratives, but
to many of us, this sometimes seemed like a slippery slope to nowhere.
Postmodernism was playful and fun, but it seemed so dangerous in its
extreme forms that I worried that it would make it impossible for me to
stake out any kind of space for advocacy. For example, I worried that my
work on South Asian religious extremists, if wholly translated through
that theoretical register, would necessarily uphold the cultural value of
their perspectives and voices, even the hate speech that was so abhorrent
to me. That was not going to work for me. I struggled to stake out a defensible theoretical position from which to make a clear moral stand. I
was thoroughly unsettled, and published my Hindutva research only later
with some sustained soul-searching on the matter.[1] As a graduate student
in training, I frantically wondered, could we assert anything anymore?
Could anthropologists make any "true" claims about a culture or the
human experience?

During that first year of grad school, the young teenage son of a professor was hanging out with grad students at a department party and drawing pictures for our mutual entertainment. A few of us chatted with him
and joked with him about his doom and gloom subject matter: guts and

gore, accidents waiting to happen, and already mangled bodies. One of the pictures caught my attention; it was a picture of a girl(?) in a canoe at the very top of a waterfall about to topple over the edge. At the bottom of the waterfall, he had drawn a slew of very treacherous, jagged rocks, but back up at the top, she was being chased by sharks and piranhas and a swooping bird with a sharp beak. She was literally between rocks and a hard place. This is it, I suggested to my friends, this is the squeeze we feel in pro-sem, the one that we talk about over beers and agonize over as we try to find our own happy place in an inhospitable theoretical landscape. Like the condemned figure, we were suspended between the hazards of metanarratives (the gnashing teeth and sharp threat of "social facts," "structure," "totalities," and other impossible certainties) at the top and the fragmented destructive rocks of postmodernism that we will dash ourselves to death against at the bottom. The teen was quite pleased that we paid so much attention to the picture, and he gave it to me; he signed it before handing it over, like a rock star. I have faithfully carried that picture around for the past ten years as an artifact of graduate school socialization. I am looking at it right now, as I write. Did I mention that the teen had titled the picture, "Amazonian Doom!" and underscored the danger with a capitalized, "AHAHA"? This stark, terrifying, and literally cartoonish binary resonated deeply with my anxiety about theoretical engagement at the time.

The sporting aspect of theoretical engagement in graduate school emerged as we watched the games unfold before us, learned the rules, and started playing. Arrayed before us, our professors wore their theoretical affiliations like fan paraphernalia. We had some time to find ourselves, but eventually we had to choose sides. By my second year of grad school, many of us had factionalized, and some of my cohort were such enthusiastic cheerleaders for their theoretical teams that it became a primary identity marker. I am talking missionary zeal. I chose sides too, yet, like so many others before me, I strained against the boundaries of my favorite theories and sought space for creativity.

As I write articles now, I engage with theory ritually. I do the necessary oblations and make the necessary offerings of citations and references. It is not that theory is not valuable—it does important work for us. It does enact and perform order out of chaos. But my agnostic sensibilities have affected my relationship with anthropological rituals. I do not have unquestioning faith in anything anymore. Capital-T Theory is not capital-T True. God is dead—and so is our theoretical pantheon. Any number of anthropologists and other social scientists, our senior interlocutors foremost among them, have discussed this state of "crisis" and how we might move forward. Like many others, I have taken refuge with my informants themselves. I used several Madhyamika Buddhist analytics as choice theoretical frameworks for my dissertation on Madhyamika Buddhists (Falcone 2010c). I let them tell me how to order the chaos.

Once I thought it would be fun, playful, and irreverent to bring back data from the field and then run it through a whole gamut of theoretical cookie-cutters: everything from functionalism to structuralism to feminist theory to Derridean postmodernism. Could any culture be put into conversation with any theory? Whether productively or unproductively as regards the actual subject matter was beside the point because it seemed to me that the exercise would at least tell us something constructive about our methods, theories, and epistemologies. The idea was a half-baked one to begin with, and I did not pursue it, but I always wondered what such a project would look like. Later, I realized that to some extent at least our theoretical predispositions delimit the kinds of data we seek and the kinds of questions we ask. That is, the theoretical recipes we bring to the field with us may in some part determine the ingredients we elicit for our raw material. This recognition was both provocative and disillusioning, and it was one of the reasons that in my dissertation I sought to temper this problem by referencing the theories of my Buddhist informants at least as often as I did our own. Now I wonder if the new cookie-cutter is not that very move, that very swivel to our informants . . . ? And if we have begun to play instead of preach, is the former really better than the latter? Regardless, I do not think we play out of disrespect or because we have given up, but we do it because it feels like the most honest engagement possible right now.

Hunting and Gathering

Cultural anthropologists today are foragers. We borrow compulsively and shamelessly. I actually love this about us—we transcend our disciplinary boundary walls so effortlessly. Setting aside the four-fields goliath, cultural anthropology alone is a rather shapeless, amorphous creature. The world is ours, literally. Our subject matter could be, well, anything, anywhere. And then when we come home and it is time to sit down and write, what discipline have we not raided for its theoretical contributions? I have to do a full circumambulation in any used bookstore because our subjects and theoretical findings overspill the tiny section relegated to anthropology: sociology, gender studies, religious studies, psychology, political science, development studies, critical studies, art, media, science and technology studies, philosophy, history, and so on. Are we inclusive or greedy?

Now we are also organizing more often through the lenses of our informants. Is para-ethnography not an effort to borrow analytical framings from our informants? Or collaborate in theory making with them? More borrowing, more collaborating, and I am all for it. In the end, we engulf and swallow everything in our path—it all belongs to us. We hope no one will accuse us of intellectual property infringement. I am not suggesting that our theoretical borrowing is destructive, like a retro horror movie Blob that consumes everything in its path, but sometimes I wonder. Even if we do not devour their ideas to death, we may alter, mangle, or transform them beyond recognition.

When I deployed Tibetan Madhyamika analytics in my study of Madhyamika Buddhist converts, I argued that this served to decenter anthropological authority and explicate even more about my informants than my more customary ethnographic content had already revealed. Because I was studying a Western Buddhist group (the Foundation for the Preservation of the Mahayana Tradition) that had itself liberally borrowed, translated, and reworked a more traditional, heritage Tibetan Buddhism, my own borrowing mirrored and echoed the cultural work of my informants. My borrowing served to make my representation more robust, but it certainly was as much an act of cooptation as adaptation. And, my work, like most anthropological writing, doubtlessly exposes at least as much about my own anthropological theoryscape as it does about my informants' worldview.

A Dose of One's Own Medicine

I have long been fascinated with academic culture itself and, especially, with the use of theory in our anthropological subcultures. I suggest that we need more institutionalized spaces for discussion of theory within our academic cultures. This intergenerational conversation itself is a wonderful acknowledgement of the need for such reflection. I suspect that I was invited to join this conversation in large part due to the fact that I wrote an essay in graduate school that essentially used anthropological gift theories to analyze the ways that anthropologists circulate, gift, and exchange our theories.[2] I stand by that piece, and I could and would go further to suggest that many of our theoretical frames could be usefully or at least enlighteningly deployed on our own cultural work of reading and making theoretical framings. As I sift through bodies of theoretical literature on globalization, commodification, social stratification (gender, ethnicity, class), power, and so on, I argue that each body of literature has something to tell us about ourselves, our academic culture, and our use of theory. How is theory made, circulated, and reproduced? Who decides what is most compelling or fashionable at a particular moment? How do we strategize and plan the circulation of theoretical gifts? How do we compel and convince? How much are our engagements dictated and delimited by socioeconomic needs for publications and the jobs, tenure, and promotions that depend on them? What are the mechanisms for change and temporalities involved in our changing theoryscape? Does the impetus for making new theory actually come from the shortcomings of what came before, or is it inspired more by the fame and accolades that comes with being at the leading edge of theory making? What is the economy of theory sharing versus theory making? Are we not obligated to look more closely at the phenomenology of theory exchange? Not just to understand the cultural conditions in which our knowledge is produced, but also to do justice to our craft, to the very integrity of the theories and ethnographies we produce? Why is this conversation often backstage rather than in the foreground; what are we afraid of?

In sum, I advocate for the explicit use of anthropological theory (past, present, and future) as a meditative framework for engaging with our own academic cultures.[3] I would teach theory and use it right away to look at the historical and cultural milieu in which that theory emerged and continues to be shared. We can use our own tools to get to know ourselves better. Omphaloskepsis of the worst kind, or a healthy dose of our own medicine? I assert the latter. Note that the deep and sustained meditation I am prescribing is different than the off-handed, surface observations about academic cultures that we all make from time to time. As a pedagogy or a practice, it would need to be regular, disciplined, and fearless.

People in Glass Cages (Shouldn't Throw Theoretical Stones)

Jamer Hunt

1

Theory came to me out of the mists of Europe in an undergraduate semiotics class during my first semester at college. Barely eighteen years old, fresh out of public school, I took the class because I liked the idea of watching Alfred Hitchcock movies in class. Little did I realize that it was a fifteen-week scuffle with the titans of structuralism and poststructuralism (Saussure, Lévi-Strauss, Lyotard, Kristeva, Lacan, Foucault, Derrida . . .). Theory, as the instructor presented it, was inscrutable, almost unreadable, and thoroughly mystifying—and very continental. Unexplainably, in my next semester I signed up for the sequel to the class, which focused more specifically on cinematic narrative. In it we used theory as a hermeneutic strategy, opening up secret realms beyond the visible and the manifest.

Although I turned away from semiotics eventually, I was not uninfected by the virus. I drifted toward more ethnographic interests, but still I carried with me a few key insights: that the real was not self-evident but constructed; that meaning was slippery and unstable; and that life was like a text, waiting for keen minds to unravel its discursive structure. My first encounters with anthropologists such as Clifford Geertz and Victor Turner only reinforced these assumptions. Even in their work (which was much more deeply grounded in empirical observation and cross-cultural encounter), all facts, all details, and all inconsistencies capitulated to the power of a bigger, more grandiloquent explanatory mechanism. In these days—somewhere in the 1980s—theory had gained an uppercase T and had become the lord of all social science methods.

Thus, when I entered graduate school in anthropology, Theory was the only real game in town. It was where the smart kids hung out. The others went off and did things that looked woefully similar to Evans-Pritchard and Margaret Mead. In these arrogant days, theory *was* method, which is to say that few had an interest in methodological inquiry. As a result, anthropology started to look a lot more like intellectual history. All methods (what methods?) served the master, Theory. And in those days, that seemed enough.

2

Theory became a crystal palace in which I happily lived for most of my doctoral education in anthropology. Increasingly, however, I became disillusioned with Theory's (and my own) hermeticism. The palace had become a prison. My dissertation project was thus an explicit attempt to confront Theory—in complicating ways—with the lived experience of its practitioners. It was also an attempt to make theory into a form of material practice that one could empirically investigate in the same way that one might engage with the material and immaterial culture of the Yanomami. In this process, I reframed Theory from an overpowering analytical construct to a contested field of forces (material, ideological, psychical, social, and symbolic). I repurposed traditional ethnographic methods (interviews, fieldwork, and kinship research) to interrogate and embody Theory.

As my work has shifted from an anthropology of French psychoanalysis, surrealism, and gender to design as a method for animating public participation, the role of theory has moved as well from a starring to a supporting role. Attracted to the ways in which design animates ideas within the public realm, I now use theories in a more tactical manner: they are explanatory mechanisms (and there are many of them) that can illuminate complexity and context while providing insight into paths forward through "wicked problems." In shifting its role from an end to a means, in dropping the uppercase T, I am now more pragmatic in how I use theory. Theory, for me, is a set of contested and contestable suppositions that animate my practice; they lead to informed action in the face of radical uncertainty. I am no longer content to allow theory to end with radical uncertainty itself.

3

I believe that we are still experiencing aftershocks from the powerful wave of energy released by our fetishism for French poststructuralism in the 1980s. For anthropology, this has resulted in two contrasting transformations: fresh energy for new fields of inquiry, on the one hand, and a drift toward a more solipsistic mode of practice, on the other.

A critique, coming from anticolonialist, civil rights, and identity politics movements, caused ruptures in the foundation of the discipline, certainly, but the seeds of opportunity implanted themselves in those cracks. The shift of the ethnographic gaze from tribal "primitives" to scientists in laboratories, financiers in boardrooms, or cyborgs in cyberspace, for example, has animated the profession and redrawn the conditions of possibility of the ethnographic project. This recalibration has not necessarily eliminated the need to continue to contest the disequilibria in power, agency, and narrative control that endure, but it has emboldened practitioners to explore new thresholds and horizons for practice. In unexpected ways, this shift in the ethnographer's focus has dovetailed with the rise of actor-network theory (again, imported from France). Just as anthropologists had redrawn their fields of inquiry to include nontraditional and even nongeographically bound sites, actor-network theory reconfigured the material and symbolic relationships between human and nonhuman actors, ascribing inventive forms of agency to a host of new and compelling "actors" in the field—from microbes and genes and test tubes to bankers and benches and tables. The sum of these two seismic shifts—the anticolonialist and the actor-network—has resulted in an ethnographic pluralism that holds the promise to produce fresh forms of ethnography in utterly surprising places.

There is still, however, a power that theory holds over anthropological discourse that distorts its own relevance. Too many projects move from theory to observation and back to theory again—with an overweening emphasis on theory before, during, and after. In these cases, fieldwork serves only to validate or invalidate a preciously held theory—about the subaltern, power, or subjectivity—with little openness to the vicissitudes of chance, randomness, or uncertainty. Narratives play out according to a script that theory drafts.

From my vantage as an insider who is now quite an outsider, this all feels like the end of something. The absence of new metanarratives in anthropology combined with a fealty to the energy of the cultural studies–poststructuralist moment has led to a mustiness within the profession. The conversations have become insular, as if the windows and blinds are drawn shut and practitioners are unaware of their isolation. Embracing new modalities of the ethnographic project has been a salutary shift; clinging to the vestiges of a theoretically driven agenda has been less so.

4

The graduate students that I encounter in anthropology programs are eager to tether their intellectual obsessions to their agendas for social change. They understand the quandaries and the risks of engagement, but they do not see this as a reason to step back from the fray. They also possess an openness to connecting up with other disciplines, modes of thought, and ways of acting in the world. Having grown up in an environment of flash mobs, user-generated content, remixing, blog making, start-ups, hacking, and do-it-yourself (DIY) culture, they are less troubled by remaking their world. Moreover, deep, entrenched social and environmental crises of a global scope have vividly framed their entire lives, and many are eager to roll up their sleeves and get to work. They may sometimes lack a *theory* of action but not a plan of one.

At the same time, graduate programs in anthropology are overproducing doctoral candidates at a time when the opportunities for full-time teaching are drying up. The profession needs to take a cold, hard look at the model of a successful career that is built only on a full-time teaching job, publishing, and tenure. It is becoming unethical to continue to generate graduate students who look to this as the only model of success. At the same time, many anthropologists are finding roles in alternative types of professional work, and increasingly, this may be the case. Looked at differently, this tectonic shift in the profession is an opportunity, not a crisis.

After almost fifteen years on the edges of and outside the discipline of anthropology, I see its practitioners intermittently paralyzed by theory and distanced from the world they observe. What is missing is a more generative and productive tension between theory and engagement. How can we tie theory more tightly to action (however we define it) and not just to the production of more theory? It is possible to imagine a form of pedagogy in anthropology that moves dynamically between the two ends of engagement and theory. Action and theory are two sides of the same coin, I argue, and to fixate on only one side is to miss the essential tension between the two. Design, conversely, has the opposite problem: a gung-ho commitment to intervention with too little critical reflexivity—no theory of action. Engagement, which is something that designers do with little hesitation, has long been anathema to anthropologists, and for very good reasons. But this, I believe, is an overreaction to theory; theorists were simply so good at revealing the perils of the charged ethnographic encounter that practitioners retreated back behind the glass, where they could do no harm. But any form of fieldwork and publishing reconfigures the field and alters relations on the ground, whether anthropologists choose to acknowledge it or not.

In the end, innovation in methods may be one way to navigate more effectively between theory and action. Methods by their very nature draw theory into enactment. Anthropology could draw from other fields and import new approaches into its usual modes of practice. These methods could be:

Collaborative: small teams of investigators, not all necessarily from the same field, structure their research inflected by each other's commitments and critical perspectives.

Participatory: the research subjects become involved in the design of the research plan and the data collection.

Distributed: tools and mechanisms are provided at the granular level for research subjects to generate their own narratives.

Hypertextual: a wiki-style ethnography is created that is never complete and that invites diverse contributors to continuously rewrite it.

Algorithmic: sentient technologies are configured to sample, evolve, and learn how to collect and analyze data.

This list is by no means exhaustive but is, instead, a sketch of strategies that an ethnographer could use. Each of these methods raises its own ethical and political predicaments, but they all also de-center the role that theory plays in the development of the ethnographic project. The objective in experimenting with them would be to foreground and lay bare the process by which an ethnographer engages research subjects and theoretical assumptions. By adopting more participatory modes of inquiry, the ethnographer would displace the structuring role that theory plays and open up a more negotiated space for the production of knowledge. In doing so, this project-centered approach might better balance theory with engagement and ideas with action. Thirty-plus years in the starring role as the suave, continental rake is enough for Theory.

Ethnography and Social Theory:
A Dialectic to Hang Our Hats On

Townsend Middleton

1

Remarkably, *theory* was never formally defined for me—this despite training that included a BA in anthropology, an interdisciplinary master's degree, and a PhD in anthropology. My understanding of what theory is, and its place in the discipline, has instead taken shape through an array of experiences—some of them pedagogically oriented, others not. The following are particularly memorable moments of my socialization into the world of anthropological theory.

Moment 1. (BA-level work—Charlottesville, Virginia, 1997) The scene was a core undergraduate course for anthropology majors. I was a junior. For some time, I had been learning to think critically about social forms, yet, as I was about to discover, I was hitherto unaware of this thing called theory. Notice was served not by my professor but by a fellow student. Following a lecture on our reading for the week, a senior classmate asked, "Yes, but aren't we, as anthropologists, at this point, trying to get over structuralism?" Structuralism? I had never heard the term. The rapid exchange that ensued between the professor and precocious undergrad suggested I was missing something important. Their conversation seemed to be operating on an entirely different intellectual register, replete with its own idioms, figures, and camps. Listening to this new language of thought, I began to feel very lost. Although I sensed they were talking about real-world things (which surely could not be so foreign), I could not yet translate this theory-talk into any fathomable empirical application.

Moment 2. (MA-level work—Chicago, 2001) My classmates (one hundred strong) were packed into a crowded auditorium for our weekly Perspectives in Social Science Analysis class—a core component of the University of Chicago interdisciplinary Masters Program in the Social Sciences. Each week, the course frog-marched us through a particular body of theory (psychoanalysis, structural functionalism, etc.). Having just received a riveting lecture on structuralism, my friend Nick (himself a budding anthropologist) leaned over and whispered in my ear, "Towns, I think I am a structuralist." I smiled, chuckling to myself about my friend's newfound identity. Subsequent conversations would yield the consensus that, yes, as a theory, structuralism made a good deal of sense. The following week, the syllabus offered us readings in practice theory. Following an equally fascinating lecture on Bourdieu, suffice it to say, my friend Nick had himself a new identity—this one altogether better than the previous week's.

Moment 3. (PhD-level work—Ithaca, New York, 2004) The second semester of my Proseminar in Anthropology at Cornell proved an intimate affair, lorded over by an elder statesman of the discipline. Earlier in the semester, I had run into minor trouble with this professor by mentioning Foucault on several occasions. The professor's angered, dismissive responses made it clear that, with him, theory was a loaded, potentially dangerous terrain to explore. On the day in question, we had read Hanks's *Language and Communicative Practice* (1996), a book of stunning coverage, albeit with one exception: there was no mention of Derrida. It seemed a conspicuous absence, so I piped up to ask why a book dealing with theories of language would not include Jacques Derrida, one of the preeminent philosophers of language of the twentieth century. At the mere mention of Derrida, my professor's face suddenly began turning darker and darker shades of red. An awkward silence fell on the class. Knowing I was in for it, I braced myself for what was to come—an angry diatribe on the "intellectual scandal" that was Jacques Derrida. My innocuous, fair question had been taken as a grievous affront to the professor himself *and* the integrity of the discipline.

Spanning a decade of training, these moments instilled important lessons regarding anthropology and theory. *Moment 1* opened my eyes to the function of theory as a register of intellectual exchange—albeit a register with particular touchstones, dividing lines, and histories. *Moment 2* entailed a young anthropologist being swayed by the heuristic value of one theory and then the next. *Moment 3* revealed the identificational adherence to theory—the camp effect, if you will—within anthropology and the human sciences more generally. As the reddened response of my teacher made affectively clear, expert identities were deeply invested in the dividing lines of theory. Traversing this terrain, whether as a curious graduate student or later in my career, would require care and sensitivity, not just epistemologically but professionally.

To my eye, these moments figure theory three ways: (1) as a register/ economy of intellectual exchange; (2) as a heuristic and analytical resource; and (3) as an identification matrix, generative of inter- and intradisciplinary identities. How the proportions of these qualities vary across the generations remains a question worth exploring and which, I hope, this volume will bring to light. My personal experiences suggest a significant reweighting of these attributes from one generation of scholars to the next.

2

Theory exerts overt and covert influence on my research. Although my writing does engage theory directly, the greatest impact of theory has been in the way it shapes my methods as a researcher. For example, my work on the politics of tribal recognition in India clearly lends itself to Foucauldian optics. After all, "tribe" is a category largely born of the checkered colonial and postcolonial history of ethnology on the subcontinent. Figured accordingly, India's affirmative action system for Scheduled Tribes may be read, in Foucauldian terms, as a conspicuously ethnological form of governmentality. And, indeed, I have evoked the term throughout my work. That said, my engagements with the uncanny return of "tribe" to the lives and politics of

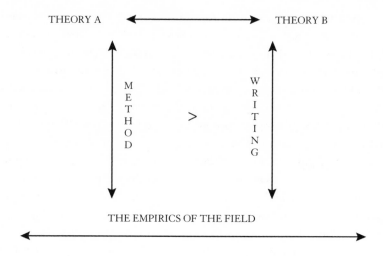

Figure 1. Negotiating theories, fieldwork, and writing

contemporary India are guided, methodologically, by a more Marxian concern with the real-time dynamics and agents of knowledge production. I have accordingly concentrated as much on the capillary diffusion of ethnological knowledge-power as I have on the ways in which minorities, activists, and civil-servant anthropologists alike negotiate state-sanctioned ethno-logics.[4] This more dialectical approach enables me to ask how particular ethnological paradigms do—and do not—shape the social and political possibilities of the communities with which I work. Theory, in this regard, profoundly affects where I focus my attention in the field, and with whom, and with what I engage.

Foucauldian and Marxian analytics both work in this case. I therefore continue to explore their recombinatory potential in my research and writing. Co-mobilizing these theoretical concerns requires a concentrated sorting out of their epistemological in/commensurabilities. This sorting out is not something I take lightly. But, when fueled by ethnographic empirics, it is intellectual work that I find worthwhile and illuminating.

As a heuristic device, theory serves important—but always limited—analytical functions. Whether a matter of scale, ontological presuppositions, or epistemological blind spots, each theory has its explanatory capabilities and deficiencies. How, then, might we play off the differences between theor*ies* to constitute a more productive dialectic between ethnography and social theory? Dominic Boyer's (2010) work on multiattentional method gives us a start. Multiattentionality, for Boyer, involves incorporating multiple theoretical engagements into a single project to balance and stabilize their respective strengths, weaknesses, attentions, and inattentions. Working with theor*ies* provides a means to innovate and diversify not just our analytical capacities but also our research techniques and findings. This concept work (indicated by the top line of figure 1) can thus productively inform our work in the field and on the page.

3

Thanks to the contingency of ethnographic knowledge production, I believe there is something distinctive about the relationship of anthropology to theory. The distinction, however, is one of degree, not pure difference. More so than most, anthropologists' concerns with social theory retain an empirical imperative. Even for the most wonkish theoreticians within the discipline, theory is never enough. As an intellectual practice, anthropological theory-talk distinguishes itself by its persistent return to ethnographic experience.

Let me provide a counterexample. Just the other day, I found myself sitting at a Durham coffee shop, with a lively discussion of theory going on at the table to my right. In play were philosophical luminaries Wittgenstein, Husserl, and others. For twenty minutes, the professors (not anthropologists) debated the ins and outs of theory, never once mentioning anything of empirical note. The lively conversation struck me precisely for its contrast to anthropological theory-talk. It is hard to imagine a twenty-minute conversation between anthropologists operating solely on the register of pure theory and not taking a turn to the vibrancy of social life.

But it is not merely the empirical groundedness of anthropology that sets it apart. It is also the nature of fieldwork. Protean, contingent, and emergent by nature, the ethnographic field is a categorically unstable referent. As such, the interplays between theory and ethnographic practice are never stable. This is intellectually productive in a number of ways. First, not unlike Kant's retrieval of empiricism to check the hubris of pure reason, ethnography checks the hubris of pure theory. Conversely, the changing morphology of any given field of investigation may demand theoretical innovation—for instance, by raising new issues to be understood, challenging normative epistemologies, and beckoning alternative analytical vocabularies. At once generative and corrective, the field, in this sense, has a wonderful habit of exposing the explanatory capacities and limitations of theory. Doing so, it reveals the fundamentally heuristic character of theory. In sum, although other human sciences also situate themselves within the dialectics of theory and empirical research, the categorically contingent, emergent, and variegated properties of the ethnographic field imbue anthropological theory-talk with a degree of dynamism that is distinctive.

4

With regard to theory, there are a number of trends among my generation that concern me. As the identificational impulse of theory has waned, the heuristic impulse has remained strong—perhaps to a fault. Given the dizzying array of theories on offer, there seems to be an increasing amount of window-shopping going on with junior scholars' deployment of theory. The tendency to sample theory only when and where it suits them is too often attended by a witting or unwitting glossing over of the deeper epistemological implications of these moves. In this regard, when senior scholars quip that the new generation lacks theoretical awareness, their claims are often warranted. This affects the way the relation of anthropology to theory is produced and understood. As one senior mentor opined to me, "Graduate students these days couldn't look at a piece of anthropology and tell you about its theoretical make-up if they had to!"

So what to do about this problem? Given the proliferation of the discipline over the past fifty years, teaching a comprehensive pro-seminar course has become impossible. Covering so much ground means devoting less time to developing students' skills in critically assessing the qualities of theory itself. Certainly, teachers are doing students no favors by turning red in the face and dismissing major intellectual figures as "scandals." But I do believe that the older generations have a passion for interrogating theory that may be productively conveyed to today's students. To hone these critical attentions, it would be useful to couple graduate-level pro-seminars with theory-specific courses of a narrower, yet deeper focus. These courses would not be topic-based; rather, they would concentrate on one or two theoretical approaches to develop students' skills in grappling with the ins and outs of theory more broadly. Having scrutinized the seminal thinkers and texts of a given theory, the course could then shift into a diagnostic mode, having students cut their teeth by diagnosing the theoretical underpinnings of select ethnographies. Pedagogically, these courses would provide a space for more focused engagements with social theory—the goal being to sharpen students' awareness of the character, stakes, and im/possibilities of various theoretical approaches, including their own.

Theory as Method

Deepa S. Reddy

The prospect of reminiscing about my first introductions to theory in relation to anthropological method is not at first a pleasant one. This is because, and it is necessary to make a critical distinction at the outset, "method" is always two things: ethnographic method, about which one expects to learn (even if it is not precisely taught), and professional method, the norms of collegiality and the etiquette and mechanics of scholarly interaction (which is not taught at all or even, for that matter, formally discussed). The two interact in ways that many graduate students will probably recognize, in ways that are overdetermined by showmanship and fraught with anxiety.

Now it is telling that the Rice anthropology program did not have a methods course. What we had, instead, in more or less practically oriented form, in *and* out of classrooms, was several doses of "theory" in the classic sense—of modernity and postmodernity, of gender kinship, religion, linguistics, and more. Reading theory here was akin to reading the gilt-edged classics, appreciating their exemplary stature, even their esoteric value. Critiques were of course welcome if we could develop them, but critiques were also somewhat beside the point. Like it or not, theory was a rite of passage into anthropological adulthood. As such, it had a commanding presence, ironically nowhere more evident than in the (roughly) extracurricular spaces of department life: hallway talk, lectures, seminars, conferences, and other informal interactions with peers and professors. Graduate school was not by any means my first exposure to classic theory. It was, after all, some combined fascination with assorted theories of virgin birth, development, feminism, colonialism, exchange, and representation that had drawn me to graduate studies in anthropology in the first place. What was different now was its reach, its permeation into the professional identity we now sought to develop and among people we were barely beginning to know, both within and beyond the close confines of the department.

Theoretical posturing was inevitable as a first demonstration of professional credibility in graduate student circles; theory making was all about identity-seeking in this context. Quickly sensitized to the use of arbitrarily defined theory as a de facto shorthand mechanism of intellectual assessment, some of us reacted badly (and probably excessively) to name-dropping and often distinguished mentors based on how theoretically adept we felt they were or on how they handled what by then had become the *problem* of "theory." The curve-ball questions of dissertation defenses were invariably theory-based. Stories of just-defended students on the job market who have to negotiate the theoretical minefields of their interview sites are commonplace. Theory in this dual sense of being that which informs what we do and that which demonstrates what we are became very charged, very much an aide or block to nascent friendships, verily a frame by which we became three-dimensional anthropologists. That process and what it demanded slid between no fun and intolerable—and probably skewed the value of theory in my mind for a good long while. [In early discussions that led up to the *Fieldwork* book, Jennifer Hamilton remarked on the "critique-critique-critique" compulsions of graduate training—a negative sort of self-making that instrumentalized theory and did not help in cultivating broad friendships either.]

None of this can easily be disassociated from the theory making that also went on as part of our own research, of course, because the two processes of professional identity construction fed into each other. Quite possibly as a result of this mutual influence, but perhaps also given my interest in experimental writing at the time, theory making was closely tied to another critical element of ethnographic method: the identification of one's authorial voice. I do not think I will ever forget the moment of my first postfieldwork meeting with George Marcus and Jim Faubion, after I had managed (I realized in retrospect) to *vomit* out some fifty-odd pages of utterly raw reactions to a fieldwork year spent steeped in debates over political and public Hindu-ness that I had then dropped in their laps. I recall their responses—together: "What [the hell] is this?" on the one hand, and "We think you need a less polemical voice," on the other—as, quite frankly, a prompt to theorize, to step back a little to figure out what, conceptually, I was trying to convey and so also to channel the rawness of my first visceral reports on fieldwork into something more distanced, reflexive, and therefore more valuable. I was jolted into the realization that theory conferred scholarly value, was critical to extracting scholarly value from the rough empirical. It was precisely the startle I needed. I turned critical attention instead to dismissive characterizations of Hindutva as pathologically extremist, reading it instead as a form of ethnicist politics that required (quite ironically, given my own recent dispositions) less reactive study. This de-pathologizing approach, as John Zavos (pers. comm.) was later to describe it, and the voice that came with it became the framework for my dissertation and the basis of much of my work on Hindutva to date.[5]

"Theory" at this stage of my professional development, it is perhaps already clear, was not the classic theory of earlier graduate training, although it did involve engagement with established frameworks and classic accounts. Here, theory was not even specifically anthropological but on some level just that measure of reflexive distance that allowed for the dispassionate articulation of critique. It became ethnographic somewhat later, in the form of a positive set of proposals for the study of public Hindu-ness as a form of (vernacularized) political praxis. Such a de-pathologizing approach as I was advocating demanded the sort of nitty-gritty attention to several things all at the same time: coincidences, circumstances, juxtapositions, flash mob–like alliances, ephemeral phenomena, controversies that did not happen, even failures, and generally the sorts of details to which I think anthropology as a discipline, and certainly anthropology at Rice, is much more willing to give credence. Measured responses to big questions, such as, What is Hindutva? over two decades since political Hinduism first caught serious academic attention, seemed possible only with the aid of ethnographic method—both data gathering and analytical, in a mutually implicated loop.

Coming to this realization, however, required the experience of interdisciplinarity, which I got in two ways: first, by being inserted into a "human sciences" pool at University of Houston–Clear Lake (UHCL) in which anthropology was consigned the marginal importance of a service discipline, and second, in the HapMap project work (which was largely the subject of my essay for the *Fieldwork* volume; Faubion and Marcus 2009) to which some stereotypically distilled version of anthropological praxis was central. Interdisciplinarity was a mix of insult and adulation: deans who challenged us and the fate of our programs during annual reviews to distinguish ourselves from investigative journalists; students who were variously wowed by "culture" or could not at all see the difference between anthropology and social psychology; peers in other sciences, both human and biological, who quite respectfully recognized the instrumental value of ethnography in politically affirming diversity or in opening community doors, thus paving the way for other sorts of nonanthropological research. In most of these interactions, what was distinctive about anthropology was not theory but method—participant observation, mainly, of the sort Malinowski might cringe to acknowledge—and the application of this method to elucidating cultural difference on a global scale, enough to keep area studies demarcations very much alive. What was useful about these interactions was the way in which they drew attention to powerful models of anthropology that were nothing like what we recognized, forcing an articulation of what it was, in the end, that made anthropology distinctive if it was not the "over a hundred-year-old" methodology of participant observation. The push came, too, from the "cultural turn" in disciplines such as psychology, and more forcefully, sociology (more recently, for instance, in the work of such authors as Syed Ali—coincidentally, a friend from fieldwork days in Hyderabad—Shehzad Nadeem, and Smitha Radhakrishnan, to name only South Asianists). If ethnographic methods stripped bare and taken in isolation turned anthropology into something unrecognizable to anthropologists, and then if ethnography was available to all disciplines to emulate, then what was it that made anthropology distinctive after all?

I do not presume to have *the* answer to that question, although the answer for my circumstances zeroed in on analytical method. Some three years after the culmination of the community consultation work for the HapMap project in Houston, the traditional project paper that reports key research findings is yet to be published. Whatever other personal/idiosyncratic reasons there are for this, it is also the case that the final take-home points for bioethics were entirely anticlimactic and, apparently, lacking in theoretical value: the Indian community in Houston was fully supportive of genetic research of the sort the HapMap represented; there were no controversies to report; and the value of Knowledge with a capital K was affirmed. Further, because there were no red-flag issues, it appeared as though there was almost nothing to report—aside from some insights on the particular community cultural views of genetics, viewed through the twin theories of karma and reincarnation (Hutchinson and Sharp 2008).

But was that it, really? From my perspective as a cultural anthropologist, the stated cultural views that were to formally constitute the output of the project were by-products—the price to be paid for the opportunity to position oneself in the context of such research in the first place, the price to be paid for gaining access to a reflexive vantage point that allowed the observation of several disciplinary commitments, objectives, and methods. What was fascinating was the project itself: its genesis, its management of interdisciplinarity (here extending to the physical sciences), and the ways in which it created a moment for cross-disciplinary conversation—one premised on certain staid notions of what mattered about the other disciplines but that nonetheless opened out a space where new sorts of affinities could emerge. And then also the data, which were not limited to interviews or focus-group transcripts but included *all* project-related interactions: how asking questions about participation in genetic research pointed to ways of thinking about civic-ness, how certain sorts of gifts enable a rethinking of certain sorts of commerce, the value(s) of life itself, and the role of science and medicine in defining our common humanity. In other words, what made the project anthropologically interesting was an involved-but-distanciated reflection on its process and what the data we sought were leading us to, well beyond themselves. "Where is your 'Methods' section?"

both the project lead and our medical/physical anthropologist colleague asked in response to an early draft of what would become the "Good Gifts" and "Commons" papers (Reddy 2007, 2013). Jennifer Hamilton (then project manager) and I looked at each other, smiled, and responded quite in unison: "There isn't one." The point was that, in this case, method was analytical method, which *was* in fact laid out in some detail: the extension of Mauss's theory of the gift via Parry's re-reading into an interpretation of commonplace affirmations of the value of science research as themselves generating contemporary theories of what gifts should be but are not/ cannot be. Method was also embedded in textual strategy, a way of *reading* the data for what we did find, as opposed to what we set out to find, and a way of *writing* the data in a way that recognized interdisciplinary disjuncture but also the possibilities for ethnography to emerge anew precisely as a result of interdisciplinary overlaps and interactions. It is this interaction, for example, that prompts, first, a social science articulation of science as irrevocably political but, then, in response, a conception of "good science" that transcends both markets and politics but works practically within the limits set by each. Acknowledging scientists' response to social science critique—acknowledging the emergence of new data sets and new theories from sometimes unexpected places—is possible only if one operates within an analytical space committed to critical (self-)reflexivity and multisited (Marcus 1995a) multiattentionality (Boyer 2010), which to my mind are far more the signatures of anthropology than its famed participatory research method.

What is invaluable to me about ethnographic method, further, is its route to addressing the theoretically oriented "big questions" from within layered, contradictory, richly detailed descriptions of particular scenes and often with the aid of data that would otherwise have been discarded as uninteresting or otherwise marginalized. But recognizing that what is falling through either traditional or predefined data-collection sieves remains particularly challenging, all the more so in a human subjects era of institutional review board (IRB) protocols that seek to rein in and streamline data-collection processes. What are data? How can we teach ourselves to keep sights on the topic and its methods that funding agencies, IRBs, our peers, and informants demand in pithy preformatted summaries while also thinking of these as simply placeholders for projects that search out "data" in more wide-ranging ways? For wide-ranging data will then (one hopes) demand wide-ranging, equally multiattentional organizing/classificatory mechanisms, and other interpretive tools that press the question (whether one uses coding software or post-it notes): What theory matters? What concepts and critiques, what intellectual trajectories, whether originating in dusted-off gilt-edged volumes or elsewhere, help to discipline and focus analytical attention simultaneously on the "big" and "little"? What are the media by which data can be conveyed from rawness into value?

And then, one hopes too, that the posing of the "What theory matters?" question serves also to preemptively displace the dominance of theory in any singular genealogical sense, to open it out as a space of possibility and interpretive innovation, and to disturb its default functions in the angst-ridden processes of professional self-making enough to embolden new sorts of more open, more honest conversations.

8

DIALOGUE

Encountering and Engaging Theory (or Not)

James Faubion: So we'd like to begin by inviting you to react to the responses. Who's going to be the brave, the proud, and the few here? Go.

Lisa Breglia: Well, maybe I'll just say something about the emergence of a couple of themes that characterize a lot of our responses. They are two really different themes, I think. One would have to be the profound effect of poststructuralism on all of us as a body of theory and what that meant for all of us. A second thing, which is perhaps related, would be the emergence of a certain kind of—well, several kinds of tropes, really, in the narration of our experiences with theory. It wasn't consistent across all the comments, but it was there maybe 90 percent of the time—I don't know really exactly how to put it—first there was anxiety, resistance, and then moving into not embracing but coming to terms with theory, and finally going to the field and then having some kind of movement through theory in another way. Maybe we could talk about that emplotment of our engagement with theory. I thought that was really interesting, interesting in the sense that it bothered me a little bit.

James: Now, that's hardly a last line to drop. We need to hear more.

Lisa: Well, because one of the first things I studied about anthropology had to do with tropes of narrating experiences in fieldwork. I mean how we talk about these things isn't neutral.

James: Your implication being that what we're calling theory somehow disrupts the project of narrativization, or—?

Lisa: More that we're creating a narrative.

James: And how do you see theory informing or perhaps lacking in the narratives that we create via fieldwork?

Lisa: This was addressed in the introduction and in a couple of the pieces as well: that sort of "thingness" of theory that is outside of a natural orientation to the process of anthropology or ethnography, as though it were something that we have to encounter.

Jamer Hunt: If I understood your comment, Lisa, I like the way you left it hanging as being slightly disturbed by it. What it made me think was that in some ways there's a kind of pathetic conventionality to all of our encounters with theory as you've prompted me to reflect on them.

That is, it starts to sound a little bit like what fieldwork was for an earlier generation of anthropologists, a sort of rite of passage that one had to move through in the various developmental phases of becoming professionalized. But rather than it being a kind of geographic or cultural impediment or series of tests, this is a kind of intellectual and conceptual body of gymnastic poses that one has to go through in order to come out the other end as a professionally sanctioned anthropologist.

In that sense there is a kind of woeful quality by which we all end up narrating this rite of passage through theory in our different ways, either by slaying it or embracing it or however we all manage the difficulties.

Lisa: How much better did he say that than me? [*laughs*]

Deepa Reddy: Not just woefulness, right? I mean, there's a redemptive quality to this narrative in the end, isn't there? At least for most of us.

Jessica Falcone: I think there is something redemptive about all of our stories, but what I thought immediately when Lisa was speaking was that we're performing this in some way, and that almost makes it a little bit less authentic. It's almost as if we're being forced to tell this story in order to be professionalized anthropologists, right? That should give us a little bit of a sense of skepticism about the story. I can see why Lisa is concerned. It's a really, really interesting observation, Lisa. Thank you for getting us started.

Townsend Middleton: It's very interesting that we're all coming at these issues postfield. I think the thingness of theory was certainly part of the professionalization process coming into fieldwork; think about the type of gymnastics you have to perform for, say, a grant application. It seems to me that there is a common theme running throughout all of our narratives: in certain senses it seems like we all have come to peace with theory by working in the field, but I don't think that we have all achieved a similar peace with theory.

   I think it manifests in different forms and, Jess, reading your piece, I took you as saying that theory has emerged as anthropology's myth and you perform it ritually because it's part of the job. But I think other people have taken up different perspectives and different relationships to it. It's interesting to think about how that relationship was professionalized prior to field, but that we seem to have come out of fieldwork with more personal relationships.

Andrea Ballestero: It's really interesting to me that in order to speak about theory, in any of the multiple ways that we have, we have resorted to the notion of the field as if it was that stable place in which something happened. That's really interesting, especially given that this volume is a continuation of a conversation with different interlocutors about fieldwork not being what it used to be.

   Then there's another tension in the papers about depathologizing the raw empirical through theory, which is really telling about the ways in which we're still entangled in these ethnography-versus-theory dilemmas, even as our papers are saying that theory is more like method, more like a way of asking questions. I do feel that there's ambivalence among us about what it is that theory is.

We always talk about the gymnastics that we have to do, the legitimizing moves that we have to make when we claim a certain theoretical background, the expectations of performing that, but I always wonder when I hear people say that. What specifically are those expectations and where are they coming from? What concrete forms do they take?

Dominic Boyer: It sounds like the ball has been hit back to us here. One thing we are very interested in hearing more about are the ways in which those particular expectations for theory become internalized and when. So, for example, we're very interested in this part of the volume in pedagogy. I'll just narrate my own experience. I was trained at Chicago, where it was quite clear in terms of the internal institutional hierarchy of value that theory was the most important intellectual practice in which you could invest yourself.

We all took the same course, the famous Systems sequence, our first socialization to the discipline. It was also known as *the* theory course, the course in which we had theory handed down to us, and in my case, the course literally began with Genesis. It had a sort of biblical character: theory from Genesis up until the Enlightenment. Then we were turned out to tackle our own case studies without any sort of further—or fairly minor—interventions in formal theoretical training. I think it's not unusual that theory is treated in this way in graduate training, as this sanctified form of knowledge, set apart in a course unto itself. Would anyone want to follow up on that?

Jamer: I keep being struck by the extent to which different generations talk about the different generational investments in theory and accountability to theory. I can't help but think that we will look back at these twenty or thirty years and see them as a very peculiar kind of moment within anthropology, within social science, within academia in general, where this very strange thing called theory—nobody would defend the idea that there's Theory with a capital T, and yet we're all incredibly comfortable talking about it as if it is out there and exists and is built out of this funny combination of continental philosophers who all came over to the U.S. at about the same time.

Plus, I'm always struck, in thinking back to my own graduate experience, at how important it was to see these books that were beautifully designed by Bruce Mau for Zone [Books], for example, which looked so unlike anything else that we ever saw. Normally, books look kind of dreary, but these books looked sexy and mysterious and occult. There was a very strange set of interweaving circumstances that have, I think, created this mystique that we're now just getting to the end of, for better or worse.

James: What I'm interested in hearing a little bit more about from all of you is what kind of substantive content you're actually giving to the term *theory*. Is it a catchall term for theorists? Who's a theorist and who isn't? How do we identify them? Were they effectively identified as such or was the identification simply assumed in your training process? And I'll just say that when I teach my theory course I offer it to people not as God's truth but as the possibility of finding a muse or two or three.

Deepa: A muse?

James: Yes, not someone you necessarily think is speaking the truth, the whole truth, and nothing but the truth, but someone who sings to you, is inspiring in one or another way. All of you whose work I know have found someone or other who has functioned that way for you. I'm wondering whether it would even be possible to produce a dissertation if you didn't find that.

Jessica: I was really fascinated by what Lisa wrote in her paper about how she's moved on from dropping theories and citationality and started baking theory in a little bit more, more group theorization. I would really like to understand that in a more practical way.

Lisa: Yeah, my muses are all in the endnotes now [*laughter*].

Andrea: I could also add that the way that I see this as using the help of others who have said things in a much more clear way than I can. It's much more of a middle space, not as if there's theory at one pole and data at the other. It's a much more instrumental way to engage with theory, with theories of different and sometimes opposed traditions. I'm guilty maybe of what Townsend was noting in his paper: of being part of a younger generation of scholars who don't own up to the full epistemic implications of the theories that they use.

But that middle ground isn't really about "theory." Rather about specific snippets that have helped me ask questions about the existential engagements that I've had in fieldwork, many of which happened before the field, hence my noting the carefulness that we have to have in talking about the field. It's not a theory. It's not one muse. It's a multiplicity of them, with the danger and maybe the preoccupation being how much we have to own up to in securing epistemological foundations. How much can we just take them—the contributions that these authors have made—in different directions? Whether you can put opposing thinkers to work side by side is something I'm really interested in as a form of ethnographic endeavor and research not necessarily as a form of 'theory-making" per se.

Dominic: It would be interesting to hear others comment on whether they feel there is a need for a deeper analytic apparatus in order to operate with concepts.

Jamer: At the risk of theorizing theory, what I keep hearing and reading is a shift from theory being more in the realm of metanarrative—that is to say, a kind of grand epistemological structure that helps to explain almost everything and one develops a faith in it, which is how a lot of us might have been operating ten or twenty years ago—to theory as sort of a lever that you pick up when you need it or a screwdriver that works particularly effectively. But it's not anything much more than that. Instead it becomes—this came up a lot in the discussion of the kind of thingness of theory in various responses—a different kind of work that we're expecting theory to do. It's a pretty dramatic shift from a more cosmological, almost religious investment in theory to now a much more kind of work-a-day attitude—oh, this little bit helps me here. I'll use it, but I profess no fealty to this particular religion or to this particular kind of worldview.

There is definitely a shift going on where these things become instrumentalized, but with a very kind of low level of investment in them. They're just simple tools to be picked up. They do work and they operate in a series of relations in the same ways that other things operate in those fields of relations, and they're not much more than that. They certainly don't stand outside those sets of relations.

Andrea: Sometimes the position is that "these kids don't put enough time into figuring out what's really going on, they're just very instrumental and pragmatic and don't want to carry the weight of the intellectual work that needs to be done." I actually think that it is a much more uncomfortable and intellectually dangerous position to be in the instrumental space because you know that you're vulnerable to many people who have spent a lot of time thinking through one or two intellectual traditions in depth.

Townsend: I wonder if we could turn this conversation back to the senior anthropologists. It sounds like this idea of a toolbox with multiple theories that we can grab as needed and work with is as we find them as helpful is in certain ways a luxury but also a major conundrum of our generation. I wonder to what extent when you guys were coming up in training whether there was pressure to basically become a master of one theoretical school and to self-identify within that school?

George Marcus: Well, I don't have much to say about that because when I went to Harvard everything was in disarray. I was in the Social Relations project, so theory was Daniel Bell or theory was external to anthropology and certainly not poststructuralist. What poststructuralist theory was for anthropology students was a kind of invisible, hidden discourse that your professors didn't teach. All the works in translation were circulating among students as new, cool ways to look at the fading paradigms of kinship, ritual, etc. at a place like Harvard.

I understand that at Chicago—because of its self-esteem and image—theory was appropriated for local purposes. The professors at Harvard would never admit to not understanding Foucault, even though Foucault was not taught. There was an authority to theory in the Chicago curriculum that by this time did not exist in anthropology generally because "theory" referred to anthropological theory—which was frankly, at that time, in decay.

Dominic: But established anthropologists didn't acknowledge that anthropological theory was in decay?

George: Not explicitly.

Dominic: In the days that I was at Chicago, you could not, as a rule, make any reference to Michel Foucault's work in any paper that you wrote without receiving censure. That seems very strange by comparison today, but it was true. I think that the feeling was that it was bad theory. It was antitheory. Real theory was culture theory—anthropological culture theory and to a lesser extent linguistic theory.

That does raise a question: whether that distinct preserve of specifically anthropological theory is meaningful to the younger generation or whether that's simply been turned inside out, and this field of muses that Jim was talking about has become not only the way that we practice our work but the way that we teach it and socialize younger colleagues as well, too. Jim, what do you think?

James: Well, I began studying anthropology in the mid-1970s, the heyday of the linguistic turn, when Lévi-Strauss was in great command, as well as Mary Douglas and Edmund Leach. My attraction to the discipline was that it had a kind of intellectual command that reached beyond its boundaries, though interestingly at that moment it was still relatively well bounded. That is to say that only with the hydrogen bombs dropped in the mid-[19]80s did the field begin to open up, usually at the higher-status tiers of the university departments, to the great permeating wave coming in from outside.

In my own experience, I felt that I needed to be able to speak like all the masters, that it was a question of intellectual fluency in the different reigning imaginations. I really never felt that I had anything imposed on me. I'm speaking at the level of my college education now, actually. At Berkeley, as a matter of survival on the one hand and intellectual predilection on the other, one would drift to that professor whose intellectual inclinations were closest to one's own.

Again, I don't think the issue of compulsion affected me in the way in which it strikes me that it does affect a lot of people who are younger as the discipline has become more campish—now you'd better belong to a camp. If you don't, then you're out. Anthropology has become very sectarian to my mind. Maybe some of the anxiety—if anyone wants to reflect on that—about what you feel in your engagement with "theory" these days might have to do with that fragmentation and encampment of the discipline now.

Jessica: I talked a little bit about this in my essay. There was kind of a game being played where everyone had to really proclaim what team they were on. We would have colloquia almost every week at Cornell. Some of the graduate students would sit around and try to figure out what questions different professors were going to ask, based on what camp they had already proclaimed themselves to be in. With some folks, it was really easy. I do think that there was some anxiety about that, but I actually think that at the same time we were being socialized to have some skepticism about the game.

At Cornell—I think this is interesting—the History of Anthropological Theory class came late. Most of us took it in our third or fourth year. The introductory pro-seminar was a really open space where there was Heidegger and Freud and Lacan and Marx and Derrida. There was really no emphasis on anthropological antecedents. We were looking at theorists from all over, from philosophy and sociology and psychology. I think there was a tension—we were being encouraged to pick sides, but we were also being exposed to an amazing breadth of theory from outside of our discipline that made it difficult, I think, to pick sides without feeling that you were closing important doors.

I definitely think that I was one of the people who had a lot of trouble proclaiming myself. I had trouble with the idea of guru devotion in the theoretical realm. I wasn't ever able to say okay, I'm a Lacanian and that's what I am. Instead, I wrote one article where I used Lacan and that was very productive, but I don't think I'm ever going to use him again. Towns seems to feel that this might be a problem that our generation faces, but I'm just not sure. I have a lot of skepticism about the missionary view that I saw with certain faculty and certain graduate students that become devotees, actually, of particular perspectives. That's just to say that I'm really ambivalent about this question.

[. . .]

Theory in the Positive Sense of the Term

George: I just want to intervene at this point. Jessica's comment in connection with some of the others seems to evoke a kind of critical view of the practices of using theory in anthropology. I'm just trying to excavate, beyond that, a more positive ideology of the use of theory today—regardless of whether or not it corresponds to the kind of scholarly production that leads to adequate or successful careers—a use of theory that involves the real stakes in the game for most of you in your work.

Not to go on too long about this, but let me just draw a couple of lines that struck me in Jamer's essay that I could also pull out from the others. By the way, just to bracket this, a lot of people use "toolbox" or "tools" when they talk about theory. It irritates me. I understand the usefulness of this metaphor, but it makes something flat that's really committed and exciting, I'm sure, in your work.

Anyhow, Jamer is more eloquent on this [*reading from the response draft*] "I am no longer content to allow theory to end with radical uncertainty itself." Well, that's what theory produced. It produced forms of argument that depended upon the sustaining of uncertainty and multiplicities. I don't think we want to close that off, necessarily, so what do you think about, "I'm no longer content to allow theory to end with radical uncertainty itself."

Two, "this has resulted in two contrasting transformations"— this is the hopefulness—"fresh energy for new fields of inquiry on the one hand, and a drift toward a more solipsistic mode of practice on the other." Well, we've talked about the latter; what about the former? The idea that what is really pushing anthropology today are "new objects of study," new fields of inquiry in which there's not an established anthropological tradition yet in which there is a desire to move in and make a distinctive anthropological contribution. Is theory somehow related to this enterprise of moving into new fields of inquiry? Is the use of theory, theory that we're taught, old theory, new theory, whatever we want to mean by or practice as theory, related to that?

One more comment is enough: "The graduate students that I encounter in anthropology programs are eager to tether their intellectual obsessions to their agendas for social change." Is there something distinctive about the contemporary use of theory in that context? Then the last thing—I see this in a number of the papers—the idea that theory has something to do today with the license to experiment. It's connected to the legitimation or the attractiveness—aesthetically or otherwise—of the notion that the work we do as research is experimentation.

I want to push it in the direction of the more hopeful, positive, committed, and invested in uses of theories today, despite what it's been in the past and how we've been required within the paradigm of anthropology of the last twenty years to teach it.

Dominic: Reactions?

Deepa: You are thinking of theory as a license to experiment or providing a sort of rationale for experimentation. Is that where you're going with this, George?

George: Yes, and also the legitimation for you as an anthropologist, like you did in the medical center with that example you gave, to move to new objects of study beyond the ones you were recruited to engage. For instance, as you said, it wasn't very interesting— what they wanted you to find out for them in the study—with respect to the way anthropologists think. What you thought was interesting was something far different, and you realized that that surprise or that novelty or that pleasure in finding the blood types, that project that you found somehow through theoretical inspiration. What we share in common is the aesthetic pleasure in surprise that a number of people have ideologized.

The field today is not a dour, hard place where you collect data on other people and then try to explain it with concepts. It's a place where it's not what you thought it was. I want to keep Jamer's point in mind not to accept that theory justifies you in just ending up in radical uncertainty. But I also want to ask you to discuss how various kinds of theory provide you with the frameworks that engage you in some way that is much more committed. That's the arena in which I want to talk about theory. How theory is generative for you all.

Deepa: There are two ways in which theory functions. One of the ways it functions is as a validation of experimentation and is much more familiar. I mean the sort of citational practices that we have that in order to be able to do anything new with our material, with our discipline, with our arguments, we have to justify it in terms of the theoretical approaches that people have taken before. I gather what you're talking about is something a little bit different, actually.

It's the sort of theory finding, the theory making that, for example, I had in the medical center, where our research basically produced nothing that was really of much value for the bioethicists, but if you looked at it in another way, it was actually a very interesting project. I actually looked at that as analytical method. I mean, I didn't think of it as theory per se. Maybe I was just horribly biased given the sort of struggle that theory had represented for me before, but I took it as being a methodological strategy, as a way to read data. The theory making came out of the method.

This goes back to something else that I wanted to say in response to Jim's comment about muses, which resonates in our papers. The location of theory was not always or necessarily or even primarily in the textbooks. It was in fieldwork. I remember George commenting at some point about the role that my father-in-law had played in my dissertation fieldwork. He was a muse. I think my inspirations have, by design or by default, quite honestly come from the context of field circumstances and of needing to make sense of all its jumble. Theory was a commitment to one's fieldwork, one's subjects, one's family, and so on and so forth. All that went into the making of theory.

Jessica: In some of our writing you also find this idea that theory can be paralyzing as well as playful. I just want to put it out there that there are both sides to consider.

Deepa: I take George's point about the limits of the toolbox metaphor. But to get back to Jamer's earlier point, he was saying we should not normalize theory, right? Theory functions in all those different ways, sometimes it's just a crutch, a tool one uses to make a point. Or to address the anxieties about the potential reviewers of an article.

Dominic: Towns, you had an interesting research project in the sense that you really were studying anthropological theory at work in the world. It really did conflate the sort of usual theorem/datum relationship. What's your reaction to this?

Townsend: Well, I've thought a lot about George's ideas of para-ethnography and the para-site. For me, my research was full of uncanny encounters with forms of ethnological knowledge and ethnological theory that I didn't condone. I have always struggled to try to find a space to work collaboratively with the people I've been researching because they are so invested in a particular type of theory that, to me, seems very dated but for them really holds the key to a lot of current political possibilities and possibilities of social justice.

In a certain sense, I think they could use a healthy dose of post-structuralism, but at the same time, it makes for very difficult encounters. It does problematize the relationship between theory and the field. There are certain types of theories I deploy to try to understand what's going on, that allow me to look in a differ-ent way at, for example, certain types of unexplained structural arrangements. This gets back to one of Andrea's points: whether theory is to serve only an analytical purpose or can also be a way of looking at things, a way of seeing.

I think it helped me as a fieldworker to think about whether taking on a certain type of theoretical inclination would lead me to look at the situation differently. I think that has enabled me to kind of grapple with some of these found forms of anthropology that I've investigated, to see them from different angles and to try to understand where the people are coming from and to account for their different motivating logics.

But, as far as finding a collaborative space to work in a kind of a para-site mode, it's been very difficult for me.

Andrea: We've talked mostly about theory and the field, or theory in the moment of fieldwork, but we have talked very little about theory and—if you will—the moments of problem design. The moments when you're in the field or when you're starting to write a paper, when you're thinking about your book. Those other moments are important to come to terms with because it's not just that citational practices are all that is going on.

It's not very much use to arrange neatly and very cohesively all of the Foucault or Lacan you want to use at the moment in which you're trying to figure out what it is that you're doing with a paper or with your whole project. There's a moment in which you make a first attempt to clarify what it is that has captured your attention. At such moments it's been really useful for me to think about theories in that very mundane instrumental kind of way, in the sense of really thinking through how would this look if I were to think as author X, which might be one of the theory guys of the poststructuralist turn. Or in my case, it has been people like Evans-Pritchard, the old stuff that's supposedly not so theoretical that has been really influential in the way in which I think about my project and the way in which I push myself to remain vigilant of my own thinking practices.

At those moments, the frame is not necessarily citational strategy but how you're grappling with in the world.

James: I have to ask you: What it is about Evans-Pritchard that's not so theoretical?

Andrea: No, it's not that I think that. That's the way in which he has been normalized. That's my point—when we talk about theory, we go mostly nowadays in anthropology to Foucault, Marx, and Lacan, maybe Geertz, to more explicitly theoretical arguments. People are not really thinking of the older work when they talk about theory, in general. I might be wrong, but that's my perception.

James: I see what you mean. I completely agree. Nobody would dare confess to be a structural-functionalist or a Durkheimian any more, absolutely, but that is a theory at work in Evans-Pritchard, to be sure.

Lisa: To go back to more positive ideologies regarding the use of theory that George was talking about. I think another element is the dialogues between anthropology and the other human sciences that use theory as a medium, theory as an argot really. Those help to keep anthropology as a discipline—especially our ethnographic work—-very relevant.

Deepa: Do you think it's the data, Lisa, or is it method, or both maybe?

Lisa: I don't work in anthropology now, so I use words like *data*. We contribute empirical stuff that also fits in similar theoretical models in other disciplines and in an interdisciplinary context. We might be working with the same theoretical models, but we have done it as anthropologists.

Jessica: As other disciplines start to use ethnography more, are we going to be able to continue to claim that this is an anthropological contribution?

George: Well, we've returned long after the 1980s to the question of the forms of anthropological authority that we have now and what sustains them. Those are the questions that you two have just raised, and the question of how theory operates in that is a very interesting question. Once you've historicized the theory period, as many of you do, now what is anthropological authority? That's what we're exploring. As anthropologists diffuse their interests into various new objects of study, would you have to engage in the languages of other domains of expertise?

Following ethnographic method, you have to create communicational means to create bodies of reception for what you're doing. Perhaps what theoretical discourse is doing after the period that you've historicized—one thing it's doing—is maintaining certain kinds of authorities and solidarities in a field that is prolific in its expansion into arenas that are already filled with other kinds of discourses with which it has to relate.

My point—a bit different from the previous two—is that it's not that theory is going to give you authority in other fields of the social sciences. Although it may be that anthropology does ethnography plus theory and that makes it different from others. Rather, that theory actually creates certain kinds of solidarities and authority among anthropologists themselves as they diffuse and explore new arenas of study and practice.

Jamer: I think one thing that I can add to completely support your point is the really remarkable proliferation of ethnography and ethnographic methods within various kinds of corporate practices. These are cases where theory is actually disparaged and really would marginalize a practitioner working, say, for Intel. I think in those environments there's much more of an old-fashioned interest in pragmatic analytic insight. When it's frosted with some sort of connection to a larger theory, that actually handicaps it a little bit because nobody there is interested in the debates over whether this is a proper use of Foucault or not.

What gets left over is a more raw and quite mongrel form of ethnography where people videotape users using toothbrushes for a week and a half and consider that a complete ethnography and then try to glean some sort of insight that they can then use in reorienting a product or service. It is interesting because it's a version of the ethnographic method that has moved outside of anthropology, at least in the corporate contexts that I'm familiar with. But it's completely abandoned any kind of theoretical, and really almost any kind of methodological, discussion or rigor. In many instances, it actually does provide pretty substantial and profound insight, but it is completely walled off from the theoretical discourse that has traveled with anthropological ethnography for at least the last thirty or forty years.

Andrea: Can I offer a little bit of a different perspective? The conversations I have had in those environments go in the opposite direction. The reason why they have wanted to talk to me is not to help them provide some method by which they can figure out how people in China use the cell phone or anything like that, but instead they are asking me about what theoretical trends I see in the field. So I think that we might be at a point in which the nature of ethnography outside of academia might also be changing.

I completely agree with you, Jamer, that whether Foucault is appropriate or not for a certain type of microchip is not going to be a conversation that you hear in the boardroom with the people who make choices about products. But at a lower organizational level, I've found that it's actually the more theoretical discussions that people are interested in.

[. . .]

Teaching Theory and Analytical Method

Dominic: Let me pull together a couple of points. I was very interested in Jim's remark about how theoretical sectarianism is on the rise in anthropology today. That connected also to Jessica's sense of paralysis and being disabled in the face of identifying with theory, and also to Deepa's point about thinking about theory as analytical method. Analytical method is an idea I'm interested in.

Could it help us to teach theory better? In other words, would it help to teach theory as analytical method? Are there strategies that you may be working on right now or thinking about right now—let's say if you were asked to teach the "theory course" in your department—that would make an impact in that way?

Obviously, theory is laden with authority. We've all been talking around that issue: there's power involved and power that is used often in a very nakedly disciplinary sense. That was my experience in graduate school—to socialize people into certain camps in order to reproduce or build a school of some kind.

At the same time, to address what George is talking about, to get to these more positive ideologies, it sounds like we have institutional and professional work to do to avoid exercises in socialization in that disciplinary sense. Is there another way of socializing ourselves in which we wouldn't end up feeling that theory is an external force that is commanding us?

Deepa: I think it would have definitely helped me if theory had been taught as analytical method. I won't say that it wasn't. I mean, I think we did have many moments of that, but I don't think I realized that that's what was happening until much later—so it needs to be made explicit.

Then to tack on to something that Jessica said a while ago about not all of us having theoretical gurus any longer. I think that thinking of theory as analytical method would have actually helped me bring a lot of theorists into conversations, perhaps across time and across schools, and would have therefore then deflected some of the camp-oriented pressures that we felt at the time. But I don't know that that's the case for everybody.

I remember many moments in graduate school reading things and thinking, okay, why exactly is it that I'm reading this? I'm just supposed to appreciate the logic of it. It's beautiful thinking, but I wasn't exactly able to deploy what I was reading for a very long time. I think I still struggle with that, and so somewhere I wished that there had been some part of my training actually devoted to the deployment of these theories more explicitly than it had been.

James: Do you mean deployment in a sense of for what purposes, for what one or another of them can do? I had a sense when you were talking about analytical method that you actually wanted a more explicit pedagogy about, say, how to go about constructing a theory as a design instrument. Or are you talking about both?

Deepa: Yes, both. I remember so many of us as graduate students—I'm sure this is an experience that we all share—having come away from fieldwork with so many bits and pieces and having no idea for a long time how to string these things together. What I am imagining is just somewhere a theoretical recognition that fieldwork is really hard [*laughter*] and that figuring out how to make sense of it is really difficult, and that we could be making more use of theory to be able to pull those pieces together, if that makes sense.

Dominic: Any other thoughts on this?

George: I'll just throw one more bomb out. Do you think that the limits of theoretical discourse today are set by the paradigm of fieldwork? Because I'll remind us that there was a long history of anthropology before the fieldwork paradigm and that back then anthropology was often driven, sometimes irresponsibly, by theoretical discussion. The key point that you've raised, Deepa, is that perhaps there's no way to think about theory that isn't tied in some way to its role in graduate pedagogy in preparing someone for fieldwork. Is that the constraint on our thinking about theory?

Jessica: I was just going to reiterate something that I wrote about. I feel that when I was being trained as a graduate student no one ever talked about the whys and the wherefores of academic culture in any kind of meaningful, sustained way. I think that a project like this one would be a useful thing to add to courses about theory. Let's talk about it. Let's try to feel it and understand it as a cultural artifact of our academic culture. Theory is otherwise so taken for granted.

This might do some of the work that Deepa was asking for—if in our classes we actually turned the theories that we were talking about on ourselves. Again, this may not really reverberate for anyone but me, but that certainly would have been something that I would have welcomed in terms of socialization and pedagogy.

Dominic: I'll note one of the things I think is distinctive about your work, Jessica. You've engaged theory with much more performativity than most people have. In your dissertation (Falcone 2010), you adopted the strategy of performing a Buddhist analysis of Buddhism, and that produced a recursive effect, which I certainly sought, or rather fell into, with my own work in Germany too, which in turn necessitated a more creative engagement with theory (Boyer 2005). But I've worried as I've returned to this mode again and again (Boyer 2013) just what can you really get out of it. I mean, there's a pleasure to trying to understand a theory form from within. It's like a very specific and curious form of performance art. That's a different metaphor for theoretical practice than the instrument, the toolkit. Instead, it's something that you inhabit in a more theatrical mode. On the one hand, this is enlightening. On the other hand, it could also be viewed as rather precious.

Jessica: In a Buddhist discourse they would suggest that that sort of meditation is really important in order to move forward with any sort of self-knowledge about the world that you're in.

James: To put it in a semi-slogan-like manner: courses in theory should always enfold in a dimension of *Homo Academicus* (Bourdieu 1988).

Jessica: Absolutely. That worked for me.

Deepa: Just to add that our training at Rice wasn't absent of self-reflexive moments. Jim, I think the kinship volume was one of those moments (Faubion 2001), at least in my mind, where we actually had a course with you, or some sort of a mini-version of a course, that was a crash course on all the classic theories of kinship. Then we were encouraged to rethink them in more contemporary cosmopolitan terms, right?

James: Right.

Deepa: The data, the empirical material, the ethnographic material that we were using in those cases was not fieldwork per se. It was autobiography or auto-ethnography. So there were those moments. I just wish that there had been more of them, and I wish that there had been more of them when we were talking about other theorists as well.

Townsend: I wonder if there's a broader issue here about teaching theory prefield. At that stage, graduate students by and large don't have anything to apply the theory to, so, yes, these types of autobiographical reflections through theory are actually quite helpful because all of a sudden it feels more applicable. I think the danger of having no empirical material to which to apply the theory is that theory becomes this pure realm of "high theory," a purely conceptual place.

I think one of the reasons that the field is so transformative is that all of a sudden we have something to apply the theory to. That's where there's a very productive dialogue that emerges between what you've encountered in the field and the types of theory that you came into the field with. But it is the pedagogical challenge, I think, to find ways to make theory applicable so that people can work through its strengths and weaknesses.

Lisa: I have to say that that's not the only thing that theory is for because I think that's falling back into the toolkit idea or into using things as expedience, solely as means to ends. I think that's really dangerous because theory is something else too, and learning theory is something else too. It's also a way to learn how to think. It's sitting in classes reading things that are really way too hard for you [*laughter*]. It's something that is part of the experience of being a graduate student. Being a student in those kinds of classes is also a way to teach you how eventually, if this is your goal, to be a professor.

Dominic: Lisa has a great point, and I'd like to dwell on it for a second because I think that's the story oftentimes we tell ourselves about why it's important to teach theory prefield. It helps to refine the intellect. It sharpens people. It makes them more rigorous.

Because it's challenging them it forces them to pay greater attention. My question is whether the placement of theory within a single "theory course" is the best or only way of teaching theory within the course of graduate training. It's something that I think a lot about, and I wonder about alternatives . . .

Andrea: Maybe I can talk a little bit about what I've done in my class, which is to assign ethnographies and somewhat arbitrarily from all of the theoretical claims that they make or citations they make, assign also one of those supposedly theoretical pieces. So we read Julia Elyachar's *Markets of Dispossession* (2005) and then also Adam Smith. Then the discussion was at what points do they encounter each other and at what points do they depart from each other? What does this theory allow the anthropologist to say, and what kinds of things are not being said?

That explicit and staged connection between ethnographies and some of the theoretical works that those ethnographies use has been really productive for me as well, not only for the graduate students. It has been a really interesting moment to figure out when the theorist comes to save the anthropologist and the other way around.

Jamer: What I would also love to come out of this discussion is to have it reflect back on what we call theory. I'm just struck by the extent to which we abstract something called "theory," as if there were a group of intellectuals who can hover above the world and only speak in a somewhat private language divorced from any kind of empirical engagement.

You can think through how this all happened, but in some ways it helps me to reflect back on somebody like Foucault and the fact that his best and most profound work was one that was a fairly close historical, quasi-sociological intellectual history with ethnographic-like attention to practices within prisons. It was not the least bit divorced from the specifics of an encounter with certain kinds of material practices. Similarly, somebody like Derrida: we excised theories from Derrida, and then they float on their own, but Derrida was someone who was closely attached to texts and to the reading of Genet or people like that.

A lot of the theorists that we think about were actually literary critics or they were sort of sociologists. They were confusing, perhaps. They didn't fit in neat boxes. Some of the less interesting ones, like the later Baudrillard, became floating heads who spoke about the world around them with little engagement in the granularity of it.

But I think one nice thing that could come of all of this is repositioning the theories that we looked at as being theory as being instead partial and provisional and very much grounded in certain practices. In our enthusiasm for them, we turned their provisionality into something that very different from what they originally were. I think that, if we could now look back with some distance and ask, okay, are there ethnographic-like moments within these texts that we can utilize as we start to think through our own projects, it would allow us to demythologize theory as such by putting the texts into more historically appropriate sorts of frameworks.

George: So there is an anthropological approach to the use and care of theory that has not yet been generated in anthropology that would be worth articulating. That's interesting. It's not just about understanding Foucault. I mean, of course, one might want to understand Foucault, but there could be a kind of anthropological interest in the assimilation, learning, and understanding of broader theory forms, the universal theories that affect our societies.

Dominic: And also precisely in this way, an attempt to think about theory as a kind of epistemic practice, an intellectual practice unto itself—or unto themselves because it's plural—something against which we can triangulate our own efforts. I think that's a very helpful point.

Jamer: Just to add a quick point to that as well, what really gets elided in conversation is that Lacan was a practicing analyst. He was not only a theorist. Foucault was an activist and someone who was working on behalf of prisoner's rights, not just a philosopher or thinker sitting in the university.

I think we can fill out the picture even further once we begin to realize that we've really cut these theorists off at the neck despite the fact that they are wholly embodied. If we can re-embody them, we can begin to see that their practices were much more than academic practice. They were often applied, which is a word that in contemporary anthropology is frightening to a lot of people, but in lots of these cases, these were people who tacked back and forth between theory, analysis, and practice.

[. . .]

AFTERWORD

On the Need to Reinvent Anthropological Teaching and Training in Theory

Dominic Boyer

The preceding pages contain a great many insights into the state of theory in anthropology today. I will not attempt to paper over the different visions to make of them a synthetic narrative or diagnosis. I will, however, draw attention to three common themes that echoed across the responses and discussion.

First, the observation was made several times and in several ways that different generations approach "theory" as practice and object of reflection with different stakes. Indeed, there was a strong sense that much "theory talk" continues to quietly index a conceptual phase shift in the 1970s and 1980s related to a rising interest in continental (especially French and German) philosophy. This investment made good organic sense in various disciplines in the human sciences at the time. In anthropology, for example, normative holistic accounts of cultures and societies, already under pressure because of their colonialist heritage, were finally shattered and resituated by younger generations of ethnographers taking inspiration from analytical resources such as German critical theory and French poststructuralism.

This moment conjured the "thingness" of Theory as alternative to extant norms of anthropological knowledge-making.

But one of the more interesting outcomes of our exercise here is how it reveals to what extent the thingness of Theory is now itself in a state of being unwound by a younger generation that no longer feels the need to react directly to the now amply criticized colonial era of anthropology. For the "post–writing culture" generations, in other words, the promise of disciplinary redemption through theory is being questioned. The more radical position is that anthropology is now capable of developing positive new norms and forms of analysis without the mediation of philosophy and literary theory (see, e.g., the mission statement of the journal *HAU*). But even among those who believe that theoretical dialogue across the human sciences remains generative for anthropological research, one senses a general distrust of theoretical claims to accessing higher orders of truth and a greater tendency to imagine theory in its positive sense as part of a design sandbox for illuminating particular aspects of ethnographic and fieldwork engagements. Perhaps, as Jamer Hunt suggests, "having grown up in an environment of flash mobs, user-generated content, remixing, blog making, start-ups, hacking, and do-it-yourself (DIY) culture, they are less troubled by remaking their world." Thus, more and less is being demanded of "theory"—it need not provide the transcendental claims of philosophy to be efficacious in contemporary anthropology, but it does need to be more receptive to pluralization, mutation, and adaptation to a variety of fieldwork situations and ethnographic representations. In these emergent ethics of analytic work, no theory possesses a monopoly of truth any longer; but every theory creates opportunities for what Andrea Ballestero terms "parallax and provocation." Lisa Breglia concludes, "Theory (in a broad anthropological sense) can be summoned to make anthropological work increasingly flexible, nuanced, sophisticated, and complicated, yet translatable and mobile."

Second, we hear in the responses and especially in the dialogue a realization that well into the fourth decade of the "reflexive turn" we still find it difficult to talk about theory as a normalized and normalizing aspect of our intellectual practice. We lack a conceptual language specific to the reflexive engagement of theory and also the habit of engaging theory as an object of anthropological reflection unto itself. This is perhaps unsurprising given that so many of our disciplinary institutions continue to encourage us to consider theory as something that stands above or beyond our "core business" of anthropological ethnography: the "theory course" that stands alone within graduate pedagogy, the necessary performance of theoretical erudition in key sections of grant applications and qualifying examinations, the careful management of theoretical coordinates in peer review, and so on. In classic Durkheimian terms, theory is treated as a sacred in professional anthropology, it is what one imagines differentiates our ethnographic projects from those of other kinds of ethnographers such as travel writers and journalists. Thus, to treat theory as a normal aspect of knowledge-making in anthropology—one subject to manipulation, experimentation, and design by fallible human researchers rather than extending like rays of light from the philosophical pantheon down to earth—is not only counterintuitive but actually dangerous in a disciplinary sense. Subjecting theory to the typical anthropological profaning of contextual, relational analysis robs us of mana. Yet in our exercise there seemed to be a strong sentiment that this was the direction in which to push anthropological engagement with theory, as Jessica Falcone suggested, "to look at the historical and cultural milieu in which . . . theory emerged and continues to be shared." With more concerted effort along these lines to think about theory in the way anthropology has long considered other forms of knowledge and ways of knowing, one hopes that the reflexive dimension of our "theory talk" will become subtler and more rewarding.

But perhaps the strongest commonality that emerged from this exercise was affective: how advisors and advisees alike recall a troubled sense of alienation in their early professional exposure to theory. Theory is recalled principally as an authoritative discourse (whether a disciplinary authority or some other kind) and as a medium of allegiances, identities, and loyalties. In some cases, theory was acknowledged as a necessary intensification of intellectual attention and virtuosity. But this virtuosity was also obviously linked to a competitive politics of belonging in which limited theoretical competence could be used to delegitimate one's anthropological merit (despite the fact that how theory actually was supposed to contribute to the making of anthropological knowledge seems to have very often remained opaque). In the worst cases, theory is recalled as a powerful instrument for "missionary work" or "sectarianism," defining right from wrong intellectual practice, inscribing the tension and battle lines between different communities of anthropological practice. Perhaps such uses of

236   *Dominic Boyer*

theory to mark in-groups and out-groups have intensified the suspicion that theory is just one academic power game among others. But even if one resists that simplification of the social life of theory, it is hard not to feel that the place of theory in teaching and training could be improved, perhaps dramatically, by developing new ethics and institutions to challenge the claim that a nonreflexive authoritative discourse represents the greatest way of knowing to which young anthropologists might aspire.

What Is the Matter with the Conventional Forms of Graduate Pedagogy and Graduate Training in Theory?

Pedagogy emerged in our discussion as a key site of intervention for improving the relationship of anthropology to theory. Because graduate pedagogy typically represents the first intense phase of disciplinary professionalization, it represents an ideal opportunity to present alternative ethics of theoretical engagement to anthropologists-in-the-making. Pedagogy, of course, is a complex phenomenon, at once a matter of individual orientations (e.g., particular teachers' favored teaching strategies) and transindividual institutions (e.g., departmental and collegiate expectations for pedagogical content and performance). Both individual and transindividual dimensions of pedagogy need to be addressed to improve earlier experiences of theory, especially when so many problematic memories are related to particular personalities. As Towns Middleton put it bluntly, "teachers are doing students no favors by turning red in the face and dismissing major intellectual figures as 'scandals.'"

But one would imagine that there is nothing specific to anthropology about ungenerous teaching. In academic life, beyond even the desire for intellectual reproduction and extension (e.g., building a school and dominating a field in Bourdieu's sense), there is a more basic desire for recognition. One wishes to explain to students the ideas and approaches one finds animating and to see them equivalently enchanted. But if students seem fascinated, instead, by work that one finds inscrutable or troubling, it becomes all too tempting to wish to portray that work in an unflattering light.

The more specific problem—from the point of view of the trinitarian commitment of anthropology to fieldwork, ethnography, and theory—is the conventional institution of a "theory course" in which two of the three essential elements of anthropological knowledge are routinely trivialized or abandoned. The theory courses referred to in this volume generally involved the serial presentation and discussion of works of theory (whether originating in anthropology or elsewhere) relatively disconnected from their biographical, social, and political contexts of origin. Moreover, how to link this absorption of theory to the practices of ethnography and field research remained, in most cases, quite obscure. Discussions instead focused on understanding theorists' key arguments and concepts, and on comparing these to other key arguments and concepts. Given the constant rotation of texts, the arguments and concepts typically arrived without extensive commentary on genealogies and contingencies but, rather, as it were, as fully formed epistemic schemata springing sui generis from the genius of their makers. Students often report feeling overwhelmed and lost in these contexts, vulnerable and humbled in the face of textual authority (Thorkelson 2008). Teachers often argue that the challenge of grappling with writing that is "too hard" is positive as exercise in developing "intellectual rigor." Rigor may indeed follow—but also a tendency toward obeisance and imitation of authoritative discourse that is insulated from the contingencies of its contexts of production as well as from its pragmatics of application. One can imagine how, even were such a course to be made more canonically unconventional (e.g., by featuring all women or all non-Europeans on its roster), it could still reproduce the conventional pedagogical model by presenting a carousel of disembodied "thinkers."

Decontextualizing and disembodying any form of knowledge would seem to violate every rule of anthropological engagement. Yet this kind of syllabus is familiar in every graduate curriculum. Obviously, in the design of doctoral training, it is reasonable to look for efficient ways to expose students to the wide range of conceptual and discursive coordinates that we feel they may be accountable to—all education, in other words, necessarily involves language learning. Yet the experience of stand-alone "theory courses" send signals to young professionals that naturalize the typical modes of engaging theory diagnosed in the introduction: either (a) theory is allowed to exist as a status-laden authoritative discourse floating above the domains of anthropological fieldwork and ethnography or (b) it is treated as a citational afterthought to the ethnography-fieldwork relation. Theory, to reiterate the premise of this volume, can be more than (a) + (b). But for it to be so, we need to explore alternative modes of teaching and training.

What Might Training in "Analytical Method" Look Like, Practically Speaking?

The proposal to teach "analytical method" rather than "theory" emerged in the course of our exercise. What could this mean? The conversation felt toward an alternative pedagogy of conceptual/analytical/theoretical engagement. Falcone suggested the image of theory as "meditative framework"; Faubion offered the prospect of finding conceptual inspiration through muses; Ballestero described a studio course that prompts experimentation via "conceptual iterations of the possible avenues" that students might explore in their research projects. A move toward "analytic method" is clearly not programmatic in a singular sense—no one felt, for example, that replacing a stand-alone "theory course" with a stand-alone "analytical method course" is the answer.

The most important principle is that theory be treated in graduate pedagogy and training as a methodological phenomenon as well as, for example, a conceptual phenomenon. Theory is not, in other words, simply a matter of concepts and arguments to be absorbed and deployed, but it is, rather, a matter of epistemic dispositions shaped by life and experience that we operationalize to gain insight within and across our fieldwork and ethnographic engagements. Analytical method could thus be viewed as the processual and experiential counterpart to theory imagined (critically) in our dialogue as "thing-like" authoritative discourse. Analytical method is something one *does*, a process of exploratory sense-making that is itself nothing new but an aspect of research practice that is too often obscured or subverted by the hegemony of the theoretical concept. A reframing of anthropological theory work in terms of method means, as we have sought to accomplish in this volume, to call attention to the processes through which concepts, narratives, and arguments are formed, authorized, and circulated.

As something one does, a formative process in need of recognition, a successful institutionalization of analytical method would mean a commitment substantially greater than a single lecture in a "methods course" or even a single course on its own. To become "habit" rather than simply "insight," analytical method would have to appear and be reinforced throughout a program of graduate training. It could receive recognition in courses such as Ballestero's studio, and then it might also receive reinforcement in other courses that contained substantial attention to the historical and social contingencies of the formation of anthropological knowledge and to "theory" as a practice in the human sciences. In my current pro-seminar course, for example—a course that has evolved over the past fifteen years from a conventional theory course to a historically sensitive theory course to a reflexive diagnostic "walk-through" of the conditions and expectations of anthropological professionalization—analytical method is integrated into a more general discussion of staging an intervention in a field of anthropological knowledge. The idea is to iteratively perform the analytical process of attending to emergent phenomena and relations in the world, assaying a domain of disciplinary activity, and imagining how particular lines of inquiry (research questions) can reveal significant novelties that will provoke further dialogue and reassessment. And, needless to say, if the ethics of theoretical engagement in anthropology are to be changed, then this will have to occur not only in formal pedagogical settings but also through the myriad informal encounters in offices, meetings, and social events in which professional socialization also takes place. The abstraction and frequent valorization of theory will have to change as an everyday norm of conduct.

In other words, ethics and institutions of analytical method will operate most effectively if all coursework is allowed to contain opportunities for methodological training and experimentation in addition to, or better yet in place of, the absorption of epistemic ready-mades. The methods course might thus be considered as the rule rather than as the exception to graduate pedagogy. "Teaching" should be refunctioned as "training," and "training" should be expanded to include engagement beyond the boundaries of academic institutions. We are, after all, committed to the practice of a field science. There are, thus, limits to what we can really learn and teach of anthropology within the environment of a research university or college.

There is always the anxiety with proposals for greater methodological attention that truly "sophisticated" training (e.g., the dutiful study of the masters) will take a back seat to the dull application of method. But method is dull in contemporary anthropological training only because of how it has been formalized and ghettoized institutionally with such limited imagination. On the contrary, it seems to us that there could be no more exciting and generative intellectual exercise than involving anthropologists-in-the-making immediately and directly in the process of making anthropology, of bringing to life the processes of inquiry and analyses from the first day of professional training. The theoretical intelligence of anthropology will not suffer. Indeed, however we wish to objectify analytical method, we think its outcomes will become more interesting and relevant in the engagement of contemporary life, a lively anthropological afflux into the practice of theory across the human sciences.

NOTES

1. Portable Analytics and Lateral Theory

1. http://www.haujournal.org/index.php/masterclass/pages/view/endorsements.

2. On Programmatics

1. See also Rabinow and Bennett's work, en.scientificcommons.org/paul_rabinow.

3. The Ambitions of Theory Work in the Production of Contemporary Anthropological Research

1. To foreshadow a bit: my point will be that anthropology cannot simply rely on its professional community in reception only to do or shape this programmatic work. Somehow, reception must be blended granularly into the classic practice and expectation of fieldwork research and method. For me, in recent years, this operation means linking or extending the intellectual functions of the professional community of anthropologists into the field of inquiry in research projects themselves. What forms of new assemblages of methods and research practices this would require, and what their feasibility and political problems would be in implementation, have been a primary and growing interest of mine over the past decade (Marcus 2012).

2. I offer an anecdote here about how a certain programmatic influence of theory/theories in the training of anthropological graduate students manifests itself as a literal, perhaps eventually productive (!), contradiction in the process of making anthropologists. If I were producing this anecdote as a short essay, I would entitle it "Beautiful Theories and the Precipice of Fieldwork." "Beautiful Theories" refers to a brilliant book by Elizabeth Bruss (1982), deserving to

be remembered, which questioned the programmatic authority of theories and theoretical discourse that were very much then in fashion in shaping the doing and discourse of literary criticism. In anthropological graduate training today, the centrality of the "theory course" and the prominence of theoretical exegesis in almost all other courses (along with the absence of rigorous field methods courses) communicate the importance and authority of theory as a programmatic construction or pillar in the otherwise diffuse curricula of training in many departments. I learn this repeatedly in attending the unfolding minidramas of oral examinations as they are conducted in my present department. The department to which I moved from Rice—anthropology at the University of California, Irvine—schedules oral examinations at the conclusion of two or three years of coursework before the student leaves to do a year or more of fieldwork. The basis of the orals are elaborate documents consisting of a research proposal and two synthetic papers on topical and theoretical subjects that define the research. This moment of oral examination is pivotal because upon the graduate student's return and writing up, our department has no oral defense of the dissertation. The returned student works mainly with his or her supervisor and upon committee approval of the dissertation exits the program. What I have noticed in our oral examinations is almost a ritual undoing of the theoretical language of the student on his or her way to the field in favor of a much more pragmatic prompting to speak literally about what he or she anticipates doing in fieldwork: a kind of compensatory focus on operationalizing the thinking that has gone into the project that is likely to be wound in theoretical circles, rationales, and key concepts. Recently, I personally found this pulling back on the theory elegance of a particular student, especially gifted in this way, in favor of prodding about how he or she anticipates collecting data in a literal field of neighborhoods and marketplaces to be a bit harsh but also supremely evocative of widespread contradictions in pedagogical practice. In anthropology, mastering theory (and its beauty!) is extremely important in training and evaluating students—as a mode for demonstrating intellectual capacity—but it threatens as well producing fieldwork, which notoriously, as a method, is not taught, as theory is, in most anthropology departments.

This divide between the programmatics of theory and the lack of such programmatics in the technology of question asking before or after fieldwork is something that I regularly see students—especially those with an affinity for theory—being caught in, at least temporarily, as they move between the seminar room and fieldwork. And I am regularly reminded of this by the ritual of the particular oral examination that we schedule in our department. Interestingly, orals that come at the end, on the submission of the dissertation, have a different quality in the way they manage the theory-fieldwork divide (for a memorable, personal anecdotal example of this, see Marcus 2010, 38–40). By then the tendential crafting of theory specific to the analytics of a dissertation is clearly in play, and the programmatics of theory substituting for the programmatics of research is less dramatic than when the orals occur before fieldwork.

3. It is worth mentioning an evolution in the work of Michel Callon, one of the founding thinkers of what became influential actor-network theory. His work on markets and his argument that economic theory (the science of economics) does not describe or explain markets from a intellectual distance, but actually participates in their making, has similarities to the movement of theory that informs ethnographic research into the immersed dynamics of fieldwork itself envisioned in this chapter. To argue in this way, Callon depends on an attractive and significant notion of "theory in the wild" as the kind of stuff that research is after and engages with. In an unpublished paper, Andrew Barry (2013) traces a late-1990s, early-2000s distancing by both Bruno Latour and Callon from what they wrought and had become canonical actor-network theory. Latour's movement away had complex trajectories (his movement into collaborations with artists and his concern with design are of interest as well to my argument in this chapter), but Callon's development seems even more instructive for the direction in which this chapter is moving. Theory in the wild led Callon for a time to explore forms, which Andrew Barry describes as "hybrid forums," composed of intellectuals, researchers, activists, social movement organizers, and a more

diffuse public. The suggestion is that they were efforts to practice, investigate, and explore the construct of theory in the wild, to understand theory as social effects, to realize in another sphere an insight parallel to the one that theory did not analyze markets but made them. Interestingly, Barry remarks that what Callon in fact created was "social movement theory/practice for the age of experts." The implication is that these were less experiments in form in the immersion of investigation that sought to study theory in the wild while participating in it than they were a rationale or ideology for the merging of expertise—its forms of theoretical, conceptual thinking— with activist projects. Frankly, I know little more about this move in Callon's work than what I learned from Barry's very brief treatment. Still, without the activist or social movement associa- tions, hybrid forums seem close to how interventionist forms are being conceived by those who are indeed experimenting with theory in the wild as the core production of ethnographic research built around diagnoses circulating and morphing in circuits of reception that themselves become the data of scholarly research enterprises that programmatically organize their activity, indepen- dent of identification with activist or social movement goals.

4. To give a sense of the difference of a Boasian paradigm of ethnographic/field research and its resonance for conceiving an alternative mise-en-scène of the contemporary, I quote Bunzl:

> In Boas's fieldwork, a constitutive epistemological separation between ethnographer and native was absent. . . . From Boas's perspective, neither anthropologist nor informant had immediate access to the history he hoped to reconstruct. In this situation, anthropologist and informant were united in a common epistemological position vis-à-vis the real Other of Boasian anthropology. That Other, ultimately, was the history that had generated the present condition, a history that eluded immediate description due to the absence of writ- ten records. In practice, this meant that Boas was just as happy if Native Americans gen- erated ethnographic data themselves. . . . (2004, 438)

Then,

> Insiders and outsiders were thus differentially positioned at the onset of the ethnographic project. What is central in the present context however, is that Boasian ethnography not only did not rest on that distinction but was also designed to efface it. Guarding against alternating sounds, outsiders would produce the same ethnographic data as insiders; at the same time, the critical awareness of secondary explanations would guide insiders (and the anthropologists who derived their information from them) toward the actual histories of contemporary ethnic phenomena. Conceptually, this meant that insiders and outsiders would generate the same kind and attempt the same kinds of historical recon- structions. . . . (2004, 439)

While the particular kinds of knowledge quests have changed considerably in contemporary ethnographic research, the core Boasian relation in fieldwork inquiry, as evoked by Bunzl, is certainly close to the kinds of prototypes of collaborative thinking (Marcus 2014) on which a diag- nostic programmatic guiding contemporary ethnographic research would depend. Beyond this neo-Boasian mise-en-scène, fieldwork would progress in the contexts of circulations and recep- tions of the collaborative thinking that fieldwork produces. By a quite transitive relation between insider and outsider, in sum, the Boasian style of fieldwork gives the programmatic construc- tion of contemporary anthropological research more to work with than what is imagined in the Malinowskian alternative.

5. Certain earlier, ambitiously programmatic projects of anthropology entertained notions of the ethnographic field that extended from investigations in cultural settings elsewhere seam- lessly to receptions in the context of everyday work in the university—I have in mind here the

Notes to Pages 57-63

ethnoscience/cognitive program in U.S. anthropology of the 1950s and 1960s—but they developed within a referentialist commitment to the programmatic that constrained what could be data from the field.

The question in the same experimental or interventionist ethos is what would work today. The disciplinary apparatus simply does not exist in anthropology, as it does in the sciences, to produce such a referentialist programmatics. Of course, I do not believe this is circumstantial. Anthropology itself does not have the means or the apparent will and inspiration, in its own court, to produce a rigorously referentialist programmatics. What is open to it, not as a consolation but as a strong alternative, is what I have been labeling, following Faubion, a programmatics of the diagnostic, built out of the persistently and creatively strong theory-driven interpretive character of ethnographic research.

    6. "The Asthma Files," theasthmafiles.org.

    7. "The Theory of the Case"

On 25 June 2013, Lamy wrote:

Good piece, thanks. See also, as a confirmation of your analysis, a recently published report on "the future of world trade: the challenges of convergence", which can be seen as an attempt to overcome the mercantilist approach of trade offs. PL

-----Original Message-----

From: marcus [mailto:gmarcus@uci.edu] Sent: 24 June 2013 23:18
To: Lamy, Pascal Cc: Jae Chung; Christine Hegel; gmarcus@uci.edu
Subject: Our Theory of the WTO Case . . . In Conclusion

Dear DG Lamy,

    As our anthropological project draws to a close, it seems to be the right point to present to you, from those of us who have continued after 2010, our theory of the WTO case. It was a rare gift to have open access to the DG Cabinet and the Secretariat. And, the rules of social relations dictate that one gift must be answered with another. Although we have very little to offer that can be considered a gift that the WTO would value highly, we do have a story to tell. But, first, thank you. No one else would have been creatively confident enough to let the anthropologists roam among the rather tough legalistic crowd of the Secretariat, but you did. Some time after 2004/2005, and certainly after 2008, the organization, mostly the DG Cabinet, realized that impediments to negotiation consensus were multiplying in structural, political and cultural ways: the triple digit membership introduced unmanageable complexity to the interest based negotiation calculations; the US, once a leader in the system, had become distracted, defensive, and rigid in its offers; the growing assertive confidence of middle power Members, while a great moral victory, slowed down the process by bringing the negotiation down to deeply contested details; the NGO-led discourse of equity, meant to be productive, deepened the suspicion of any proposal from certain Members. So fractured, there was no organizing leader, and thus no agency, in the system. Denied leadership and shared values, the system had to decide to redesign itself but it turns out that the problem of decision making was the very problem it had to solve first. There was no system, just individual parts in it. Given this tautological problem, once defined by a retiring DSB judge as "many hands but no one voice", the DG innovated (a problematic word we know) by redesigning the forum, without rewriting the rules, to bind the Members to multilateralism. So the project of change of culture from within began as a means to create a new community of trade. How to bind the Members as a community? The new forum a) What kind of problem is this? The anthropological case emerged after the July 2008 Ministerial when a deal among the major Members, seemingly so close, vanished. After this heartbreak, what was the prognosis for WTO, for multilateralism without the forward energy of the successive Rounds? In one sense, nothing: its future remains its present. Ships come and ships go, carrying goods to their destinations across borders. Post 2008 crisis numbers suggest only a slight and benign growth in protectionism, a sign of the vitality of the current WTO framework. But, as you know better than any one of us, while the work of TRP and DSB continued unabated, new trade issues found their consensus elsewhere. The resulting siphoning of personnel, political interest, and "energy" from the WTO Geneva suggests that perhaps the new danger to multilateralism might be found not as a competition among nations, but among trading blocs. If the optimists have it right, the bilateral agreements will return to the multilateral forum, and all will be well. If the pessimists are right, the competition to create the new standards on trade issues, like IP, may spark friction and worse, and trade will become again overtly a political tool. As a keeper of the system, what to do? The textbook answer is clear. As some in the Secretariat told me, almost in rebuke, the system was designed to have only one source of agency, the members, so the responsibility lies with them. While that is a good enough of a procedural answer, that is not good enough for operational intervention. For those who understand themselves as caretakers of the system, the task was to untie the knots and to push the levers. Was one lever at the level of the domestic lobby groups, as is in the case of the United States? Or was an important knot the complexity of the negotiation process among one hundred fifty some ministers? The case is then: how does a system, designed to be spoken in the passive voice, change actively? It was time to tap into the power of the weak. To experiment with lateral strategies of organizational movement. b) Why was it necessary to deploy the lateral move? Of course, there is no WTO as a coherent, independent organization. It is a linguistic and legal fiction, made of parts coordinated through the rules of the organization. Members decide and the organization, DSB, DG Cabinet, and Secretariat, execute that decision within the framework of the Agreements. Change in any legal sense can come only from the Members, but the question that occupied the DG was, can there be any other source of change? c) Why do the Major players not initiate change? It is the tragedy of the commons. In the past, the leaders either offered concessions to Members to overcome their defensive positions, or they moved with such speed, others felt compelled to follow. But recently the "owners" suddenly found themselves in a house they thought they owned but only leased. Due to domestic governance difficulties and realignment of trade powers, the major players adopted a pure defensive position and no longer offered concessions on desired issues. Instead they introduced counter moves elsewhere. Importantly, the United States must have seen that now is the last instance in which they could move to create another US centered trade regime and the WTO impeded that goal. As a result, in the absence of that ownership or power, defensive interests remain interests and do not coalesce into what the system calls consensus. d) With no leaders, what are the organization's options? As a response, the DG Cabinet seems to have engaged in three different genres. The first, the game of diplomatic persuasion, of exerting "peer pressure." The second is to embed the WTO within the network of IOs. The third, which is the art of the 'nudge,' to move things along incrementally, even glacially, as a strategy of the long game, one of change in the culture of the organization. This one requires faith, hope, and charity, and an immense tolerance for disappointment, and satisfaction with private pleasure in small apparent forward moves. 1) Expanding the language of trade to reimagine it as a system of shared values in the speeches of the DG and the visual, photographic history of multilateralism since 1947 2) Speaking a vocabulary of contemporary openness, an homage of architecture stripped of British club ambiance as a way of reforging the narrowly legalistic and procedural idea 3) Bringing and binding the members into the building as an act of communitas, if only to share open meeting spaces and improved amenities 4) Recreating the Secretariat in the image of the globe and not so much the anglo past 5) Negotiating the resistance within the ranks of the GATT based contingent, who saw the lateral strategy as the recasting trade from a pure economic issue to an interrelated one. The game has changed. It is no longer possible to calculate the offensive and defensive interests of the entire trading nations within the purely transactional framework of GATT. In recognizing this fact and the undeniable weak powers of the organization, the end game was to change the practices at the WTO, so that the organization may help bind the separate Members into a trade community whose commitment to multilateralism can transcend the interest-based calculations. It was a long term gambit to create the opportunity for the emergence of trust by forging a shared experience in the off chance that shared values can decrease negotiating complexity by increasing trust, and community can calculate the costs and benefits over a longer durée. In other words, to change the system without changing its rules required an investment in manifesting a utopic dream of a new political and cultural unit. Its actual emergence is slow and tenuous but the articulation of this dream may defend an increasingly vulnerable space of multilateralism. To those who see GATT as a way of defending against the nightmare of nationalism, aligning the weak powers may be the organization's best chance to move the organization from within.

Sincerely,
Jae Chung
Christine Hegel
George E. Marcus

8. These lines evoke for me my own personal history with the multisited construct of the emerging future for ethnographic research that I introduced in 1995 (Marcus [1995] 1998a)—basically one of a number of reflections constructed at that moment that put ethnographic research in motion, the most prominent and successful of which was actor-network theory. Mine had the misfortune (but my own fault) to be understood in a literal way as the reproduction and multiplication of sites of research where the modes and standards of inquiry applicable to one would be produced in each. Of course, this was open to obvious critiques of feasibility, which I anticipated in the original article. What I was personally more interested in was how work in one place evoked often hidden routes to others precisely through the theory or concept work that the ethnographer could do with specific subjects and not others (the key informant becoming an epistemic partner in complicit relations—a construct with which I was working by the late 1990s (Marcus [1997] 1998b). In this trajectory, I indeed saw the multisited construct becoming something like the emergent connectivities and paths of recursion that were generated by collaboratively produced and distinctive ideas of ethnography emerging in the scenes of fieldwork—as a technology of question asking that sent one on a trajectory that was in fact multisited. What was missing was thinking about the literal forms that might materialize this sense of fieldwork process then. Changes in the way the world presents itself to ethnographers for fieldwork projects and dramatic changes in media and communication technologies have finally made the question of doing things differently with the classic method explicit and pressing. In the original multisited formulation, this question was not far under the surface, but it became only gradually (and never clearly) sayable in the present and the recent past.

4. Theorizing the Present Ethnographically

I extend my warm thanks to Dominic Boyer, James Faubion, and George Marcus both for organizing the stimulating Rice University conference on which this contribution was based and for keeping faith with this volume through all these years.

1. In part, the history of the relationship between social theory and politics becomes visible in shifting concept names for both its objects and its scholarly study. I have therefore inserted a set of footnotes to comment on these shifts in names and their meaning.

2. The differentiation of the *social* from the *political* is originally the consequence of introducing society as a new object of study in the eighteenth and early-nineteenth centuries. It was

then used to refer to the domain of voluntary associations conceived to mediate between state and families (e.g. Ferguson [1767] 1995; Hegel [1820] 1986; cf. Wagner 2000). Later, however, the semantics of *social* has come to include the economic and the political, much in the same way in which the Greek understanding of *political* once included not only issues of governance but anything that pertained to human life in the company of others. In fact, the contemporary word *society* maps more closely on the Greek word *politeia* than any of the currently favored translations of the latter, such as "state," "republic," or "constitution." Here, I continue to speak of the social in this inclusive sense.

3. The well-known historical exemplars are post–Peloponnesian War Athens (Plato and Aristotle), the disintegrating late Roman Empire (Augustine), condottieri-ravished late-Medieval and early-Renaissance Italy (Dante, Marsiglio, and Machiavelli), the post–Reformation wars-of-religion Europe (Bodin, Hobbes, deGroot, and Pufendorf), absolutist Europe (Locke, Montesquieu, Rousseau, and Kant), post–French Revolution Europe (Burke, Fichte, Schelling, and Hegel), and finally industrial revolution Europe (Smith, Ricardo, Malthus, and Marx). The fact that there have been many major crises in many parts of the world without producing social theory indicates that to make such bursts happen it also takes, in the very least, an institutionalized set of practices geared at the conceptualization of social life.

4. There was a locally perceived respite from the modality of crisis only. But even the years from the mid-1950s to the mid-1960s, often celebrated as "golden," were dotted with experiences of crisis on the international level that, at least in Europe, had profoundly disquieting domestic repercussions (e.g., Algeria 1954–1962, Suez 1956, Sputnik 1957, Berlin 1961, Cuba 1962, and Vietnam) with consequences for theorizing practices.

5. Indeed they founded a club with the telltale name Club of the Friends of the Eternalized, whose members edited Hegel's oeuvre notably by adding Hegel's own marginal notes as well as explanatory additions taken from Hegel's lectures to his originally taut published texts, published as supportive scaffolding for his lectures. This group later famously split into left and right Hegelians over David Strauss's (*The Life of Jesus*) interpretation of Hegel as a pantheist, which the left shared and the right rejected.

6. Radical theologies leading to altered or new rituals and subsequently breakaway churches are historically the closest precursor of ideologies. Cathars and Waldensians are good examples (Cohn [1957] 1980). They, however, were operating with a scriptural truth regime, whereas ideologies all claim to be grounded in science.

7. Just to stay with the examples provided in note 1: Aristotle was suspected of Macedonian sympathies and had to flee Athens; Dante and Marsiglio were seen as members of the Ghibelline party (pro-empire) and had to flee to Verona and to Munich, respectively; Machiavelli was ousted from his job, imprisoned, and later put under house arrest; Bodin was variously enmeshed in the complicated politics of his day and at times imprisoned; Hobbes fled Civil War England to France and then from Catholic France to the Netherlands.

8. As in the case of the classical Greek *politeia,* the translation of the Latin *civitas* poses considerable problems because our whole institutional fabric as well as our social imaginaries have changed. Although *city* nicely betrays the etymological roots, the word means today something totally different than *civitas*. Augustine had, inspired both by the historical experience of the *imperium romanum* as an at least potentially world-encompassing political order as well as by the universalism of Paulinian Christianity, an encompassing, indeed global set of orders in mind, driven by very different principles of organization.

9. Still, Hobbes dedicated the entire third part of his *Leviathan* to justify the first two parts in terms of scripture and dedicated the fourth part to the denouncement of heresies. When the link to scripture is subsequently less obvious, it still remains central for the proper historical interpretation of authors' works. Kant's grounding of his moral and political philosophy in knowledge a priori is *historically* incomprehensible without references to a transcendent deity.

10. The figure of the social contract is a peculiar reinterpretation of the Sinai covenant as the initiating moment of statehood but now articulated in a very Greek way, as a collective of equal citizens driven by their own reason, which is thought of (to make this thought Christian again) as an inborn repository of divine law.

11. In introductory classes taught at institutions of higher learning, such theories are often bundled with the help of a disciplinary ribbons that may or may not bear a deeper meaning grounded in practices of concept formation. Economic theory is today overwhelmingly developed from a unifying philosophical perspective and preferably expressed in formal languages. Sociological theory is a basket designator for any conceptualization sociologists may undertake or prescribe as necessary in the formation of neophytes.

12. Pre–French Revolution political philosophy of course makes no distinction between explanatory and normative concerns. Among the modern directions of social concept formation, boundaries between these two tendencies are also by no means clear cut. There is a thoroughly rationalist branch of economic theory that aims at explanation; some authors have split their contributions between genres and others have continued to mix them, as Habermas ([1963] 1990) did or with the more recent trend to suffuse political philosophy with more realism (e.g., Rawls [1993] 2005; or most recently, Honneth 2011).

13. Thus, Hayek's eponymous book ([1944] 1991) could easily discern some of the limits of socialist reasoning, but he could of course not identify its own.

14. How poisonous and far-reaching this ideologization was can be illustrated with a trifle. Previously, I have used the word *autonomization*. As a native German speaker, I am often tempted to craft words in English to match concepts. Because I know that English is much less forgiving of such idiosyncratic operations, I look up my mental concoctions in the hope that they reflect proper English usage. Punching *autonomization* into Thefreedictionary.com, accessed April 9, 2015, I was immediately referred to the encyclopedia with the following warning underscored with a gleaming red triangular warning sign: "**Warning!** The following article is from The Great Soviet Encyclopedia (1979). It might be outdated or ideologically biased."

15. In many ways, the liberal reverse of critical theory was Karl Popper's critical rationalism (1934, [1945] 1971) which, inspired above all by Kant's rigorous attempt to define the limits of reason, took aim at Hegelian and post-Hegelian "historicism." Popper saw the latter defined by two assumptions: that all forms of social life are relative to circumstance and that it needs to be analyzed in totalities. At the same time, however—and this is the reason why I do not discuss it in the main text—critical rationalism continued to naturalize liberalism. Moreover, Popper could not see the totalization inherent in liberalism, which is, ironically, the effect of its ahistorical views.

16. Deconstruction's direct, publicly avowed impact on U.S. sociology and political science remained much more marginal.

17. In anthropology, this term is mostly associated with the aforementioned works of Clifford, Marcus, and Fisher, but also with Capranzano, Rabinow, and others. In sociology, reflexivity has more recently been associated with Bourdieu and his school (e.g., Bourdieu and Wacquant 1992), but it is in many ways prefigured in the ideal-typical approach of Weber (e.g., 1904) and in the whole project of a sociology of knowledge.

18. Naïve scientism characterizes most of normal science, both in the social and the hard sciences.

19. Even though the reifying characteristics of naïve scientism are routinely blamed on the nineteenth century, it has deep roots in the ontological biases of post-Socratic classical Greek philosophy, which consistently valued permanence, the unchangeability of substances over the variability of processes. It has further roots in the Biblical creation myth centering on an entitizing divinity. In addition Whorf ([1939] 1956) has suggested that the noun phrase centricity of Indo-European languages supports reifying thought.

20. Whitehead ([1927–28] 1979) coined the term *misplaced concreteness* for much the same phenomenon.

21. This false certainty was as much a feature of Soviet-style socialisms as it is of contemporary economistic liberalism (for this term, see note 33).

22. In what follows, it will become clear that I follow neither Marx ([1867] 1963) nor Lukacs ([1924] 1972) in their analyses of the epistemic and ethical effects of reification because both analyses depend on romantic epistemologies beholden to the possibility of comprehending totalities of particulars and contexts (Althusser 1971; Honneth 2005). This critique notwithstanding, the epistemic effects of reification remain important and, in many ways, the basis for the ethical and political consequences of reification.

23. In what follows, I am indebted to U.S. pragmatism (e.g. James [1907–1909] 1975; Dewey [1925] 1927) and to the later work by Wittgenstein ([1957] 1984) as well as the work on metaphor by Whorf ([1939] 1956), Ricoeur ([1975] 1977), and Lakoff (1993).

24. The need for alterity is, incidentally, the reason why mathematics and logic or other highly abstract bodies of theory *can* function as formidable tools for empirical work. This is, of course, also the reason why relevance is never clear for any conceptual framework and why it is important to not dismiss sheer intellectual play out of hand.

25. Max Weber ([1904] 1988) made this point, of course, long ago. He spoke of the necessity that scholarly pursuits proceed from a particular "value perspective."

26. Ricoeur's ultimate project moves in the opposite direction, concluding from the centrality of narrative in fiction and history that narrativity describes a human existential, a fundamental and universal dimension of being human in the world.

27. Aristotle's notion of mimesis shows consistent emphasis on the characteristics of the medium in which mimesis takes place. This shows, for example, in his consideration of the various advantages and disadvantages of various media (verse, prose, music, painting, and implicitly stage acting as opposed to writing) for mimesis. In other words, Aristotle is quite aware that the iconicity of relations is proximate and never complete. But that would mean that he sees mimetic relations as metaphorical in the way I have used the term previously (and in spite of his warning against metaphor later in his text). Ricoeur's interpretation of Aristotle as suggesting a triple mimesis from closing the circle from life to text, from text to stage, and from stage back to life makes excellent sense of Aristotle's (and Plato's) concerns with the political role of the arts (see also Havelock 1963).

28. Hegel's theory of recognition (cf. Honneth 1992) is in fact a dynamization and generalization of older legal models that systematically relate institutions to institution-initiating interlocking actions (Justinian [533] 1987). What the legal perspective does not make explicit (but has always assumed implicitly for the proper functioning of any legal institution) is that the unique public performance of initiating actions (often, but not exclusively, speech acts) has to be followed up by continuing recognition in mundane practice. Roman law was aware of the import of legal means of redress in cases of breech, but this is once more the depiction of a punctual intervention necessary only in cases of last resort, precisely when recognition breaks down.

29. It is telling in this context that practice theorists have, by and large, failed to account for the institutionalization and transformation of practices. Among the best and still frustrating accounts available are Sudnow [1978] 1993 and Wacquant 2004.

30. I provide a more detailed discussion of the advantages and disadvantages of various activity concepts in Glaeser 2014.

31. With Ricoeur, one could say, then, that every act is a synthesis of the heterogeneous, that every act has a story. For the social scientist, it can pay to take it as the corpus delicti.

32. Typically the same action partakes in the reproduction of several institutions. If my neighbor and I are on "greeting terms" with each other, each greeting exchanged reproduces that mini-institution and, at the same time, the cultural form of "being on greeting terms." It also reproduces

me and her as particular individuals, as well as the greetings we choose to exchange as formulas employable in the language in which we choose to communicate with each other, and so on.

33. Unfortunately I cannot use the term "neoliberal" here, because it is simply too narrow. The neoliberal is often invoked in opposition to the Keynesian, which, however, remains entirely within what I call here economistic liberalism, in which the two are marked by merely gradual differences in their understandings of the role of the state and the potential for market failure.

34. To understand the appeal and hegemonic hold of economistic liberalism in our time, one has to consider the fact that all holders of stocks and mutual funds and those parts of society that have pension plans are among the clients of managers and as such beholden to them and to their performance.

5. Trans-formations of Biology and of Theory

1. Donna Haraway, personal conversations at "Lively Capital" conference, November 7, 2004, Irvine, CA. The papers presented at this conference have since been published and, I hope, reflect something of the ethos that Haraway was calling for at the conference (Sunder Rajan 2012).

2. https://www.marxists.org/archive/marx/works/1845/theses/theses.htm (accessed April 19, 2015).

3. My reading of the XIth Thesis on Feuerbach owes much to Etienne Balibar (1995), who reads it for its implications for the history of philosophy and the break that Marx as a philosopher achieves from that history in *The Philosophy of Marx*.

4. There are by now a number of famous examples of "translationally derived" anticancer therapeutics. For instance, to provide just three well-known examples: herceptin (trastuzumab) is a monoclonal antibody that interferes with the HER2/neu receptor, which is overexpressed in certain breast cancers; Gleevec (imatinib mesylate) inhibits bcr-abl, a tyrosine kinase whose overexpression leads to chronic myeloid leukemia; and Avastin (bevacizumab) acts through effecting endothelial vasculature by inhibiting vascular endothelial growth factor (VEGF). Peter Keating, Alberto Cambrosio, and their colleagues have studied translational research in cancer in Euro-American contexts (Keating and Cambrosio 2012). For an account of the challenges involved in taking research on angiogenesis into the clinic and therapeutic development, see Michael Fischer's (2012) account of Judah Folkman, who was the researcher involved in the elucidation of mechanisms of angiogenesis and its inhibition that would lead to the development of Avastin.

5. For the notion of "mangle of practice," see Pickering 1995.

6. For the notion of co-production in science and technology studies, see Jasanoff 2004. For the elaboration of its utility in theorizing contemporary biomedicine, see Sunder Rajan 2012.

7. For two volumes at the intersections of science, technology, and society (STS) and anthropology that deal with notions of imaginary, see *The Late Editions* collection on "Technoscientific Imaginaries" (Marcus 1995) and *Dreamscapes of Modernity* (Jasanoff and Kim 2015).

8. In 1995, a business component was added to this. Now, MBA students from the MIT Sloan School of Management can also enter the HST track.

9. Both Sengupta and I were undergraduates in human biology at AIIMS. Since then, Sengupta has studied pharmacology, obtained a PhD at Cambridge University, and completed a postdoctoral fellowship at MIT. He was then hired as assistant professor in HST.

10. Traditionally, public institutional development in medicine was under the purview of the Indian Council for Medical Research (ICMR). There has tended to be little conversation or collaboration between DBT and ICMR. Indeed, the two organizations come under the purview of separate ministries, DBT being under the Ministry of Science and Technology and ICMR under the Ministry of Health. This implies entirely separate budgets and bureaucratic governance structures. In Indian hospitals, it was (and still is) rare to find serious research programs. The Pediatrics Department at AIIMS is one of the few exceptions, and Bhan himself is in large measure responsible for that.

11. As a joint Harvard-MIT program, HST has one director from each of the universities. Gray was the director from MIT.

12. Two who are often referenced in Gray's own talks about HST are Bruce Rosen, who developed functional magnetic resonance imaging (fMRI), and David Ho, who was involved in the development of HIV Protease inhibitor and was named *Time* magazine's man of the year in 1996.

13. Fischer was my PhD dissertation advisor and chair of the program when I joined it in 1998.

14. This is a fundamental difference in the tenor of this account from early articulations of actor-network theory, as in the work of Bruno Latour (1988a, 1988b) and Michel Callon (1986), which have been powerful foundational methods for STS. Latour and Callon tend to assume that the end-game of scientific negotiation and controversy is consensus and stabilization. For such an assumption to work, one has to imagine a shared set of contexts or backgrounds against which conversations, negotiations, and controversies unfold. My point, precisely, is that these never existed within a complex emergent organizational milieu such as THSTI, which is also trans-national in its conception and implementation.

15. Examples of biotech parks in China include the Life Sciences Park in Beijing and the Shanghai-Zhangjiang Hi-Tech Park in Shanghai.

16. For the articulation of an anthropological problem of contemporary technoscience as being one that has to simultaneously make sense of its structures and its peopling, see Fischer 2012a. For an elaboration of a theoretical process that takes into account a scalar analysis of the macro, meso, and micro in relation to ecoinformatics, see K. Fortun 2012a.

17. For a longer analysis of the attempt by India to be a global player through initiatives in the life sciences, see *Biocapital* (Sunder Rajan 2006, chap. 5).

18. I am grateful to Rajeswari Sunder Rajan for helping me think with and through Rushdie. Sunder Rajan is currently working on a book manuscript, "The Burden of the Nation," which traces the influence of Rushdie on the contemporary Indian novel in English. My drawing on Rushdie here owes much to her manuscript in progress and to conversations with her about Rushdie.

19. For an elaboration of Marcus's pedagogical sensibility and its relationship to questions of method, see Sunder Rajan 2011.

20. Marcus, especially, has thought about para-sites in relation to graduate student dissertation projects and has supported a number of them through the Center for Ethnography at the University of California, Irvine. See http://www.ethnography.uci.edu/ethno_para-site (accessed July 13, 2013).

21. Here is the full list of participants and their affiliations at the time of the para-site: Kaushik Sunder Rajan (associate professor of anthropology, University of California, Irvine; anthropologist of science and technology); Martha Gray (J. W. Kiekhefer Professor of Medical and Electrical Engineering, MIT; director of the HST Division, MIT from 1995 to 2008); Michael M. J. Fischer (Andrew W. Mellon Professor of Humanities and professor of anthropology and science and technology studies, MIT; current research project on the institutionalization of global biomedicine with a focus on Singapore); Mriganka Sur (Sherman Fairchild Professor of Neuroscience and Head, Department of Brain and Cognitive Science, MIT; basic research on developmental plasticity and dynamic changes in mature cortical networks during information processing, learning, and memory); Adam Drake (postdoctoral associate in the lab of Jianzhu Chen at MIT; development of humanized mouse models to study immune responses); K. Vijayraghavan (director of the NCBS, Bangalore; basic research on the developmental neurobiology of animal movement, in particular the formation of muscles in *Drosophila*); Satyajit Mayor (professor in the area of cellular organization and signaling, NCBS, Bangalore; basic research on mechanisms of endocytic trafficking of transmembrane and lipid-anchored proteins); Chetan Chitnis (research

scientist in the malaria group at the International Center for Genetic Engineering and Biotechnology [ICGEB]), New Delhi; research on erythrocyte invasion by malarial parasites, involved in developing antimalarial vaccines); Sunil Shaunak (professor of infectious diseases, Division of Investigative Science, Imperial College, London; research involves developing drugs against hepatitis C; cofounder of a start-up, PolyTherics); Fiona Murray (Sarofim Family Career Development Professor of Management of Technological Innovation and Entrepreneurship, Sloan School of Management, MIT; studies on science commercialization, the organization of scientific research, and the role of science in national competitiveness); Ganesh Venkataraman (chief scientific officer and senior vice president of research, Momenta Pharmaceuticals Inc., Cambridge, Massachusetts; research faculty member, Harvard-MIT division of HST); Joe Smith (vice president of emerging technologies, Corporate Office of Science and Technology, Johnson & Johnson); Nimish Vaccharajani (vice president of pharmaceutical development, Advinus Therapeutics Private Limited, Bangalore; previously, director of clinical development, Bristol-Myers Squibb Pharmaceutical Research Institute); Shiladitya Sengupta (assistant professor of medicine and HST, Harvard Medical School, Brigham and Women's Hospital; research on developing engineering and nanotechnology solutions for complex diseases; founder of three start-up companies, in the United States, United Kingdom, and India); Mehmet Toner (professor of surgery (biomedical engineering) and HST, Harvard Medical School, Massachusetts General Hospital; research focusing on the physiochemical aspects of freezing cells and engineered tissues); Brian Seed (professor of genetics and HST, Harvard Medical School, Massachusetts General Hospital; research on using new technologies to couple rapid identification of interesting genes with methods to study their consequences in an organismic context); Beth Karlan (director of the Women's Cancer Research Institute, Cedars Sinai Medical Center, Los Angeles, and professor of obstetrics and gynecology, Geffen School of Medicine, University of California, Los Angeles; surgeon and research on the genetic definition and phenotypic determinants of human ovarian carcinomas, molecular biomarker discovery, and inherited cancer susceptibility); Alok Srivastava (professor and head of the Department of Hematology and head of the Centre for Stem Cell Research, Christian Medical College, Vellore; research on and treatment of hemophilia); K. Srinath Reddy (president, Public Health Foundation of India; previously, head of the Cardiology Department, AIIMS, New Delhi; clinical cardiologist with a career commitment to preventive cardiology and public health); Uma Chandra Mouli Natchu (Department of Biotechnology Ramalingaswamy Fellow, THSTI; completing a PhD in public health at the Harvard School of Public Health; trained as a pediatrician; research on pediatric malnutrition); Michael Montoya (assistant professor of anthropology and Chicano/Latino studies, University of California, Irvine; medical anthropologist researching the relationship between biomedicine and social indictors such as race and poverty); Gopal Dabade (medical doctor, community health activist, and convener of the All India Drug Action Network [AIDAN], Dharwad, Karnataka; actively involved in public advocacy around access to essential medicines in India); Sarah Kaplan (associate professor of strategic management, Rotman School of Business, University of Toronto; author of the *New York Times* business best-seller, *Creative Destruction* [with co-author Richard Foster], which studies the culture and systems of long-established companies and how those often result in their underperforming in the market over time); Bhaven Sampat (assistant professor in the Department of Health Policy and Management and in the School of International and Public Affairs, Columbia University; research at the intersection of issues in innovation policy and health policy); and Thomas Pogge (Leitner Professor of Philosophy and International Affairs, Yale University; has written extensively on political philosophy and more recently on extreme poverty and global justice; involved in the establishment of Health Impact Fund, which is an attempt to provide an incentive structure through international governments for pharmaceutical companies to provide medicines and treatments for developing countries at an affordable cost).

22. Martha Gray, letter to Indo-US Forum, 2009.

6. Figuring Out Theory

1. I use the term *refraction* to point to the way theory can "deflect (light, for example) from a straight path" and "alter by viewing through a medium" ("Refraction" 2000), which synchs well with a goal of producing "kaleidoscopic insight" (called for later in this chapter). Writing about "the promise of monsters," Donna Haraway casts the term *refract* differently (setting it against *diffract*). Ethnography, it seems to me, needs both. In Haraway's rendering, "Diffraction does not produce 'the same' displaced, as reflection and refraction do. Diffraction is a mapping of interference, not of replication, reflection, or reproduction. A diffraction pattern does not map where differences appear, but rather maps where the effects of difference appear. Tropically, for the promises of monsters, the first invites the illusion of essential, fixed position, while the second trains us to more subtle vision" (1992, 300).

2. Marcus notes that "this neat image certainly does not correspond to the experience of reading *Naven* for the first time as one moves through Bateson's tortuous, uncertain narrative progression" (1985, 69).

3. In my view, the anthropology of science has been so lively over the past two decades because it has both drawn on established methods in anthropology and been compelled to innovate new approaches to deal with new kinds of ethnographic materials and engagement with interlocutors. As Sharon Traweek (2002) has taught, the anthropology of science happens on "faultlines" where different things come together, often producing transformative disruption.

4. Over the years, I have become increasingly convinced that research skills and sensibilities are a key educational goal and political good in students of all ages because so many problems we face today have far from straightforward solutions, making most jobs research-intensive. Research sensibilities also counter the shrill anti-intellectualism that characterizes so much political discourse today. I have directed undergraduate research for many years, and in 2013 I taught "Figuring Out Methods" to undergraduates for the first time, as the first semester in a two-semester thesis sequence. I have also developed a nine-week program that draws even younger students into research, mentored by university students. We started with middle school students, added high school students, and then in 2014 added upper elementary students. Our youngest researchers were eight years old.

5. The conception and practice of punctuation in experimental ethnography deserves much more elaboration. Some sense of the potential can be drawn from this succinct explication in *No Subject: An Encyclopedia of Lacanian Psychoanalysis*:

> Punctuation is one of the forms which the intervention of the analyst may take; by punctuating the analysand's discourse in an unexpected way, the analyst can retroactively alter the intended meaning of the analysand's speech: 'changing the punctuation renews or upsets' the fixed meaning that the analysand had attributed to his own speech. [1] Such punctuation is a way of 'showing the subject that he is saying more than he thinks he is.' [2] The analyst can punctuate the analysand's discourse simply by repeating part of the analysand's speech back to him (perhaps with a different intonation or in a different context). For example, if the analysand says *tu es ma mère* ('you are my mother'), the analyst may repeat it in such a way as to bring out the homophony of this phrase with *tuer ma mère* ('to kill my mother'). ("Punctuation")

6. I use the term *care* here with Mike Fortun's forthcoming writing on care (of data) practices in genomics in mind. Care, in this expansive articulation, involves knowledge production acutely and iteratively attentive to context (and the inevitable double binds of context).

7. The concept of "light structure" has also come to be important in efforts to build digital infrastructure for ethnography in the Platform for Experimental and Collaborative Ethnography

(PECE)—calling for new ways of thinking about computation, supporting ontologies, controlled vocabularies, and so on (Poirier, DiFranzo, and Gloria 2014). I write further against too much structure in "From Latour to Late Industrialism" (Fortun 2014).

8. Note that the notion of a set used here plays off Bateson's (1972) engagement with set theory in his theory of communication and the double bind. Also consider how the sketching structures are like the walls of the labyrinth described by Borges (1962) and, in turn, by Hans-Jörg Rheinberger (1998) in his conception of experimental research systems, set against "testing devices."

9. I elaborate on the urgency of attending to discursive gaps and risks in contemporary ethnography in a previous essay, addressing the continuing significance of "writing culture" (Fortun 2012b).

10. Mike Fortun (2005) has theorized this as a mode of friendship, drawing on Derrida's writing on the "Politics of Friendship" (1993).

11. I have learned to anticipate the paralysis so often provoked when students are asked to articulate social theoretical questions—and have worked to understand and deflect it. Anxiety in part stems from persistent mystification of what "theory" *is*. Anxiety can also stem from a sense that, once articulated, theory is set, cemented, rather than something that should shift as a project progresses. Sketching, and continually revising one's sketches, helps offset this.

12. In an earlier essay titled "Figuring Out Ethnography" (Fortun 2009), I describe a sketch that I use to help students explicate their own style—building on oppositions written about by Evelyn Fox Keller (1985), a historian (between a compulsive obsessive disorder and a paranoid disorder), and by Roman Jakobson, a linguist (between two types of aphasia).

13. Gayatri Spivak suggests a potent connection between theory and political mobilization, arguing that the critical scholar is to create infrastructure such that the subaltern "gains access to metonymization" (2008). Rather than speaking for the subaltern, the scholar helps create discursive structure with space *for* the subaltern. In the theory of theory articulated here, this would be called theorization; to create infrastructure for collaboration—whether in the formation of an academic panel or for political work—is to theorize. This is a different way to theory than that described (and critiqued) by Spivak (1998) earlier, analogous to capital formation. In the latter mode, one theorized by imposing a homogenous reading (a gold standard) across heterogenous material, such that history drops from view (and political possibility).

14. In a set of memos not described here, I ask students to design covers for the books they will write, and to imagine and lay out how the text will move readers—literally—from cover to cover, from X to Y (recognizing that imaging a reader itself takes ethnographic insight). What is X, I ask, the place you imagine your reader will start? And what is Y, where you want to take her? *How* are you going to move her? Is the way forward straight? Are there repetitions or turns that the readers needs to make so that the readerly effect of the text is more than cognitive?

7. Responses

1. For more, see the articles that emerged from that body of research about Indian-American Hindutva groups (Falcone 2010b and 2012).

2. For more, see the recently published version of this essay, Falcone 2013.

3. I present a more detailed extension of this idea in Falcone 2010a.

4. See, for example, Middleton 2011a, 2011b, 2013.

5. Including my involvement in the "Public Representation of a Religion Called Hinduism" collaborative network project, which has resulted in an *International Journal of Hindu Studies* journal special issue on "Temple Publics," a series of three essays surveying "Hindutva" (Reddy 2011), and an edited volume, *Public Hinduisms* (Reddy et al. forthcoming).

Bibliography

Abélès, Marc, ed. 2011. *Des anthropologues à l'OMC*. Paris: CNRS Press.

Althusser, Louis. 1971. *Lenin and Philosophy and Other Essays*. New York: Monthly Review Press.

Aristotle. (322 BCE) 1970. *Poetics*. Translated by Gerald F. Else. Ann Arbor: University of Michigan Press.

Asad, Talal, ed. 1973. *Anthropology and the Colonial Encounter*. New York: Humanities Press.

Auerbach, Erich. (1946) 1994. *Mimesis: Dargestellte Wirklichkeit in der abendländischen Literatur*. Tübingen: Francke.

Bakhtin, Mikhail. 1981. *The Dialogic Imagination*. Austin: University of Texas Press.

Balibar, Étienne. 1995. *The Philosophy of Marx*. Translated by Chris Turner. London: Verso.

Barry, Andrew. 2013. "Translating Actor-Network Theory: Resistances of Music." Unpublished manuscript prepared for the MusDig Conference, St. Anne's College, Oxford, July 11, 2013.

Bateson, Gregory. 1935. "Culture, Contact and Schismogenesis." *Man* 35: 178–83.

———. (1936) 1958. *Naven: A Survey of the Problems Suggested by a Composite Picture of the Culture of a New Guinea Tribe Drawn from Three Points of View*. Stanford: Stanford University Press.

———. 1972. *Steps to an Ecology of Mind: Collected Essays in Anthropology, Psychiatry, Evolution, and Epistemology*. Chicago: University of Chicago Press.

Bateson, Gregory, Don Jackson, Jay Haley and John Weakland. 1956. "Toward a Theory of Schizophrenia." *Behavioral Science* 1: 251–64. Reprinted in Gregory Bateson, 1972, *Steps to an Ecology of Mind,* 201–27. Chicago: University of Chicago Press.

Beck, Ulrich. 1992. *Risk Society: Towards a New Modernity*. Translated by Mark Ritter. New Delhi: Sage.

Beck, Ulrich, Anthony Giddens, and Scott Lash. 1991. *Reflexive Modernization: Politics, Aesthetics and Tradition in the Modern Social Order*. Stanford: Stanford University Press.

Benedict, Ruth. (1934) 1989. *Patterns of Culture*. New York: Houghton Mifflin.

Benjamin, Walter. (1936) 1977. "Der Erzähler." In *Illuminationen: Ausgewählte Schriften*, 385–410. Frankfurt: Suhrkamp.

Bennett, Jane. 2010. *Vibrant Matter: a Political Ecology of Things*. Durham, North Carolina: Duke University Press.

Berlant, Lauren, and Michael Warner. 1998. "Sex in Public." *Critical Inquiry* 24(2): 547–66.

Bhabha, Homi K. 1994. *The Location of Culture*. London: Routledge.

Blanchot, Maurice. (1980) 1995. *The Writing of the Disaster*. Translated by Ann Smock. Lincoln: University of Nebraska Press.

———. 1986. *The Writing of the Disaster*. Translated by Ann Smock. Lincoln: University of Nebraska Press.

Blumenberg. Hans. 1979. *Die Lesbarkeit der Welt*. Frankfurt: Suhrkamp.

Boellstorff, Tom. 2008. *Coming of Age in Second Life: An Anthropologist Explores the Virtually Human*. Princeton: Princeton University Press.

Borges, Jorges Luis. 1962. *Labyrinths: Selected Stories and Other Writings*. Translated by Donald Yates and James Irby. New York: New Directions.

Bourdieu, Pierre. 1977. *Outline of a Theory of Practice*. Translated by Richard Nice. Cambridge, UK: University of Cambridge Press.

———. 1988. *Homo Academicus*. Trans. Peter Collier. Stanford: Stanford Univ. Press.

———. 1989. "Social Space and Symbolic Power." *Sociological Theory* 71(1): 14-25.

———. 1990. *The Logic of Practice*. Translated by Richard Nice. Cambridge, UK: University of Cambridge Press.

———. 1991. *Pascalian Meditations*. Trans. Richard Nice. Stanford: Stanford Univ. Press.

Bourdieu, Pierre, and Loïc J. D. Wacquant. 1992. *An Invitation to Reflexive Sociology*. Chicago: University of Chicago Press.

Boyer, Dominic. 2003. "Censorship as a Vocation: The Institutions, Practices, and Cultural Logic of Media Control in the German Democratic Republic." *Comparative Studies in Society and History* 45(3): 511–45.

———. 2005. *Spirit and System: Media, Intellectuals and the Dialectic in Modern German Culture*. Chicago: University of Chicago Press.

———. 2006. "Ostalgie and the Politics of the Future in Eastern Germany." *Public Culture* 18(2): 361–81.

———. 2010. "On the Ethics and Practice of Contemporary Social Theory: From Crisis Talk to Multiattentional Method." *Dialectical Anthropology* 34(3): 305–24.

———. 2013. *The Life Informatic: Newsmaking in the Digital Era.* Ithaca: Cornell University Press.

Boyer, Dominic, and Alexei Yurchak. 2010. "American *Stiob*: Or, What Late Socialist Aesthetics of Parody Reveal about Contemporary Political Culture in the West." *Cultural Anthropology* 25(2): 179–221.

Brown, Donald. 1988. *Hierarchy, History and Human Nature: The Social Origins of Historical Consciousness.* Tucson: University of Arizona Press.

———. 1991. *Human Universals.* New York: McGraw-Hill.

Bruss, Elizabeth. 1982. *Beautiful Theories.* Baltimore: Johns Hopkins University Press.

Bunzl, Matti. 2004. "Boas, Foucault, and the 'Native Anthropologist': Notes toward a Neo-Boasian Anthropology." *American Anthropologist* 106(3): 435–42.

Calhoun, Craig. 1995. *Critical Social Theory: Culture, History and the Challenge of Difference.* Oxford: Blackwell.

Callon, Michel. 1986. "Some Elements of a Sociology of Translation: Domestication of the Scallops and the Fishermen of St. Brieuc Bay." In *Power, Action, and Belief: A New Sociology of Knowledge?* Edited by John Law. London: Routledge & Keagan Paul.

Cerwonka, Allaine, and Liisa H. Malkki. 2007. *Improvising Theory: Process and Temporality in Ethnographic Fieldwork.* Chicago: University of Chicago Press.

Choy, Timothy, Lieba Faier, Michael Hathaway, Miyako Inoue, and Anna Tsing. 2009. "A New Form of Collaboration in Cultural Anthropology: Matsutake Worlds." *American Ethnologist* 36(2): 380–403.

Clifford, James. 1988. *The Predicament of Culture: Twentieth-Century Ethnography, Literature, and Art.* Cambridge, MA: Harvard University Press.

———. 1998. "Notes on Travel and Theory." http://culturalstudies.ucsc.edu/PUBS/Inscriptions/vol_5/clifford.html (accessed June 5, 2015).

Clifford, James, and George Marcus, eds. 1986. *Writing Culture: The Poetics and Politics of Ethnography.* Berkeley: University of California Press.

Cohen, Cathy. 2005. "Punks, Bulldaggers, and Welfare Queens: The Radical Potential of Queer Politics?" In *Black Queer Studies: A Critical Anthology,* edited by E. Patrick Johnson and Mae G. Henderson, 21–51. Durham: Duke University Press.

Cohn, Norman. (1957) 1980. *The Pursuit of the Millennium: Revolutionary Millenarians and Mystical Anarchists of the Middle Ages.* Rev. ed. Oxford: Oxford University Press.

Coleman, E. Gabriella, and Alex Golub. 2008. "Hacker Practice: Moral Genres and the Cultural Articulation of Liberalism." *Anthropological Theory* 8(3): 255–77.

Comaroff, Jean, and John L Comaroff. 2011. *Theory from the South: Or, How Euro-America Is Evolving toward Africa.* Boulder: Paradigm.

Crenshaw, Kimberlé W. 1990. "Demarginalizing the Intersection of Race and Sex: A Black Feminist Critique of Antidiscrimination Doctrine, Feminist Theory and Antiracist Politics." *University of Chicago Legal Forum* 1989: 139–67.

———. 1991. "Mapping the Margins: Intersectionality, Identity Politics, and Violence Against Women of Color." *Stanford Law Review* 43: 1241–99.

———. 2010. "Close Encounters of Three Kinds: On Teaching Dominance, Feminism, and Intersectionality." *Tulsa Law Review* 46: 151–89.

Daston, Lorraine, and Peter Galison. 1992. "The Image of Objectivity." *Representations* 40: 82–128.

Deeb, Hadi, and George E. Marcus. 2011. "In the Green Room: An Experiment in Ethnographic Method at the WTO." *Political and Legal Anthropology Review* 34(1): 51–76.

Derrida, Jacques. (1967) 1976. *Of Grammatology*. Translated by Gayatri C. Spivak. Baltimore: Johns Hopkins University Press.

———. 1978. "Structure, Sign and Play in the Discourse of the Human Sciences." In *Writing and Difference*, 278–94. Chicago: University of Chicago Press.

———. 1982. "Différance." In *Margins of Philosophy,* translated by Alan Bass, 3–27. Chicago: University of Chicago Press.

———. 1993. "Politics of Friendship." *American Imago* 50(3): 353–91.

———. 1994. *Specters of Marx: The State of the Debt, the Work of Mourning, and the New International*. Translated by Peggy Kamuf. New York: Routledge.

Dewey, John. (1925) 1927. *Experience and Nature*. 2nd ed. Chicago: Open Court.

Duggan, Lisa 2003. *The Twilight of Equality?: Neoliberalism, Cultural Politics, and the Attack on Democracy*. Boston: Beacon Press.

Dumont, Jean-Paul. 1978. *The Headman and I: Ambiguity and Ambivalence in the Fieldworking Experience*. Long Grove, IL: Waveland Press.

Edelstein, Dan. 2009. *The Terror of Natural Right: Republicanism, the Cult of Nature, and the French Revolution*. Chicago: University of Chicago Press.

Elyachar, Julia. 2005. *Markets of Dispossession: NGOs, Economic Development, and the State in Cairo*. Durham: Duke University Press.

Fabian, Johannes. 1983. *Time and the Other: How Anthropology Makes Its Object*. New York: Columbia University Press.

Falcone, Jessica. 2010a. "A Meditation on Meditation: The Horizons of *Meditative Thinking* in Tibetan Monasticism and American Anthropology." *Michigan Discussions in Anthropology* 18(1): 402–41.

———. 2010b. "'I Spy . . .': The (Im)possibilities of Ethical Participant Observation with Religious Extremists, Antagonists, and Other Tough Nuts." *Michigan Discussions in Anthropology* 18(1): 243–82.

———. 2010c. "Waiting for Maitreya: Of Gifting Statues, Hopeful Presents and the Future Tense in FPMT's Transnational Tibetan Buddhism." PhD diss., Cornell University.

———. 2012. "Putting the 'Fun' in Fundamentalism: Religious Extremism and the Split Self in Hindu Summer Camps in Washington D.C." *Ethos* 40(2): 164–95.

———. 2013. "The *Hau* of Theory: The Kept-Gift of Theory Itself in American Anthropology." *Anthropology and Humanism* 38(2): 122–45.

Faubion, James D., ed. 2001. *The Ethics of Kinship: Ethnographic Inquiries*. Lanham, MD: Rowman and Littlefield.

———. 2009. "The Ethics of Fieldwork as an Ethics of Connectivity or, the Good Anthropologist (Isn't What She Used to Be)." In *Fieldwork Is Not What It Used to Be,* edited by James D. Faubion and George E. Marcus, 145–66. Ithaca: Cornell University Press.

———. 2011. *An Anthropology of Ethics*. Cambridge, UK: University of Cambridge Press.

Faubion, James D., and George E. Marcus, eds. 2009. *Fieldwork Is Not What It Used to Be*. Ithaca: Cornell University Press.

Feld, Steven. 1995. "From Schizophonia to Schismogenesis: The Discourses and Practices of World Music and World Beat." In *The Traffic in Culture: Refiguring Art and Anthropology,* edited by George E. Marcus and Fred R. Myers, 96–126. Berkeley: University of California Press.

Ferguson, Adam. (1767) 1995. *An Essay in the History of Civil Society*. Cambridge, UK: Cambridge University Press.

Fine, Gary Allan. 1995. *A Second Chicago School? The Development of a Postwar American Sociology*. Chicago: The University of Chicago Press.

Fischer, Michael M. J. 2003. *Emergent Forms of Life and the Anthropological Voice*. Durham: Duke University Press.

———. 2007. "Culture and Cultural Analysis as Experimental Systems." *Cultural Anthropology* 22(1): 1–64.

———. 2012. "Lively Biotech and Translational Research." In *Lively Capital: Biotechnologies, Ethics and Governance in Global Markets*, edited by Kaushik Sunder Rajan. Durham: Duke University Press.

Fortun, Kim. 2001. *Advocacy after Bhopal*. Chicago: University of Chicago Press.

———. 2003. "Ethnography in/of/as Open Systems." *Reviews in Anthropology* 32(2): 171–90.

———. 2009. "Figuring Out Ethnography." In *Fieldwork Is Not What It Used To Be: Learning Anthropology's Method in a Time of Transition,* edited by James D. Faubion and George E. Marcus, 167–72. Ithaca: Cornell University Press.

———. 2012a. "Biopolitics and the Informating of Environmentalism." In *Lively Capital: Biotechnologies, Ethics and Governance in Global Markets*, edited by Kaushik Sunder Rajan. Durham: Duke University Press.

———. 2012b. "Ethnography in Late Industrialism." *Cultural Anthropology* 27(3): 446–64.

———. 2014. "From Latour to Late Industrialism." *HAU: Journal of Ethnographic Theory* 4(1): 309–29.

Fortun, Mike. 2005. "For an Ethics of Promising, or, a Few Kind Words about James Watson." *New Genetics and Society* 24(2): 157–73.

———. *Minding Genomics: Care of the Data in Contemporary Sciences* (forthcoming).

Fortun, Mike, and Herb Bernstein. 1998. "Muddling Through." In *Muddling Through: Pursuing Science and Truths in the 21st Century,* chap. 9. Washington D.C.: Counterpoint.

Foucault, Michel. 1976. *"Society Must Be Defended": Lectures at the Collège de France, 1975–1976*. Translated by David Macey. New York: Picador.

———. (1984) 1998. "Polemics, Politics and Problematizations." [Interview Conducted by Paul Rabinow.] In *Essential Works of Michel Foucault, Vol. 1: Ethics: Subjectivity and Truth,* edited by Paul Rabinow, translated by L. Davis. New York: New Press. http://foucault.info/foucault/interview.html.

———. 1997. "Polemics, Politics, Problematizations: An Interview with Michel Foucault." In *Essential Works of Michel Foucault, Vol. 1: Ethics: Subjectivity and Truth,* edited by Paul Rabinow, 111–19. New York: Zone Books.

———. 2005. *The Hermeneutics of the Subject: Lectures at the Collège de France, 1981–1982.* Edited by Frédéric Gros. Translated by Graham Burchell. New York: Palgrave Macmillan.

Fourcade, Marion. 2009. *Economists and Societies: Discipline and Professions in the United States, Britain and France, 1890 to 1990.* Princeton: Princeton University Press.

Geertz, Clifford. 1973. *The Interpretation of Cultures.* New York: Basic Books.

———. 1983. *Local Knowledge: Further Essays in Interpretive Anthropology.* New York: Basic Books.

Giddens, Anthony. 1986. *The Constitution of Society: Outline of the Theory of Structuration.* Berkeley: University of California Press.

———. 1991. *Modernity and Self-identity: Self and Society in the Late Modern Age.* Cambridge, UK: Polity Press.

———. 1993. *The Transformation of Intimacy: Love, Sexuality and Eroticism in Modern Societies.* Stanford: Stanford University Press.

Glaeser, Andreas. 2005. "An Ontology for the Ethnographic Study of Social Processes: Extending the Extended Case Method." *Social Analysis* 49(3): 18–47. Reprinted in Terry M. S. Evens, and Don Handleman, eds. 2006. *The Manchester School: Practice and Ethnographic Praxis in Anthropology,* 64–93. New York: Berghahn.

———. 2011. *Political Epistemics: The Secret Police, the Opposition and the End of East German Socialism.* Chicago: University of Chicago Press.

———. 2013. "Theorizing Modern Politics and Its Ironies of Control through the Case of East German State Socialism." *Interdisciplines* 2(2): 119–66.

———. 2014. "Hermeneutic Institutionalism: Towards a New Synthesis." *Qualitative Sociology* 37: 207–41.

Golub, Alex. 2011. "Big Content Runs 66% of Our Journals but the Open Access Shortfall Is Our Fault." Savage Minds. http://savageminds.org/2011/09/08/big-content-runs-66-of-our-journals-but-the-open-access-shortfall-is-our-fault/ (accessed April 20, 2015).

Graeber, David. 2011. *Debt: The First 5,000 Years.* Brooklyn: Melville House.

Gunn, Wendy, Ton Otto, and Rachel Charlotte Smith, eds. 2013. *Design Anthropology: Theory and Practice.* London: Bloomsbury.

Habermas. Jürgen. (1963) 1990. *Strukturwandel der Öffentlichkeit: Untersuchungen zu einer Kategorie der bürgerlichen Gesellschaft.* Frankfurt: Suhrkamp.

———. 1984. *Theory of Communicative Action, Vol. 1: Reason and the Rationalization of Society.* Translated by Thomas McCarthy. Boston: Beacon Press.

———. 1987. *Theory of Communicative Action, Vol. 2: Lifeworld and System: A Critique of Functionalist Reason.* Translated by Thomas McCarthy. Boston: Beacon Press.

Hanks, William F. 1996. *Language and Communicative Practices.* Boulder: Westview Press.

Haraway, Donna. 1991. *Simians, Cyborgs and Women: The Reinvention of Nature.* New York: Routledge.

———. 1992. "The Promises of Monsters: A Regenerative Politics for Inappropriate/d Others." In *Cultural Studies,* edited by Lawrence Grossberg, Cary Nelson, and Paula A. Treichler, 295–337. New York: Routledge.

———. 1997. *Modest_Witness@Second_Millennium.FemaleMan©_Meets_OncoMouse™: Feminism and Technoscience.* New York: Routledge.

Hardt, Michael, and Antonio Negri. 2000. *Empire*. Cambridge MA: Harvard University Press.

Harvey, David. 1990. *The Condition of Postmodernity*. Oxford: Blackwell.

Havelock, Eric. 1963. *Preface to Plato*. Cambridge, MA: Harvard University Press.

Hayek, Friedrich August von. (1944) 1991. *The Fatal Conceit: The Errors of Socialism*. Chicago: University of Chicago Press.

Hegel, Georg Wilhlem Friedrich. (1807) 1986. *Phänomenologie des Geistes*. Frankfurt: Suhrkamp Verlag.

———. (1820) 1986. *Grundlinien der Philosophie des Rechts*. Frankfurt: Suhrkamp.

Helmreich, Stefan. 2009. *Alien Ocean: Anthropological Voyages in Microbial Seas*. Berkeley: University of California Press.

Hoffman, Lynn. 1981. *Foundations of Family Therapy: A Conceptual Framework for Systems Change*. New York: Basic Books.

Holmes, Douglas. 2009. "The Economy of Words." *Cultural Anthropology* 24(3): 381–419.

Honneth, Axel. 1992. *Kampf um Anerkennung: Zur moralischen Grammatik sozialer Konflikte*. Frankfurt: Suhrkamp.

———. 2005. *Verdinglichung*. Frankfurt: Suhrkamp.

———. 2011. *Das Recht der Freiheit: Grundriß einer demokratischen Sittlichkeit*. Berlin: Suhrkamp.

Horkheimer, Max. (1937) 1992. "Traditionelle und Kritische Theorie." In *Traditionelle und Kritische Theorie: Fünf Aufsätze*, 205–60. Frankfurt: Fischer.

Horkheimer, Max, and Theodor W. Adorno. (1944) 1988. *Dialektik der Aufklärung: Philosophische Fragmente*. Frankfurt: Fischer.

Howe, Cymene. 2013. *Intimate Activism: Sexual Rights in Postrevolutionary Nicaragua*. Durham: Duke University Press.

Hutchinson, Janis Faye, and Richard R. Sharp. 2008. "Karma, Reincarnation, and Medicine: Hindu Perspectives on Biomedical Research." *Genomic Medicine* 2: 107–11.

Hymes, Dell, ed. 1972. *Reinventing Anthropology*. New York: Random House.

Ingold, Tim. 2011. *Being Alive: Essays on Movement, Knowledge and Description*. New York: Routledge.

Iser, Wolfgang 1976. *Der Akt des Lesens*. München: Fink.

Jackson, Jason Baird. 2012. "We Are the One Percent: Open Access in the Era of Occupy Wall Street." http://www.anthropologiesproject.org/2012/03/we-are-one-percent-open-access-in-era.html (accessed April 20, 2015).

Jakobson, Roman. 1956. "Two Aspects of Language and Two Types of Aphasic Disturbances." In *Fundamentals of Language*, edited by Roman Jakobson and Morris Halle. The Hague: Mouton.

James, William. (1907–1909) 1975. *Pragmatism and the Meaning of Truth*. Cambridge, MA: Harvard University Press.

Jasanoff, Sheila. 2004. "Ordering Knowledge, Ordering Society." *States of Knowledge: The Co-production of Science and Social Order,* edited by Sheila Jasanoff. New York: Routledge.

———. 2005. *Designs on Nature: Science and Democracy in Europe and the United States*. Princeton, NJ: Princeton University Press.

Jasanoff, Sheila, and Sang-Hyun Kim, eds. 2015. *Dreamscapes of Modernity: Sociotechnical Imaginaries and the Fabrication of Power*. Chicago: University of Chicago Press.

Johnson, Stephen T. 1995. *Alphabet City*. New York: Viking Children's Books.

———. 1998. *City by Numbers*. New York: Viking Children's Books.

Justinian. (532) 1987. *Institutes*. Translated by Peter Birks and Grant McLeod. Ithaca: Cornell University Press.

Keating, Peter, and Alberto Cambrosio. 2012. *Cancer on Trial: Oncology as a New Style of Practice*. Chicago: University of Chicago Press.

Keller, Evelyn Fox. 1985. "Dynamic Objectivity: Love, Power and Knowledge." In *Reflections on Gender and Science*. New Haven: Yale, 1985.

Kelty, Christopher M. 2008. *Two Bits: The Cultural Significance of Free Software*. Durham: Duke University Press.

———. 2009. "Collaboration, Coordination, and Composition: Fieldwork after the Internet." In *Fieldwork Is Not What It Used to Be,* edited by James D. Faubion and George E. Marcus, 184–206. Ithaca: Cornell University Press.

———. 2012. "The Disappearing Virtual Library." *Al Jazeera*. March 1, 2012. http://www.aljazeera.com/indepth/opinion/2012/02/2012227143813304790.html (accessed April 20, 2015).

Kelty, Christopher M., Michael M. J. Fischer, Alex Golub, Jason Baird Jackson, Kimberly Christen, Michael F Brown, and Tom Boellstorff. 2008. "Anthropology of/in Circulation: The Future of Open Access and Scholarly Societies." *Cultural Anthropology* 23(3): 559–88.

Kluckhohn, Clyde. 1959. *Mirror for Man: The Relation of Anthropology to Modern Life*. New York: McGaw Hill.

Kluckhohn, Clyde, Leonard McCombe, and Evon Vogt. 1951. *Navaho Means People*. Cambridge, MA: Harvard University Press.

Kojève, Alexandre. (1947) 1980. *Introduction à la lecture de Hegel: Leçons sur la Phénoménologie de l'Esprit professées de 1933 à 1939 à l'École des Hautes Études*. Paris: Gallimard.

Lacan, Jacques. 1977. *Écrits: A Selection*. Translated by Alan Sheridan. London: Tavistock.

———. 1988. *The Seminar, Book I: Freud's Papers on Technique, 1953–54*. Translated by John Forrester. New York: Norton.

Lakoff, George. 1993. "The Contemporary Theory of Metaphor. *Metaphor and Thought*, 2nd ed., edited by Anthony Ortony, 202–51. Cambridge, UK: Cambridge University Press.

Latour, Bruno. 1988a. *The Pasteurization of France*. Translated by Alan Sheridan and John Law. Cambridge, MA: Harvard University Press.

———. 1988b. *Science in Action*. Cambridge, MA: Harvard University Press.

———. 2011. *An Inquiry into Modes of Existence: An Anthropology of the Moderns*. Cambridge, MA: Harvard University Press.

Luhmann, Niklas. 1989. *Ecological Communication*. Translated by John Bednarz. Chicago: University of Chicago Press.

———. 1996. *Social Systems*. Translated by John Bednarz, Jr., and Dirk Baecker. Stanford, Stanford University Press.

Lukács, Georg. (1924) 1972. "Reification and the Consciousness of the Proletariat." In *History of Class Consciousness: Studies in Marxist Dialectics*, 83–222. Translated by Rodney Livingstone. Cambridge, MA: MIT Press.

Lyotard, Francois. (1979) 1984. *The Postmodern Condition: A Report on Knowledge.* St. Paul: University of Minnesota Press.

Mackenzie, Donald. 2008. *An Engine Not a Camera: How Financial Models Shape Markets.* Cambridge: MIT Press.

Magnússon, Haukur S. 2010. "What Are You Voting For, Reykjavík?" *Reykjavík Grapevine,* May 25. http://www.grapevine.is/Features/ReadArticle/Feature-What-Are-You-Voting-For-Reykjavik.

Malinowski, Bronislaw. 1935. *Coral Gardens and Their Magic II: The Language and Magic of Gardening.* Indianapolis: Indiana University Press.

Marcus, George E. 1985. "A Timely Rereading of Naven: Gregory Bateson as Oracular Essayist." *Representations* 12: 66–82.

——. 1995a. "Ethnography in/of the World System: The Emergence of Multisited Ethnography." *Annual Review of Anthropology* 24: 95–117.

——. 1995b. *Technoscientific Imaginaries: Conversations, Profiles, and Memoirs (Late Editions: Cultural Studies for the End of the Century).* Chicago: University of Chicago Press.

——. (1995) 1998a. "Ethnography in/of the World System: The Emergence of Multi-Sited Ethnography." In *Ethnography through Thick & Thin,* 79–104. Princeton: Princeton University Press.

——. (1997) 1998b. "The Uses of Complicity in the Changing Mise-en-Scène of Anthropological Fieldwork." In *Ethnography through Thick & Thin,* 105–132. Princeton: Princeton University Press.

——. 2000. *Para-Sites: A Casebook against Cynical Reason.* Chicago: University of Chicago Press.

——. 2008. "The End(s) of Ethnography: Social/Cultural Anthropology's Signature Form of Producing Knowledge in Transition." *Cultural Anthropology* 23(1): 1–14.

——. 2010. "Holism and the Expectations of Critique in Post-1980s Anthropology: Notes and Queries in Three Acts and an Epilogue." In *Experiments in Holism,* edited by Ton Otto and Nils Bubandt, 28–46. Oxford: Wiley-Blackwell.

——. 2012. "The Legacies of Writing Culture and the Near Future of the Ethnographic Form: A Sketch." *Cultural Anthropology* 27(3): 427–45.

——. 2014. "Prototyping and Contemporary Anthropological Experiments with Ethnographic Method." *Journal of Cultural Economy* 7(4): 399–410.

Marcus, George, and Michael J. Fisher. 1986. *Anthropology as Cultural Critique: An Experimental Moment in the Human Sciences.* Chicago: University of Chicago Press.

Marx, Karl. (1852) 1977. *The Eighteenth Brumaire of Louis Bonaparte.* Moscow: Progress Publishers.

——. (1857) 1974. *Grundrisse der Kritik der politischen Ökonomie.* Marx-Engles Werke Vol. 43. Berlin: Dietz.

——. (1867) 1963. *Das Kapital.* Vol. 1. Berlin: Dietz.

Maurer, Bill. 2005. *Mutual Life, Limited: Islamic Banking, Alternative Currencies, Lateral Reason.* Princeton: Princeton University Press.

Mead, George Herbert. 1934. *Mind, Self, and Society*. Chicago: University of Chicago Press.

Merchant, Carolyn. 1980. *The Death of Nature: Women, Nature and the Scientific Revolution*. New York: Harper Collins.

Middleton, Townsend. 2011a. "Across the Interface of State Ethnography: Rethinking Ethnology and Its Subjects in Multicultural India." *American Ethnologist* 38 (2): 249–66.

——— 2011b. "Ethno-logics: Paradigms of Modern Identity." In *Handbook of Modernity in South Asia: Modern Makeovers*, edited by Saurabh Dube, 200–213. New Delhi: Oxford University Press.

———. 2013. "Scheduling Tribes: A View from Inside India's 'Ethnographic State.'" *FOCAAL: Journal of Global and Historical Anthropology* 65:13–22.

Miller, Daniel. 2011. *Tales from Facebook*. Malden, MA: Polity.

Ortner, Sherry B. 1984. "Theory in Anthropology since the Sixties." *Comparative Studies in Society and History* 26 (1): 126–66.

Papastergiadis, Nikos. 2012. *Cosmopolitanism and Culture*. London: Polity Press.

Perrow, Charles. 1984. *Normal Accidents: Living with High-Risk Technologies*. New York: Basic Books.

Pickering, Andrew. 1995. *The Mangle of Practice: Time, Agency and Science*. Chicago: University of Chicago Press.

Peirce, Charles Sanders. 1998. *The Essential Peirce: Selected Philosophical Writings*. Bloomington: Indiana University Press.

Poirier, Lindsay, Dominic DiFranzo, and Marie Joan Kristine Gloria. 2014. "Light Structure in the Platform for Experimental Collaborative Ethnography." Paper presented at the Tetherless World Constellation, Web Science Conference, June 23–26, Indiana University, Bloomington.

Popper, Karl. 1934. *Logik der Forschung: Zur Erkenntnistheorie der modernen Naturwissenschaft*. Tübingen: J. C. B. Mohr (Karl Siebeck).

———. (1945) 1971. *The Open Society and Its Enemies*. 2 vols. Princeton: Princeton University Press.

Povinelli, Elizabeth. 2002. *The Cunning of Recognition: Indigenous Alterities and the Making of Australian Multiculturalism*. Durham: Duke University Press.

"Punctuation." *No Subject: Encyclopedia of Lacanian Psychoanalysis*. Last modified November 12, 2006. http://nosubject.com/index.php?title=Punctuate. (Drawing from Lacan 1977, 99, 269; 1988, 54.)

Rabinow, Paul. 1977. *Reflections on Fieldwork in Morocco*. Berkeley: University of California Press.

———. 1988. "Beyond Ethnography: Anthropology as Nominalism." *Cultural Anthropology* 3(4): 355–64.

———. 1999. *French DNA: Trouble in Purgatory*. Chicago: University of Chicago Press.

———. 2003. *Anthropos Today: Reflections on Modern Equipment*. Princeton: Princeton University Press.

———. 2007. *Marking Time: On the Anthropology of the Contemporary*. Princeton: Princeton University Press.

Rawls, John. (1993) 2005. *Political Liberalism*. New York: Columbia University Press.

Reddy, Deepa S. 2007. "Good Gifts for the Common Good: A Story of Blood in the Market of Genetic Research." *Cultural Anthropology* 22(3): 429–72.

———. 2013. "Citizens in the Commons: Blood and Genetics in the Making of the Civic." *Contemporary South Asia* 21(3): 275–90.

Reed, Isaac. 2011. *Interpretation and Social Knowledge: On the Use of Theory in the Human Sciences*. Chicago: The University of Chicago Press.

"Refraction." 2000. *The American Heritage Dictionary of the English Language*. 4th ed. New York: Houghton Mifflin.

Rheinberger, Hans-Jörg. 1998. "Experimental Systems, Graphematic Spaces." In *Inscribing Science: Scientific Texts and the Materiality of Communication*, edited by Timothy Lenoir, 285–303. Stanford: Stanford University Press.

Rich, Adrienne. 1980. *Compulsory Heterosexuality and Lesbian Existence*. London: Onlywomen Press.

Ricoeur, Paul. (1975) 1977. *The Rule of Metaphor*. London: Routledge.

———. (1983–1985) 1984–1986. *Time and Narrative*. 3 vols. Translated by K. McLaughlin and D. Pellauer. Chicago: University of Chicago Press.

———. 1991. "Life in Quest of Narrative." In *On Paul Ricoeur: Narrative and Interpretation*, edited by David Wood, 20–33. London: Routledge.

Rorty, Richard. 1979. *Philosophy and the Mirror of Nature*. Princeton: Princeton University Press.

Rubin, Gayle. 1975. "The Traffic in Women: Notes on the Political Economy of Sex." In *Toward an Anthropology of Women,* edited by Rayna Reiter, 157–210. New York: Monthly Review Press.

Rushdie, Salman. (1983) 1995. *Shame*. London: Vintage.

Said, Edward W. 1982. "Traveling Theory." In *The World, the Text and the Critic*. Cambridge, MA: Harvard University Press.

Saunders, Barry F. 2008. *CT Suite: The Work of Diagnosis in the Age of Noninvasive Cutting*. Durham: Duke University Press.

Schnädelbach, Herbert. (1999) 2011. *Georg Friedrich Wilhelm Hegel zur Einführung*. Hamburg: Junius.

Scott, James. 1998. *Seeing like a State: How Certain Schemes to Improve the World Have Failed*. New Haven: Yale University Press.

Silverstein, Michael. 1979. "Language Structure and Linguistic Ideology." In *The Elements,* edited by Paul Clyne, William Hanks, and Carol Hofbauer, 193–248. Chicago: Chicago Linguistic Society.

Simmel, Georg. (1908) 1992. *Soziologie: Untersuchungen über die Formen der Vergesellschaftung*. Frankfurt: Suhrkamp.

Sloterdijk, Peter. 1987. *Critique of Cynical Reason*. Translated by Michael Eldred. Minneapolis: University of Minnesota Press.

Spivak, Gayatri Chakravorty. 1987. *In Other Worlds: Essays in Cultural Politics*. New York: Methuen.

———. 1988. "Subaltern Studies: Deconstructing Historiography." In *Selected Subaltern Studies,* edited by Ranajit Guha and Gayatri Chakravorty Spivak, 3–32. New York: Oxford University Press.

——. 2008. "The Trajectory of the Subaltern in My Work." Lecture presented at the University of California. University of California TV uploaded February 7. https://www.youtube.com/watch?v=2ZHH4ALRFHw (accessed December 1, 2014).

Star, Susan Leigh, and James Griesemer. 1989. "Institutional Ecology, 'Translations,' and Boundary Objects: Amateurs and Professionals in Berkeley's Museum of Vertebrate Zoology, 1907–39." *Social Studies of Science* 19(3): 387–420.

Strauss, David. (1835) 1846. *The Life of Jesus, Critically Examined*. London: Chapman Brothers.

Sudnow, Robert. (1978) 1993. *Ways of the Hand: The Organization of Improvised Conduct*. Cambridge, MA: MIT Press.

Sunder Rajan, Kaushik. 2006. *Biocapital: The Constitution of Post-Genomic Life*. Duke University Press.

——. 2011. "Teaching with George Marcus (and Learning from Michael Fischer): Pedagogy as Multi-Sited Ethnography." In *Multi-Sited Ethnography: Problems and Possibilities in the Translocation of Research Methods*, edited by Simon Coleman and Pauline von Hellermann, 174–93. London: Routledge.

——. 2012. *Lively Capital: Biotechnologies, Ethics and Governance in Global Markets*. Duke University Press.

Taylor, Charles. 1989. *Sources of the Self: The Making of Modern Identity*. Cambridge, MA: Harvard University Press.

——. 2003. *Modern Social Imaginaries*. Durham: Duke University Press.

Thorkelson, Eli. 2008. "The Silent Social Order of the Theory Classroom." *Social Epistemology* 22(2): 165–96.

Traweek, Sharon. 2002. "Faultlines," In *Doing Science + Culture: How Cultural and Interdisciplinary Studies Are Changing the Way We Look at Science and Medicine,* edited by in Roddey Reid and Sharon Traweek, 21–48. New York: Routledge.

Vygotsky, Lev. (1934) 1986. *Thought and Language*. Rev. ed. Edited by Alex Kozulin. Cambridge, MA: MIT Press.

Wacquant, Loïc. 2004. *Body and Soul: Notebooks of an Apprentice Boxer*. Oxford: Oxford University Press.

Wagner, Peter. 2000. "'An Entirely New Object of Consciousness, of Volition, of Thought': The Coming into Being and (Almost) Passing Away of 'Society' as a Scientific Object." In *Biographies of Scientific Objects,* edited by Lorraine Daston, 132–57. Chicago: University of Chicago Press.

Warner, Michael. 1991. "Introduction: Fear of a Queer Planet." *Social Text* 29(4): 3–17.

Weber, Max. (1904) 1988. "Zur Objektivität sozialwissenschaftlicher Erkenntnis" *Archiv für Sozialwissenschaft und Sozialpolitik* 19: 22–87. Reprinted in 1988. *Gesammelte Aufsätze zur Wissenschaftslehre,* 146–214. Tübingen: Mohr (Siebeck).

——. (1922) 1980. *Wirtschaft und Gesellschaft*. Tübingen: J.C.B. Mohr (Siebeck).

Whitehead, Alfred North. (1927–28) 1979. *Process and Reality*. New York: Simon and Schuster.

Whorf, Benjamin Lee. (1939) 1956. "The Relation of Habitual Thought and Behavior to Language." In *Language, Thought and Reality: Selected Writings of Benjamin Lee Whorf,* edited by John B. Caroll, 134–59. Cambridge, MA: MIT Press.

Wittgenstein, Ludwig. (1957) 1984. *Collected Works, Vol. 1: Philosophische Untersuchungen*. Frankfurt: Suhrkamp.

Yurchak, Alexei. 2006. *Everything Was Forever, Until It Was No More: The Last Soviet Generation*. Princeton: Princeton University Press

Contributors

Andrea Ballestero received her PhD from University of California, Irvine in 2010 and is assistant professor of anthropology at Rice University. She has interests in sociolegal studies, economic anthropology, and science and technology studies. Her research examines the changing values of nature as expressed through legal, economic, and material means. Her work traces new (and old) forms of regulation of water in the twenty-first century, the distinctions between human rights and commodities, and the ongoing proliferation of forms of quantification. She conducts fieldwork in Costa Rica and Brazil.

Dominic Boyer is professor of anthropology at Rice University and founding director of the Center for Energy and Environmental Research in the Human Sciences (CENHS), the first research center in the world designed specifically to promote research on the energy/environment nexus in the arts, humanities, and social sciences. He is an editor of the journal *Cultural Anthropology* (2015–2018) and also edits the *Expertise: Cultures and Technologies of Knowledge* book series for Cornell University Press. His most recent book is *The Life Informatic: Newsmaking in the Digital Era* (Cornell University Press, 2013). With Imre Szeman, he is preparing *Energy Humanities: A Reader* for Johns Hopkins University Press. His next book project is a collaborative multimedia duograph with Cymene Howe, which will explore the energopolitical complexities of wind power development in southern Mexico.

Lisa Breglia is associate professor and director of the Global Affairs Program and Global Interdisciplinary Programs at George Mason University in Fairfax, Virginia. Her 2006 book, *Monumental Ambivalence: The Politics of Heritage* (University of Texas Press) examines the struggle over national patrimony between public interests and private-sector development in Maya archaeology across the Yucatán Peninsula. Her more recent book *Living with Oil* (University of Texas Press, 2013) is an ethnographic investigation of the effects of the intensive Mexican offshore oil industry on Gulf coast communities. She is currently working on a new project that looks at the relationship between resource security and citizen security in contemporary Mexico. She lives in Washington, DC.

Jessica Marie Falcone received her PhD in anthropology from Cornell University in 2010. She is currently associate professor of anthropology at Kansas State University. In 2014, she received the Edward C. Dimock Prize in the Indian Humanities for her as-yet-unpublished manuscript, "Battling the Buddha of Love: A Cultural Biography of the Greatest Statue Never Built."

James D. Faubion graduated with a BA in anthropology and philosophy from Reed College in 1980. He received his MA (1984) and PhD (1990) in social anthropology from the University of California, Berkeley. He is Radoslav Tsanoff Chair, professor of anthropology, and faculty affiliate in the Department of Religious Studies at Rice University. He is the editor of *Rethinking the Subject: An Anthology of Contemporary European Social Thought* (Westview, 1995); the second and third volumes of *Essential Works of Michel Foucault* (The New Press, 1999 and 2000); *The Ethics of Kinship: Ethnographic Inquiries* (Rowman & Littlefield, 2001); the second edition of Michel Foucault's *Death and the Labyrinth* (Continuum, 2004); *Fieldwork Is Not What It Used To Be: Learning Anthropology's Method in a Time of Transition* (Cornell University Press, 2008), with George E. Marcus; and

Foucault Now: Current Perspectives in Foucault Studies (Polity Press, 2014). He is the author of *Modern Greek Lessons: A Primer in Historical Constructivism* (Princeton University Press, 1993), *The Shadows and Lights of Waco: Millennialism Today* (Princeton University Press, 2001), and *An Anthropology of Ethics* (Cambridge University Press, 2011).

Kim Fortun is a cultural anthropologist and professor of science and technology studies at Rensselaer Polytechnic Institute. Her research and teaching focus on environmental risk and disaster, and on experimental ethnographic methods and research design. Her research has examined how people in different geographical and organizational contexts understand environmental problems, the uneven distributions of environmental health risks, developments in the environmental health sciences, and factors that contribute to disaster vulnerability. Fortun's book *Advocacy after Bhopal: Environmentalism, Disaster, New Global Orders* (University of Chicago Press, 2001) was awarded the 2003 Sharon Stephens Prize by the American Ethnological Society. From 2005 to 2010, Fortun co-edited *Cultural Anthropology*. Currently, Fortun is working on a book titled *Late Industrialism: Making Environmental Sense;* on *The Asthma Files*, a collaborative project to understand how air pollution and environmental public health are dealt with in different contexts; and on design of the Platform for Experimental and Collaborative Ethnography (PECE), an open source/ access digital platform for anthropological and historical research.

Andreas Glaeser is a hermeneutic sociologist at the University of Chicago. He has previously worked ethnographically and historically on socialist and postsocialist Germany. Theoretically, his interests have focused on processual theories of identity formation and institutional change. The results of this work have been published in two books, *Divided in Unity: Identity, Germany, and the Berlin Police* (University of Chicago Press, 2000) and *Political Epistemics: The Secret Police, the Opposition, and the End of East German Socialism* (University of Chicago Press, 2011). His current work explores the history of social imaginaries with a particular interest in the invention of absolutes in response to political crisis in ancient Israel, classical Athens, and early modern Europe.

Cymene Howe is associate professor of anthropology at Rice University and serves on the editorial collective of *Cultural Anthropology*. She is the author of *Intimate Activism: The Struggle for Sexual Rights in Postrevolutionary Nicaragua* (Duke University Press, 2013) and co-editor, with Gilbert Herdt, of *21st Century Sexualities: Contemporary Issues in Health, Education and Rights* (Routledge, 2007). Her research has centered on activism and human rights; sexuality and knowledge; and, most recently, environmental ethics, climate change, and the politics of energy transition. Her current research and forthcoming book project develop an ecologics of the anthropocene, which queries the overlapping conversations between feminist and queer theory, new materialisms, multispecies ethnography, ontologies, ethics, and imaginaries of the future.

Jamer Hunt collaboratively designs open and flexible programs that respond to emergent cultural conditions. He is the director of the Graduate Program in Transdisciplinary Design at Parsons The New School for Design and visiting design researcher at the Institute of Design in Umea, Sweden. With Paola Antonelli at the Museum of Modern Art (MoMA) he has collaborated on: *MIND08: The Design and Elastic Mind Symposium* (2008) and *Headspace: On Scent as Design* (2010); in 2013, they launched the award-winning *Design and Violence*, an experimental online curatorial project that explores the relationships among creation, destruction, design, and everyday experience. He is a *Fast Company* expert design blogger and *Huffington Post* blogger. His written work engages with the poetics and politics of the built environment, and he has been published in various books, journals, and magazines, including *I.D.* magazine, which published his *Manifesto for Postindustrial Design*.

George E. Marcus is Chancellor's Professor of Anthropology and founding director of the Center for Ethnography, University of California, Irvine. He is interested in the interfaces between ethnographic method and various design practices, on one side, and site-specific art projects, on the other. How distinctively anthropological ideas emerge in sites of intensive research and then gain salience in circulation and collaborations, independent of, and also in relation to, conventional publication, is the subject of a work in progress, *Productive Encounters*.

Townsend Middleton received his PhD from Cornell University in 2010 and is assistant professor of anthropology at the University of North Carolina at Chapel Hill. His work focuses on the politics of recognition, belonging, and autonomy in the Himalayas of India. His forthcoming book, *The Demands of Recognition* (Stanford University Press), engages communities seeking tribal status, as well as the government anthropologists handling their claims, to chart how ethnological paradigms are shaping life and politics in India in old and new ways. Sustaining these interests in the development of anthropology inside and outside the academy, he has recently co-edited a special issue of *Ethnography* titled *Fieldwork(ers): Research Assistants, Researchers, and the Production of Ethnographic Knowledge.*

Deepa S. Reddy has taught anthropology, cross-cultural studies, and women's studies at the University of Houston–Clear Lake since 2000. She now also consults for Human Factors International, a company specializing in user experience (UX) research and design. Her book, *Religious Identity and Political Destiny: "Hindutva" in the Culture of Ethnicism*, was published by AltaMira Press in 2006. She has written on caste, religious politics, and women's activism in India, bioethics and genomics among diasporic Indian communities, and the role of blood and human substance in defining Indian civic imaginaries. Her current research is on mobile lives: the impact of phone technologies on Indian social dynamics, cultural imaginaries, and work and labor. She lives in and works from Pondicherry and blogs for fun on ethnography and food at www.paticheri.com.

Kaushik Sunder Rajan earned his PhD from MIT in 2002 and is associate professor of anthropology and of social sciences in the College at the University of Chicago. He was initially trained as a biologist and works on the anthropology of science, technology, and medicine. His work has focused on a number of interrelated events and emergences: the increased corporatization of life science research; the emergence of new technologies and epistemologies in the life sciences, such as, significantly, genomics; and the fact that these technoscientific and market emergences were not occurring only in the United States but, rather, globally. His book, *Biocapital: The Constitution of Post-Genomic Life* (Duke University Press, 2006) captures a flavor of these emergences. Sunder Rajan is currently researching two new distinct although interrelated projects: one focuses on the political economy of pharmaceutical development in India in the context of changes in global capital flows and governance regimes; the second project focuses on the changing nature of the research university in India in the life sciences.

INDEX